CW00506541

Searching for Red Eagle

Searching for Red Eagle

A Personal Journey into the
Spirit World of Native America

Mary Ann Wells

University Press of Mississippi   *Jackson*

Manufactured in the United States of America

01 00 99 98   4 3 2 1

The paper in this book meets the guidelines for permanence and durability of the Committee on Production Guidelines for Book Longevity of the Council on Library Resources.

Library of Congress Cataloging-in-Publication Data

Wells, Mary Ann, 1944–
    Searching for Red Eagle : a personal journal into the spirit world of Native America / Mary Ann Wells.
        p.   cm.
    Includes bibliographical references and index.
    ISBN (invalid) 1-57806-030-0 (cloth : alk. paper)
    1. Weatherford, William, ca. 1780–1824.   2. Creek War, 1813–1814.   3. Creek Indians—Biography.   4. Indians of North America—Mixed descent—Southern States.   5. Indians of North America—Southern States—Religion.   I. Title
    E99.C9W438   1998
    975'.00497—dc21
    [B]   98-16014
                                                              CIP

British Library Cataloging-in-Publication data available

To Samuel, who listens to my dreams

Contents

Author's Note

This true story of Red Eagle-William Weatherford, a Creek mixed-blood warrior and a leader of the Red Stick faction in the Creek War of 1813–14, is told within the framework of a personal narrative: my own mystic journey into the spirit world of Native America. This journey crosses metaphysical boundaries, which, for many people, separate reality from imagination; it thereby enters the world of fiction.

A map of Georgia, in 1748, with parts of Florida, Louisiana, and Carolina. Eman Bowen, English Geographer

Chronology

1685   The British, operating out of the
        Carolinas, establish contact with the
        Alabamas (Creeks).

1699   The French arrive on the Gulf Coast.

1702   The French establish contact with the
        Alabamas.

1715–16 In the Yamasee War, fought in the
        Carolinas, the Creeks expel British
        traders.

1717   The Alabamas grant the French
        permission to build Fort Toulouse at the
        junction of the Tallapoosa and Coosa
        rivers.

c. 1724   Sehoy of the Wind clan marries François Marchand.

1729   The Natchez uprising opens the door for individual British traders to return to Creek country.

c. 1745   Sehoy Marchand II marries Lachlan McGillivray. Their children are Sehoy Marchand III, Sophia, Alexander, and Jeanette.

1756–63   The French and Indian War (the Seven Years War in Europe) pits the British against the French in other parts of North America.

1763   The wars end; the Treaty of Paris cedes French possessions east of the Mississippi (with the exception of New Orleans) to Britain.

c. 1765   The French depart Creek country, and the British take over. Over the next ten years or so, Sehoy III marries a British trader named MacFarland, is divorced, marries British army officer David Taitt, has a son, and is divorced. She then marries Scots trader Charles Weatherford, and they have four children: William, Jack, Elizabeth, and Rosanna.

1777   Alexander McGillivray (son of Lachlan and Sehoy II) returns to the Alabamas after studying at Savannah and Charleston.

1776–83   The American Revolution takes place, during which the Creeks ally with Britain.

Lachlan McGillivray returns to Scotland.

1783   The Treaty of Paris leaves Spain and the United States in dispute about the southern boundary. Spain claims all of British West Florida, which includes Upper Creek Country.

Creek country is now partly in Spanish West Florida and partly in the American state of Georgia.

Alexander McGillivray is elected chief of the Creek nation.

1785   Alexander McGillivray refuses to sign a treaty with the United States.

1787   Charles Weatherford (William's father) is in a Spanish jail in Pensacola for refusal to pay a debt to a British trading company.

1789   Alexander McGillivray again refuses to sign a treaty with the Americans because of land cessions they want in Georgia.

1790   Alexander McGillivray travels to New York City, personally meets with George Washington, signs the Treaty of New York (virtually the same treaty he had refused in 1789), is made a general in the American army, and is given a two-thousand-dollar-a-year pension.

         McGillivray continues alliance with Spain.

1791   Augustus Bowles (a white man) challenges McGillivray for leadership of the Creeks. The Spaniards capture Bowles and send him to prison in the Philippines.

1792   Charles Weatherford testifies before the U. S. Congress on the political situation in the Creek nation.

1793   Alexander McGillivray's death creates a leadership vacuum among the Creeks.

1795   The Treaty of San Lorenzo Real (Pinckney's Treaty) settles the southern boundary between Spanish Florida and the United States along the 31st parallel. Creeks still travel into Spanish territory to do business with British traders. Americans discourage this commerce, wanting the Indians to use American trading houses.

c. 1795   William Weatherford marries Mary Moniac. They have two children, Charles and Polly.

1796   Benjamin Hawkins, American Indian agent, arrives in Creek country hoping to fill the leadership vacuum and to "Americanize" the Indians.

1798   The Mississippi Territory is created; Spain withdraws to south of 31st parallel.

1799   Bowles is back in Creek country fomenting revolt.

1802   The White Sapling Conference Treaty establishes a firm border between Georgia and the Creeks.

1803   William Weatherford, his father, Charles, Sam Moniac, and several others capture Bowles and turn him over to the Spanish at Mobile for a forty-five-hundred-dollar reward.

France, having secretly reclaimed Louisiana from Spain in 1800, sells the colony to the United States. New disputes occur with Spain over whether Florida was included.

Europe is engrossed in the Napoleonic wars.

Choctaws cede the U. S. buffer zone between themselves and the Creeks along the Tombigbee. The Bigbee district, centered around Ft. Stoddert, is opened to settlers.

Indians are encouraged to run up debts with American trading houses and to give up land in payment.

c. 1804   Mary Moniac Weatherford and Sehoy III die.

Mississippi Territory organizes the Bigbee district into Washington County.

1806   Bigbee district has a population of six thousand.

1806–7   The United States opens the Federal Road through Creek country, which accelerates unpleasant encounters between Indians and encroaching white settlers.

1810   The United States seizes much of West Florida west of the Perdido from the Spaniards, but not Mobile.

c. 1810   William Weatherford marries Sapoth Thlaine.

President Madison annexes West Florida west of the Perdido to the Mississippi Territory, but still the Americans make no attempt to occupy Mobile.

American settlers and Americanized mixed-bloods begin to build neighborhood stockades as fears of Indian attacks grow.

Hawkins establishes a death squad of Americanized Indians to mete out justice as he decrees it.

Mormouth, an elderly Creek chief, accidentally shoots and kills Thomas Meredith, an American traveling on the Federal Road. The death squad executes the old man.

Soon another American, William Lott, is murdered on the Federal Road. The accused are executed immediately.

Sam Moniac and William Weatherford drive a herd of cattle into Choctaw country to sell, using the trip as an excuse to meet with the Choctaw leader Mushalatubbee. The Choctaw chief agrees to assemble the three main chiefs for a conference to discuss an alliance (against the Americans) with the Creeks.

Moniac and William Weatherford return home, round up another herd, and, on the ruse of selling it in Pensacola, meet with Spanish officials to ask for aid and alliance. The Spaniards can offer only moral support.

Spain is engaged in civil war at home, in which, aided by Britain, they hope to oust Napoleon's brother from the Spanish throne. Spanish outposts such as Pensacola and Mobile are in a diplomatic limbo with no regular provisions or communications from the home country.

1813

February   Little Warrior and a party returning from the Wabash meet some Chickasaws who tell them that war has begun between the Americans and the Creeks. They immediately attack American settlers on the Ohio River. Hawkins sentences all to death.

February 12   Congress authorizes General James Wilkinson to take possession of Mobile from the Spanish.

March 8   Wilkinson arrives in Mobile from New Orleans.

The Spanish evacuate to Pensacola.

Sporadic, independent Indian attacks on Americans begin.

At Duck River, Tennessee, several people are killed and a white woman is kidnapped by Creeks.

April 13 Hawkins declares the kidnappers guilty and as usual sentences all to death without due process of established Creek law.

Traditionalists target death squad members.

After securing Mobile, General Wilkinson is ordered to Canada to fight the British.

Major General Flournoy is ordered to Mobile to replace Wilkinson as head of the U. S. Seventh Military Division.

Flournoy orders Brigadier General F. L. Claiborne, along with six hundred Mississippi militiamen, to Fort Stoddert to protect the United States from invasion by "Spanish, British or Indian forces."

June 25 After conferring with several Americanized Indian leaders, Wilkinson writes to U.S. judge Harry Toulmin at Fort Stoddert from Sam Moniac's inn on the Federal Road (where he had stopped on his trip north) to advise the judge "to call up the volunteers" immediately.

July   Lateau, a prophet, and his followers go
to Coosa for a spiritual service, at the end
of which they attack and kill three
Americanized chiefs. In the aftermath,
Lateau and eight followers are killed.

Traditionalists murder nine members of
Hawkins's death squad.

Big Warrior invites some prophets to
Tuckabatchee, but the prophets kill the
messenger.

The prophets announce that they will
destroy Americanized towns.

Hawkins advises Americanized chiefs to
avert civil war.

All the turmoil is blamed on Tecumseh
and the British.

The Upper Creeks become "Red Sticks,"
named for the red war clubs displayed on
their town squares.

Leaders emerge among the Red Sticks—
Peter McQueen, Josiah Francis, High-
headed Jim—and go to meet with the
Choctaw chiefs. No alliance is forged.

Red Stick leaders return from meeting
with the Choctaws and set out
immediately for Pensacola. At Burnt
Corn Springs they burn the house of

death squad member James Cornells and take his wife captive.

Americans become alarmed and employ David Tate (William Weatherford's brother) to go to Pensacola and spy on the Red Sticks. Tate reports that they plan to get powder and lead, distribute it in the nation, and attack the Americans and the Americanized.

July 25 Colonel James Caller calls out the militia.

July 27 Six companies of a hundred and eighty men, top-heavy with officers, attack the Red Sticks as they prepare their midday meal at Burnt Corn Creek on the way home from Pensacola. The Red Sticks lose some two hundred pounds of powder but rout the militia. The Creek War has erupted.

Mississippi Territory militia units and U. S. regulars are sent to man the neighborhood stockades.

August 2 Sam Moniac gives a deposition to Judge Toulmin on the situation in the Creek nation. Publicly, Moniac sides with the Americans and William Weatherford aligns with the Red Sticks.

Brigadier General Claiborne visits Fort Mims, a stockade around the home of ferry operator Samuel Mims at the Tensaw, and orders the commander to strengthen the flimsy stockade. His orders are not followed.

A hundred and seventy-five Mississippi volunteers, seventy local militiamen, and sixteen regulars are in the fort to protect about two hundred local civilians.

August 20   The Red Stick army begins the march to Fort Mims.

August 30   The Fort Mims massacre occurs.

September   Major Joseph Kennedy and his detachment bury the remains of two hundred and forty-seven bodies at the fort site.

American newspapers report that four hundred to six hundred "innocent" Americans have been massacred.

The American press declares that William Weatherford is the leader of the Red Sticks.

September 24   The Tennessee legislature orders General Andrew Jackson to call up two thousand militiamen immediately to move against the Creeks.

September 29   Choctaw chief Pushmataha and a hundred and thirty-five Choctaws enlist in the American cause at Fort St. Stephens.

William Weatherford and Ochille Haujo visit Mushalatubbee again. They ask for aid and receive none.

Messages reach the Red Stick leaders that British aid will soon arrive.

October   Jackson and his militia join General John Coffee and thirteen hundred Tennessee cavalrymen below Huntsville in the Mississippi Territory.

The War Department places the operation against the Creeks under the command of General Thomas Pinckney of the U. S. Sixth Military District, though the Creek country lies in both the sixth and seventh army districts.

The East Tennessee Militia, the Georgia Militia, the third regiment of U. S. regulars, and the Mississippi Militia stand poised with Jackson's, Coffee's, Pinckney's, and Flournoy's forces to move against the Creeks.

Cherokee leader John Ridge agrees to aid the Americans.

Coffee attacks Tallussahatchee and massacres not only warriors but the elderly, women, and children.

Red Sticks besiege the Americanized town of Talladega.

November 9   Jackson, with infantry and cavalry, lifts the Talladega siege in a battle against warriors armed with bows and arrows.

November 18   Cocke's East Tennessee Militia slaughters residents of Creek Hillabee towns that have already accepted Jackson's terms for peace and have surrendered.

November 29   The Georgia Militia attacks and burns Autossee, then moves on to destroy Tallassee.

December   William Weatherford goes to Pensacola to make a plea for ammunition. British aid still has not arrived. The Spanish manage to procure three horseloads of lead and powder for the Indians.

December 23   Claiborne attacks the Holy Ground. The Red Sticks retreat across the river.

Claiborne musters out of service the Mississippi volunteers and Pushmataha's Choctaws. With the victory at Holy

Ground, the southern Mississippi Territory is considered secure.

1814

January 22	At Emuckfau, the Red Sticks attack Jackson. He retreats.
January 24	At Enitachopo, the Red Sticks win the battle with Jackson.
January 26	At Calabee Creek, the Red Sticks attack the Georgia Militia unsuccessfully.
February	A British emissary brings the Red Sticks word that supplies are being assembled in the Bahamas.
March 27	Tohopeka (Horseshoe Bend), the last stronghold of the Red Sticks, falls to Jackson.
April	Jackson moves to the Hickory Ground, site of the old French fort, Toulouse, and erects Fort Jackson.
	William Weatherford surrenders.
	Peter McQueen and Josiah Francis escape to Florida.

April 6   Napoleon is defeated in Europe. Britain can now focus on North America.

British supplies arrive in Florida.

August 9   The Treaty of Fort Jackson is signed by the Americanized Creeks.

January 8, 1815   The Battle of New Orleans, the last action of the War of 1812, ends British contact with the Alabamas and the Creeks in the Mississippi Territory.

Part One

Two Fires, One Heart

One

An Introduction

Before I had heard of George Washington, Abraham Lincoln, or even Jesus, I knew who William Weatherford was. He was Red Eagle—the icon implanted in my heart as an example of what a truly noble human being should be. He was the mythic hero who had journeyed into the abyss and returned. Detailing the facts of his life has never been easy. An Alabama-(Creek)-Scots-French mixed-blood leader of the Red Stick faction in the Creek War of 1813–14, Red Eagle began life circa 1775 as William Weatherford in the Upper Creek division of the Muskogee nation, an area the Mississippi Territory soon encompassed, and died as Red Eagle-William Weatherford-the Truth Speaker in the new state of Alabama in 1824. He left a spiritual legacy of such mythic proportions that he was long ago transformed into a legendary hero by the scattered American Indian mixed-blood communities and people of south Mississippi, Alabama, and north Florida.

As the child of a south Mississippi mixed-blood family, I

can testify that our stories of Red Eagle, whom my family usually called Billy Weatherford, reflected our collective cultural psyche and delineated our view of ourselves as a people. We also saw him more broadly as a champion of all mixed-bloods and American Indians who must eventually wage their own personal battles to define who they are. We were sure that Weatherford, a distant kinsman of my Choctaw-Alabama-Scots-French paternal grandmother, believed that being an Indian meant being a free, fully realized human being who lived in harmony with nature. In our minds, the word "Indian" translated to "true human being," a definition that was a spiritual concept. Today I consider William Weatherford's legacy to be a universal metaphor for all people struggling to maintain the dignity of their identity.

Here is a summary of what I remember of my family's highly dramatized, partisan views of William Weatherford's philosophy as told to me mainly by my uncle John Dee:

Billy Weatherford-Red Eagle-the Truth Speaker said that mixed-blood people had a right to be Indians, to live as Indians, to think as Indians, and to call themselves Indians—that being an Indian was a matter of the spirit, a decision of the heart. He said that we had to be vigilant or the Americans would claim that we never existed, that they were always promoting the theory that the people we were, were not, even though we lived, breathed air, walked the earth, and roamed the pine forests. Billy foresaw the future the Americans would inflict upon us.

Thomas Jefferson had suggested that the easiest and simplest solution to the "Indian problem" was intermarriage with whites, which he believed would bring about automatic dissolution of Indian culture and thought. Several generations earlier, the French colonial authorities in the region of the Gulf South had experienced exactly the opposite result when whites and Indians intermarried; the intermarrying

Frenchmen became Indian. The Euro-American authorities considered the Indians' cultural preference for communal living and the sharing of resources to be evil and backward. Pamphleteers and journalists of the nineteenth century called the Indian lifestyle "native communism." But it was the human condition of the early European travelers to the Indian nations and the natives whom they encountered, not government policy, that had brought us mixed-bloods into being.

The stories continued: *Billy Weatherford said that we had a right to be, that even if we were people of two bloods—two fires—we had but one heart and that heart was native. Long before we were conceived, we were native. How could anyone doubt our identity? How could anyone doubt the color of our hearts? Billy knew what the government could never grasp.*

The wild, Euro-American frontiersmen of the early nineteenth century had no patience for cultures that could not accommodate their gluttonous appetites for land ownership, personal wealth, and power; they eagerly advocated war as a chance to seize the land and bounty of the Indians and destroy the Indians' culture. The Creek War of 1813–14 became the crux of William Weatherford's war of identity, a struggle that continued for mixed-bloods long after the Creek War was lost and the peace treaty signed.

Uncle John Dee said: *Governments and wars cannot dictate a change in the color of a person's heart. So we still live, Indian souls, Indian spirits in white skins. If we were simpler organisms we would be studied scientifically and hailed for our adaptive abilities and the fact that we have sheltered the native heart against impossible odds. Across the great cosmic divide our ancestors reach back to us. We hold hands. Our hearts are one. Through their eyes we see the path.*

I do not remember when I first heard Red Eagle-William

Weatherford's name. Sometimes I imagine that it must have been when I was just a few hours old, when I was taken from the shack where I was born and was presented to the natural world beyond the four walls. I was born down on the Agricola-Latonia Road in George County, Mississippi, on July 2, 1944, in my maternal grandmother's rickety small house, to a people the white establishment said did not exist in that place or time. We were American Indian mixed-bloods, Choctaw mixed-bloods. When pressed for an explanation of their theory that we did not exist, some university professors and bureaucrats said (and continue to say) that we "might have some Indian blood" but that we did not have a viable culture separate and apart from white culture because we had not retained Indian language, customs, or even foodways, and therefore the people we said we were did not exist.

It was true that we knew only a few words of Choctaw, a language which, according to family stories, had become dangerous for our ancestors to speak, but, even as the experts expounded, we were growing and grinding our corn for grits, making hominy, and eating cornbread. We scoured the woods with our female relatives from spring through summer for wild foodstuffs such as dewberries and blackberries, Chickasaw plums, mayhaws, huckleberries, and muscadines. In the fall, we zealously collected wild sunflower tubers (Jerusalem artichokes), persimmons, chinkapins, and hickory nuts from the same woods where my father and uncles regularly visited their fish traps in the creek, ritually hunted the deer at Thanksgiving, burned the fields and forest floor in January, and played ball with an uncommon passion at every opportunity.

My family tree is a tangled maze of limbs and branches of American Indian mixed-bloods marrying American Indian mixed-bloods for as many generations as there have been mixed-bloods among the tribes and nations of the Southeast. People ask, "How much Indian are you?" I doubt that even a mathematician would be able to figure out what percentage of my blood is Indian. The other question people ask is "Which side of your family is Indian?" Both of my parents had ancestors who had been at home in the southwestern reaches of the Tombigbee River Basin long before the remnants of the ancient Nanibia, Tohomé, and Mobilian peoples who lived in the area during first contact with Europeans were absorbed into the loosely woven Choctaw confederation and became Choctaw. We were not enrolled in a tribe, nor were we members of a political entity. We suspected the government—the same government that had bedeviled our ancestors—of vile motives and avoided contact with its agencies whenever possible. For a time, blessed by the isolation of the pine forest, we were who we were, perfectly content just to be. But all too soon the isolation evaporated, and we encountered a world that demanded, in less than subtle ways, that we abandon all knowledge of our native heritage, including our traditional moral standards—basic ideas of right and wrong—and embrace materialism, the god of the white world. These pressures, which had been at work for generations, grew more intense during my childhood.

Why? Did unconscious-collective guilt over the horrendous crimes committed against American Indians by the dominant white society motivate the establishment to deny American Indian mixed-bloods their identity? By denying that a mixed-blood culture and society existed did white people distance themselves from the sins of their own ancestors? Did they unconsciously, or consciously, worry that we mixed-bloods had a spiritual lien on their souls as well as their lands? Their forebears had "removed" as many Indians as they possibly could from the lands they coveted and claimed under white laws in the Southeast, but our ancestors fell through the cracks of their laws and stayed on. Other American Indian mixed-bloods had been integrated into the dominant culture of Mississippi, Alabama, and much of the rest of the South. This had been accomplished generations before by people who had decided to "go white," to embrace materialism, to give up native thought and spiritual and moral values, and to reduce their Indian heritage to a connection with a far-distant sanitized Cherokee princess or, more rarely, a mythic Choctaw grandmother ten or twelve times removed.

Displaying souls rancid with racism, members of the white establishment often accused those of us who persisted in claiming our American Indian heritage of being "part black," people just trying "to pass" on the fringes of white society. Explored further, their theory seemed to be that a person who was part black could not be part Indian, that somehow the blackness obliterated the Indianness. In a society that considered anyone "with even a drop of black blood" beyond the pale of racial tolerance, this was the ultimate solution. The establishment acted as if we shared their racist views and would be so traumatized by being declared "part black" that we would give up our identity. Actually, my father's family did have a drop of black blood from seven generations back, courtesy of a French-Indian planter who, as the American Indian agent Benjamin Hawkins in the late 1700s carefully noted, was "mixed with a little African." My paternal grandmother had never hidden the fact and was not in the least bit ashamed of it, so the threats of the ultimate white damnation meant nothing to her. She was the first molder and shaper of my moral code. She taught by example. She lived her beliefs. As far as I could tell our drop of black blood had not dulled our senses, marred our spiritual essence, or made life any less precious. If anything, it had enhanced our feelings of compassion, empathy, and the universality of kinship. In race-obsessed Mississippi at a time when terror stalked the land, my paternal grandmother held my hand; together we looked the demon in the eye and did not blink. We just went on claiming to be who we were.

My paternal great-grandfather, with roots in the Alabama mixed-blood communities of McIntosh and the Tensaw River district, moved to the isolated wild woods near the banks of the Escatawpa River on the Mississippi-Alabama state border in the 1880s. A generation later, his son, my grandfather, journeyed to the mixed-blood community at Mount Vernon, Alabama, to claim a bride. My mother's family relocated from near Fort St. Stephens on the Tombigbee in Washington County, Alabama (a county with several mixed-blood enclaves), to Hattiesburg, Mississippi, in the late 1930s, then shortly thereafter moved again to a farm on the Agricola-Latonia Road along the Escatawpa. Slightly less Indian in their mindset than my paternal relatives, my maternal relatives were infected with a paranoia rooted primarily in miscegenation laws that the state of Alabama had as recently as the late 1920s invoked in Washington County by criminally prosecuting a mixed-blood man and a white woman for marrying. The resulting sensationalized court case convicted the mixed-blood man of being a "negro" on the testimony of two white residents who based their conclusion on the observation that the accused's grandfather had kinky hair and a "somewhat African"-shaped nose. The Alabama Court of Appeals in *Weaver et al. v. the State* upheld the Washington County verdict in a May 15, 1928, decision written by Associate Judge W. H. Samford. In everyday life this case meant that any person claiming to be an American Indian mixed-blood could have his or her identity denied and be declared black (virtually a nonperson in Alabama at that time) on nothing more than the suspicions of a neighbor. Furthermore, such a person could be criminally prosecuted and sentenced to the penitentiary if some member of the white community thought that the person's spouse looked too white.

These threats terrorized some members of the mixed-blood community and for decades left a number of my mother's relatives denying that they were American Indian mixed-bloods. In recent years, several of these relatives have become obsessed with the pursuit of genealogy, and, after several visits with Tom Goldman, a Choctaw mixed-blood lawyer in Meridian, Mississippi, have discovered that the legendary Choctaw chief Pushmataha, who lived near Fort St. Stephens when the Creek War erupted, is a kinsman. Now they have a tentative sense of pride in at least one aspect of their long-denied Indian heritage, but other areas still frighten them. When encountering one of these cousins doing some of her genealogical research at the Lauren Rogers Museum in Laurel, Mississippi, where I worked as a consultant, I said hello and introduced her as a kinswoman to the director with whom I was strolling through the library. She suffered a panic attack, gasped for breath, and denied that we were kin, making a long senseless word ramble about how mistaken I was and saying that maybe she was kin to my husband. I only smiled. Little did she know that my husband, a well-respected college professor whom she had met while he was doing research for an organized Alabama Choctaw mixed-blood group called the MOWA, is also a mixed-blood with roots in the coastal Choctaw mixed-blood community at Kiln, Mississippi.

Along our length of the isolated Agricola-Latonia Road, there was no need to deny who you were; the pine forest, the river, the bogs, the wild creatures had no racial bias. When I was born, my world, my community, my extended family stretched about a mile down that red dirt road, anchored at one end by my paternal grandmother's house and at the other by my maternal grandmother's. Halfway between the grandmothers, my father built my mother and me a shell of a house that offered adequate shelter in the summer but not in the short, wet Mississippi winter. The cold dampness flowed through the cracks, crevices, and thin walls, buffeting me repeatedly with bouts of pneumonia and inner ear infections. My parents bathed me in smoke, scraped deer antlers into boiling pots of water on the wood cookstove (to make a medicinal vapor), rolled dried rue into cigarettes, blew the smoke into my ears, and prayed. When all else failed and enough time had passed for me to become dangerously ill, they took me to the county seat at Lucedale to see the doctor in his office at the back of the drugstore. He always gave me antibiotics and immediately referred me to a specialist in Mobile.

Pneumonia always loomed as a potential death sentence. When I was five, my maternal grandfather died of pneumonia. In the time immediately following his death, I went to stay with my maternal grandmother, Mamaw, just to keep her company. She wrapped me in a cocoon of love and taught me lessons of patience and acceptance. Those days cemented our bond. We sat in the front porch swing each morning, moving gently back and forth, telling each other our dreams from the night before. Before noon we put on our wide-brimmed straw hats and went down to the mailbox. As we walked back to the house, she would read aloud the headlines from the weekly county paper, the editor's front page column, or letters from her sister or from her sons who were away in the military. When a letter came telling her one of the sons had survived a devastating plane crash, we were not surprised: she had the news almost as soon as it had happened, several weeks earlier, from a dream. Family finances offered Mamaw few options after my grandfather's death. She found temporary work as a cook. Then relatives in Mobile introduced her to an elderly widower from California who was looking for a wife. Captivated by her good nature, he proposed, they married, and he took her away to California. I accepted her departure without sadness or a sense of loss; it seemed to be part of the natural course of events, like a change of seasons. She wrote letters regularly telling us of the marvels and wonders of California and of all the appliances and conveniences populating her new life.

No electricity, telephones, radios, running water, indoor plumbing, or televisions compromised our lifestyle on the Agricola-Latonia Road during my early childhood. To outsiders our daily life might not have seemed so different from that of some of our neighbors, but our perceptions were. My mother, not my father, was the head of our nuclear family, as was the custom in matrilineal southeastern American Indian cultures. My father was never a disciplinarian; he hunted, farmed, collected turpentine, hauled pulpwood, or occasionally worked in the shipyards on the coast or the papermills in Mobile. Most important, he indulged his young children with a constant supply of small gifts, in keeping with southeastern American Indian tradition. When he was hauling pulpwood or collecting turpentine and his work took him by a country store, he always brought my younger sister and me a penny's worth of "silver bells" (chocolate kisses) or a peppermint stick. At other times, when his work was confined to the deep woods, he might bring us blue jay feathers found on the ground, a couple of stream-polished pebbles, or sprigs of wildflowers. Later, when for a brief period he worked in Mobile after I had learned to read, he would bring me a newspaper each day. A passive man who avoided assertive situations, shied way from strangers, and respected people via a personal policy of noninterference, he was rejected for military service in World War II after government psychiatrists reported that they did not believe that, in the stress of combat, he would be able to differentiate between friend and foe. With all of his positive native cultural traits, his soul was a battlefield for the ongoing war of identity and the pressures of creeping assimilation.

Our mother ruled our world. She inspired awe. Everyone feared her wrath and worked hard not to incur it as she fulfilled her traditional role in our household. As for material possessions and resources, we shared everything we had with anyone who showed up at our door. This bewildered our nonrelative neighbors more than any other of our actions. In matters spiritual and moral, the ultimate test was personal behavior. You could not claim a philosophy or theology that you did not live. Until just before I started school, our religion was a sort of homespun native spiritualism cloaked by a loosely woven mantle of Methodism useful for christening babies and burying the dead. Then my mother went to a revival meeting, "saw the light," and took us into the folds of the Church of Christ, where all teachings, ceremonies, and rituals added to the practice of Christianity since New Testament times were rejected. For a few years my mother was a true believer, personally refuting only those tenets suggesting that women should be subservient to men. Surely, she rationalized, this was so contrary to natural law that it had to be a mistranslation from the ancient languages. Asceticism became our way of life.

My identity as separate and apart from the dominant culture was reinforced before I was aware it existed. Mysticism claimed me. I was in touch with the spirit world. God dwelt inside my heart. He talked to me without words, and I understood exactly what he meant. And I did not hesitate to share my insights, especially with my father's family at his mother's house. My paternal grandfather had died before I was born, and when I knew my father's mother she lived on a largely self-sufficient farm with a multitude of adult children who had never married and never left home except for the men who served brief stints in the military. There was always a sizable gathering at the mammoth kitchen table on Sundays, and I was ready to enlighten them. My paternal uncles continued the practice of giving a child an earned name, one derived from his or her most prominent attributes. They dubbed me "the preacher"; ever afterwards when they addressed me directly they called me Preacher. Spiritually, the years have not changed me a great deal. From the seeds planted in childhood, my adult philosophy naturally metamorphosed into Taoism. My enduring spirituality and mystic experiences are rooted in solitude and deep meditation now as they were then.

The first great personal trauma entered my world when I started school. In my memory, that is the dividing line between a warm comfortable accepting world and horror.

"Who are you?" Teachers demanded as I entered the first grade at the only public school in a nearby small, rural, white community in 1950.

"What are you?" the adults assisting them mocked.

They hurled their barbed questions with the velocity of exploding bullets. They meant to maim and cripple the spirit if not kill the soul.

"I'm me," I answered with a six-year-old's candor. "I'm a girl." I was not cowered.

Up to this point I had had limited exposure to nonfamily members and to the world beyond our stretch of red dirt road and piney woods. I had the litany of William Weatherford legends and myths to forewarn me, but translating stories into the reality of people's attitudes is a formidable task for a child. The teacher, in a less-than-sophisticated passive-aggressive mode, ignored me in the classroom and left me to learn or not by my own devices. Unwittingly she pushed me into the world of the autodidact. I taught myself to read by memorizing words. Then we moved to Mobile for a few months (my father worked in a paper mill) where we lived in a transient mixed-blood enclave called the Cotton Mill Village and where I attended the last two months of the first grade and five months of the second. The school cafeteria served an institutionalized rendition of hominy at least three days a week. Hominy became my least favorite food. Soon even the smell turned my stomach.

A worse stench, that of the paper mills, sickened my mother and caused her to flee with us back to our red dirt road in Mississippi. I returned to the woods a voracious reader who already had decided to become a writer. (I had fallen in love with the newspaper in Mobile—the *Mobile Register* on weekdays and the *Press Register* on Sundays. I loved everything about it—the big, wide, crinkly sheets, the smell of ink, the carefully spaced and measured columns of words, the comics, the want ads, the photos, the stories, the immediate link with other worlds. There was a children's page on Sundays, a children's editor named "Miss Mary," and individual happy birthday wishes on the comic pages for children who belonged to the paper's Sunshine Club, as I did. I regularly participated in the essay contests—entries were printed on the Sunday children's page—occasionally winning in my age division.) Back in the woods, all the way home on the hour-long bus ride from school each day, I would try to imagine what wondrous stories that day's paper would contain.

The lessons awaiting me at my country school when I returned had little to do with academics. Arbitrarily my third grade teacher placed me in the class's poorest readers group. She knew my uneducated, barely literate father and equated his dominant native cultural traits with a lack of intellect, deciding that his daughter was incapable of learning to read, write, spell, or do arithmetic. She certainly had no intention of wasting her time trying to teach me. I was back on my own course, devouring any book or printed matter that fell into my hands. The worst humiliation was my classmates' refusal to let me join their games at recess. A day seldom passed that I did not run a gauntlet of verbal taunts. "You are nobody. You are nothing. You are trash. You are not good enough for us to spit on," the nice girls and boys said. As the years passed the more sophisticated taunts became "nigger lover" and "communist." I had ideas and ideals that my classmates considered alien. I championed causes that they did not comprehend. I asked questions that enraged teachers. I was an ascetic Christian who viewed the U.S. Constitution as a sacred document. People had strayed from those teachings just as they had strayed from the teachings of Jesus. The answers to all our social ills were available if we would just open our hearts and minds. I had the icon of Red Eagle-William Weatherford in my heart. I knew truths that I could not deny. I wanted to be accepted, but I could not disavow who I was. I had stumbled into a cultural warp and could not extricate myself from the resulting shock syndrome.

When I was in the eighth grade, a new girl came to the school all the way from Kentucky. Since she was an outsider and an unknown quantity, she was not readily accepted; for a while she was almost an outcast like me. Our paths naturally crossed, and she became my first real friend, my best friend—until her handsome blonde brother who had been away at college in Kentucky rejoined the family. With his arrival in the community, a hormonal frenzy seized the older girls at the school. Suddenly my friend was acceptable and highly sought after by a cadre of these girls. As she moved into their circle, she told me that I was the best friend she had ever had but that she could not be seen with me at school or school events anymore; we could, however, go on being friends in secret. Without the encumbrance of my presence, in a year or so she became the most popular girl in the school.

As an act of charity, the Sisters of Saint Vincent de Paul gave my mother a job at their hospital in Mobile. A relative lent her an ancient, decrepit car so that she could drive (thirty miles one way) back and forth each day. She left home early in the morning, long before the school bus came, and returned at night, long after the school day was over, just as my father did. I quit going to school more than two days a week, attending just enough to do the required work so that I would not be declared an official dropout. I simply could not bear the pain. Teachers seldom questioned my absences; when they did, I would remind them of my ongoing inner ear troubles. I did in fact suffer chronic pain and frequent episodes of vertigo. I dared my three younger sisters to tattle to our parents. The solitude of the deep woods was my true friend. I spent my days in the forest alone, thinking, reading, and dreaming. (My sisters had their own school horror experiences and coped with them in different ways. Today, they remember me as the older sister who was always disappearing alone into the woods.)

In the tenth grade, the homeroom teacher asked the twenty-five students in my class, "What do you plan to do with your life? What work will you do? Where are you planning to go to college? What will your major be? We'll start on the far side of the room and each of you will stand up and tell the class your plans. Everybody except Mary Ann. We all know she won't be able to go to college. We wouldn't want to embarrass her. Who knows? Maybe something will come up that she can do." My father worked as a day laborer for her husband, a well-to-do local farmer. One summer I had been hired for three dollars a day to assist her housekeeper in preparing for a party. That was the only worth I would ever have in her eyes. I needed her signature to verify that I was the author of a poem I wished to submit to a national student magazine. She refused to sign the verification, saying that the poem was not good enough and that I did not understand the concept of poetry, adding, "Mary Ann, you are never going to get your poetic license." She smiled smugly, celebrating her own wit. I appealed to the typing teacher, who signed the verification. The poem was mailed off, and the magazine published it as a contest winner (honorable mention), paying me a small fee. The homeroom teacher warned my father that I was behaving disrespectfully at school, that she was not going to tolerate that kind of attitude from someone like me, and that she would recommend that I be expelled. As I began the eleventh grade, I learned that a high school diploma was not necessary to enter college. With the collusion of a new high school principal who was sensitive to my plight, I shuffled courses and fluffed up my record to reflect the necessary credits for college admission, applied for and received a government educational loan, and made my escape.

A separate personal reality had orbited the space of those horror-school years, one in which I retreated into the spirit world, a dimension of thought and being that offered me a refuge, a sanctuary. For the first six years of the school nightmare, this separate personal reality had the support of my paternal grandmother, who taught by example, and of her son, my uncle John Dee, who, through his stories, musings, and kindness, profoundly shaped my perceptions. Then death claimed my grandmother and alcoholism my uncle John Dee.

Who am I?

The only legitimate answers come from the heart, they said.

Early on, Uncle John Dee taught me never to doubt or fear my heart's wisdom. Crippled in a motorcycle accident in the motorized cavalry before World War II, he came home from the army with a modest disability pension, physically unable to pursue a regular job. He made the children of the family his life's work. Beside my grandmother's kitchen fireplace in the winter or out on her front gallery in the summer, he told stories and parables. He entered into endless dialogues with me. As the outside world closed in on us, as poverty squeezed us tighter and tighter, as my parents were enslaved by an economic system they never understood, he indulged me with generous quantities of his time and thought. He taught me never to doubt any information that came straight from my heart and never to reserve thinking just for my head. He passed on details of a Native American legacy which included stories of our Choctaw heritage and a wide sweeping litany of heroic deeds performed by warriors ranging from Sitting Bull and Tecumseh to Pontiac and Geronimo (who, though a prisoner of war at Mount Vernon in my grandmother's childhood, moved about freely in her Choctaw mixed-blood community there and so seemed almost like a kinsman to us). Then there were the epic tales of our beloved William Weatherford. These stories overshadowed all the others.

One summer Uncle John Dee bought my sisters and me a set of encyclopedias for several hundred dollars on an easy-monthly-payment plan that stretched over several years. He said it was important that we expand our knowledge in all directions, but I was deeply dismayed when I looked for an entry on our hero, William Weatherford, and found none. A search for Red Eagle also proved futile. When white people and schoolteachers did speak of William Weatherford or Red Eagle, they called him a mass murderer, the mad genius of the "worst" Indian massacre in American history (the Fort Mims massacre of the Creek War), leader of a bloodthirsty band of Creek Red Sticks who took pleasure in killing white people, a senseless maniacal fanatic, a fiend. How could human hearts and souls speak so much evil of our revered Billy Weatherford? How had these jaundiced views developed? How could someone so good be considered so evil? If people could not see William Weatherford as he was, how could they ever see us in a true light? If they could not recognize good in this man, how could they recognize good in anyone? I plagued Uncle John Dee with my questions. He did not always have answers or advice that I appreciated, especially when he would say, "If you don't like it, you'll have to grow up, get educated and do something about it." Those words and thoughts, the frustration tucked away in deep memory, doubtlessly played a role in propelling me to this time and place.

A deep-seated, unreasoning hatred of William Weatherford has been a continuing legacy within factions of the Euro-American community since the Creek War of 1813–14. Others have tried to whitewash his memory by denying his willing participation in the war; some members of this group claim that William Weatherford was forced to join the Red Stick warriors in their strikes against the Euro-Americans because his family was being held hostage by the Red Sticks. This curious twist of facts has become an ongoing attempt by some highly assimilated mixed-bloods to reconcile the image of a spiritual and cultural icon that they cannot relinquish with the mores of the dominant culture. This misinformation about William Weatherford (which his own Americanized friends originally invented), as well as skewed facts about the roles blacks and native spirituality played in the Creek War, has been included in several regional histories based on secondary and tertiary sources. Careful reading of the primary source material available today offers a clearer view of the man and the war.

Considering my childhood experiences, it is not surprising that I am a revisionist. However, in a profession that usually equates linear thinking with tangible evidence, it may be surprising that I am a mystic and that I am willing to venture into the American Indian world of nonlinear thought to write about the past. Because I entered that world, this story about William Weatherford evolved to include a personal narrative and a chronicle of a mystic journey into the past. Much of the usual type of material on which a writer bases a biography is not available for William Weatherford. He did not read or write, so there are no personal journals, letters, or ledgers. Most of the primary documents that refer to him were written by enemies. However, myriad family stories have been passed on orally (and occasionally written down) for generations. I have had access not only to my own family's versions of the William Weatherford stories but also to those collected from the many descendants and kinsmen of the Alabamas Wind clan in the Wilber Stout Collection of Papers at the University of Southern Mississippi's McCain

Library in Hattiesburg. The late Dr. Stout, a professor of English at USM and kinsman of Weatherford, also included in his papers copies from the Lyman Draper Papers, State Historical Society of Wisconsin (which contain information collected from contemporary Weatherford family members), many works by archaeologists and anthropologists relating to the Creek Indians, and other miscellaneous information.

Can these meager sources balance each other and offer an honest perspective on William Weatherford? Perhaps not in a traditional biography. But in the ascetic, mystic world of American Indian thought, parallel to scientific and technological thought, such a perspective is possible. This personal narrative/chronicle requires that the reader make a journey with me into the spirit world of Native America, a place less nebulous than many imagine, a place where all stories are allegorical. My own journey there began in earnest when I was twelve years old—it was the year when I first heard of Elvis Presley and read of school integration at Little Rock, when I missed four months of school with chronic inner-ear infections, when I twice read the encyclopedia from cover to cover, and when my mother quit going to church. It was the year when my paternal grandmother died and Uncle John Dee gave up the struggle against alcoholism.

Two

The Quest

I am the deer, the big-eyed doe, the spotted fawn, the fugitive from the hounds.

The wind shouts in my ears. The woods blur. My feet find the unseen path. Run is all I know. Run.

Down the hill, away from the sudden noise, the unexpected presence, my heart eases its rapid beat. Cautiously, now I seek the spring, the cool water. Through the brush screen, the pool appears safe. I come slowly to the edge and bend down. Face meets reflection; lips touch water. Lost in the taste of liquid cool, the deer vanishes.

I am separated from what I have been. I am now the straight-haired girl reflected in shallow water.

This is the summer that I am twelve years old, a time when I can still find the place in my mind where I-am-the-deer and not ask whether this is reality. It is the summer of my vision quest, the summer my best friend is a dead Indian whom I met on that quest.

Maybe, if I had told someone, they would have said that

this friend, this dead Indian, was my spirit guide, but I told no one, instinctively knowing that what is sacred cannot be wantonly shared. Few people talked of the vision quests then. But we all knew that in the old days the people did the quests and that in the visions came the knowledge of who they were, of what their life's purpose was, and of which path they were to follow. I had read in books about vision quests; the authors seemed to have the peculiar notion that only boys sought visions, but even so there were never any valid instructions. Uncle John Dee, who remembered more about the old ways than anybody else, said he did not know exactly how the quests were done, and that if there was a formula the only place it would have been written was in a person's heart. So I surmised that the secret of the vision quest would be to listen to my own heart. If I went to the place inside my mind and heart where I-am-the-deer, I would find my vision, my path.

I was sure that my vision would only come in a special place, a place I would know intuitively. I soon found that spot in the woods, near the creek branch, where a small natural mound had a circle of trees crowning its top. I sat on the ground in the middle of the trees—magnolia, poplar, ash, and oak. Pure white sand lay in loose streaks across hard black dirt. The woods smelled of rotting leaves, wild azaleas, and wind on water. Through a low hanging branch of the magnolia, I could see a white smear of Chickasaw plum blossoms. I never doubted. My vision would come. I sat cross-legged in the sand, spread my arms out, turned my face upward toward the sun, and closed my eyes. I saw red and yellow blotches in blackness, then the grey blur of emptiness. My breath was my prayer. Time passed. When I opened my eyes, I saw an Indian's face in the air, suspended between sky and trees. The Indian was William Weatherford—Red Eagle

(Lamochattee). He had been waiting for me. We communicated without sound. Thoughts went straight from his heart to mine. If the thoughts had been words, they might have sounded something like "You are who you are. Your path is the road that beckons. Your way is the way of the people, the way of the heart, the way of the Spirit."

Billy Weatherford followed me from the time and place of our first meeting into all the dimensions of my twelfth summer. He was with me at the spring pool every day of that summer. He knew what I had yet to learn: that my vision had brought responsibility, that I would be required to make a personal journey in search of an ethereal identity which I believed was simply genetic but which was in reality spiritual, that, at the end of the journey, if my path was true, I would know that hope can be reborn from deepest despair, and that, in the rebirth, each of us can choose who and what we will be.

There are no barriers between me and the dream world at the spring. I watch the water seep up, then bubble and spill over its tiny fallen log dam into the pool, trickling out into the thin stream winding to the creek. A twisted poplar, a tulip tree, half knocked over by some long-ago storm, has gone on living by bending itself back into the dark, damp earth and sending its trunk skyward again, forming a bench between its two roots where I often sit to touch the quiet. When the wild azaleas bloomed in the early spring before the trees leafed out, this was a perfect place, nature's garden, a perfect wild garden. My heart aches at the thought. Summer now hides the perfect garden with thick green. Overhead, sunlight squeezes through the breaches in the leafy canopy of trees crowded so closely together that they weave an arcade over the spring and its branch stretching all the way to the creek. Mosquitoes swarm out of the thick tangles of brush and hum, "What's buzzin', cousin?" near my ears. I shake my head and slap them away. Time to move on.

My journey continued into other summers and winters. The path should have been clear, simple, and direct, but life is never that way. My life gained a momentum of its own, separate from my heart, that took me from the path. I became a photographer, a manipulator of light, a magician of chemical processes. With a quick shutter and fast film I endeavored to capture glimmers of spirits behind masks of reality. Sometimes I succeeded. But I was off the path. Long ago in the woods with Billy I had heard the message. The vision still talked to me in poem after poem that I hastily scribbled in journals I labeled collectively *Songs from the Choctaw Heart* and tucked away. The word-poem messages came daily, but I built a wall between myself and the vision. I married a career navy man and became a world traveler. Then the fear came.

Fear stalked my soul. Not just normal fear, but the dark terror that Black Elk, the Lakota medicine man, spoke of when relating his own experience of failing to follow immediately the true path of his vision and perform the vision on earth in some manner so that it would have real power. "If the great fear had not come upon me, as it did, and forced me to do my duty, I might have been less good to the people than someone who had never dreamed at all, even with the memory of so great a vision in me. But the fear came, and had I not obeyed it, I am sure it would have killed me in a little while."

Waking up one day in a house by the sea in Italy, stepping out onto a sunlit balcony, I felt the long stalking terror grab my heart. I was lost. I could not find the path. The fear burned in my throat, crippled my mind. The iron August heat brought lightning to compete with the fireworks igniting the *Ferro Agosto*, the last holiday of summer. My soul wandered in ever-widening circles, seeking the shade of the ancient temple walls of Jove, the tomb of Cicero, the summer palace of Tiberius. The first rains of September washed the dusty bougainvillaea vines trailing over balconies all across town. The gentle rains gave way to bombastic autumn thunderstorms. A damp chill pounded against the glass doors of my front balcony as I watched the lightning dance around a hilltop across the valley. I shivered. The lightning illuminated an ancient monastery bombed into a shell by the Americans in World War II. Townspeople said that German soldiers had taken refuge in the monastery to escape the Americans. The only sanctuary they found was death.

I shivered again as I watched the lightning. I felt and smelled the scratchy, wet wool of the German soldiers' uniforms. "Why are dead Germans calling to me?" I asked the storm. The storm did not answer.

The rain swept eastward, and the morning sun tentatively invited me outside. The question remained: why did the dead Germans call to me? I crossed the valley and climbed the hill. I squeezed through a barbed wire barrier halfway to the top, and picked my way through the briars and thistles that reinforced the barricade. The half-tumbled-down walls and roofless rooms held onto their dignity with mural fragments and fresco remnants. The long-ago monks' chants lingered just beyond hearing, cemented into the crevices and niches. A patch of prickly pear gone wild spread around pieces of tile flooring. Then, around a corner, an alcove of a chapel harbored a pile of bones, topped with human skulls. I had found the dead Germans. The bones were quiet. They had not called me here. Bewildered, I leaned against the nearest wall, searching the emptiness, no thoughts playing out a drama inside my head. I looked upward through a ragged broken arch to the sky. Billy Weatherford was there. He had been waiting for me. I knew that he would lead me back to the path.

Back at the place of the first vision I can find the path, I tell myself. I make the journey slowly, deliberately. Always a student of American Indian culture and history, I hone my knowledge along the way. In the Mississippi piney woods I reclaim a derelict Victorian house in Hattiesburg, work at a newspaper, write travel guides, become an editorial consultant and historian, coauthor a textbook, and accept a commission from the Mississippi Department of Archives and History to write a colonial history of Mississippi from a Native American point of view. I tell myself that I am in the right place and now must wait for the right time; then I will quit stalling and embark on my true journey.

I plant beans and corn and tend my squash. The right time comes upon me unexpectedly. On a late spring morning I pick cutworms off the backs of the spiny squash leaves. A voice begins to sing in the quiet of my mind, "Where are you sleeping, Billy Weatherford?" Who was this talking to me? A spirit? Or was it just a lonesome corner of my mind singing a nonsense song? The great fear still stalked my soul, still sent the terror to visit. I had waited long enough. This was the path opening, beckoning. I had run out of excuses. I must follow.

Answering the urgency of the song spinning in my head, I wash the pollen from my hair, put on my traveling clothes, and study the highway map of Alabama, the eastern half of the old Mississippi Territory where Billy lived. I circle the Little River Weatherford Monument with a ballpoint pen.

Several hours and a maze of highways later, I turn past Billy's half-brother David Tate's family cemetery into a world of dense forest and red dirt roads, rustic country churches and meager strands of electric wires running from skimpy pole to skimpy pole. I turn right when I should have turned left and drive into a dead end at a black man's yard. His dog barks fiercely. I stay in my car as the man in overalls comes to the front gate.

"I am looking for the Weatherford monument," I say.

"You should have gone left back yonder," the man says and points down the road.

"Thank you," I say.

"Don't mention it," he answers. "Lots of people get lost back here."

I wave good bye and turn the car around. Only then does the dog stop barking.

The correct turn leads to a gate in front of a barn and soybean field. To the left and under the trees, two red Catahoula sandstone monuments hide, camouflaged in the shade. Billy Weatherford's bones are sleeping here nestled close beside his mother, Sehoy. This is the place where he has become earth. Through the rectangles of the wire fence, I can see a newly sprouted soybean field stretching out. Death is quiet. Billy Weatherford's dust is at peace here. I sit on the ground and touch my face to the rough stone.

This was where Billy Weatherford camped with the Red Stick warriors in the days before the infamous attack on Fort Mims, in the nights before they plunged headlong into the conflict that would become the Creek War. The mosquitoes find me. Singing near my ears, they bite and sting. I slap at them for a while, but soon surrender the monument to them. Back in my car, windows rolled up, I head out to the main road, the paved highway that passes Davy Tate's graveyard and its neat, straight fence guarding the mown grass and grey tombstones. Billy's half-brother, who went to school in Philadelphia and Scotland and lived and died as a white man, became earth not so very far from where his Indian mother and brother turned to dust.

As I drive along certain Alabama backwoods roads for the first time, déjà vu strikes. Have I visited here at night when I sleep and my spirit travels? In these travels do I cross the time barriers and see into this world when it was Billy's? Am I seeing places from a time before my present life? I stop and study the highway map. After the Red Sticks' stop at Little River, they continued to Fort Mims. There is still some daylight left, so I, too, head there. Fishing camps now surround the site, and there is something of a village with a few stray full-time residents. Inside the dimensions of the old fort, lumps, sinkholes and almost-mounds are circled by paths and occasionally marked off by an archaeological dig. The trees stand close together. The fine white sand creeps into my shoes. The sand here along the Alabama River is never still, but is always creeping, covering, obscuring whatever it can.

I remember from Uncle John Dee's stories that when the Red Stick warriors came to attack their mixed-blood kinsmen who were turning white, who had sought refuge here during the summer of 1813, the sand had drifted against the front gate of the fort and no one had swept it back. The gate was stuck open, and the Red Sticks stormed the fort without even having to hesitate. Did the sand ally with the Red Sticks?

Uncle John Dee said that Billy sat in the woods and cried after the attack, the massacre. Some people said he threw up. (Family and clan stories cover the profane and the mundane.) Both could be normal reactions to a scene of mass murder, a battle out of control. Memories of the massacre hover here; listening closely, I think I can hear faint cries across the distance of time as the leaves tremble. I scoop up a handful of the sand that has drifted and settled trying to bury the past and hide the deeds that break the harmony of the woodland's peace. I open my fingers, and the sand slips through.

I come back to Little River many times seeking spirits and communion. I watch as friends, relatives, and history buffs erect highway markers leading directly to the Catahoula stones and then forge a miniature park out of the woods by the soybean field. I continue watching as Fort Mims, too, is reclaimed by history reenactment troupes and by Baldwin County, Alabama. Where will we build the monuments to the hearts and spirits? I ask the wind. I continue my journeys to historically connected sites, hoping to forge an ethereal spiritual chain that will link me to knowledge of Billy Weatherford's past and the spiritual identity of the people. This is my path.

In the early morning darkness of another day, I head toward the Holy Ground along the Alabama River west of Montgomery. East of Meridian, just a few miles across the Alabama state line, a panther crosses my path. Like an aberration, he darts across the highway illuminated by the car's headlights. Panthers have not officially been seen in this area for years, but state wildlife commission officials in both Alabama and Mississippi avoid saying that they are extinct. Now, I have an omen.

Later in the morning, in the broad daylight, I cross the barrier. Away from the main roads I reach the Holy Ground Battlefield Park, along the Alabama River, a place where the Creeks had prayed that they would be safe from the American army and the Mississippi Militia. We all seek holy ground, a place of peace, a place that will wrap our spirits in wonder. We seek the safety of a space where the door is open and the path across the cosmos beckons. This Holy Ground was a sanctuary, a piece of earth that embodied the sacred, a cathedral framed by water and wind. Here a warrior could become vulnerable, feel close to the Spirit. The ground had been consecrated by the converts to the movement known as the Open Door, the revived way, the new route to the eternal path, news of which had been brought to the Creek country by Tecumseh's Shawnee priests and prophets.

My journey is full of expectations. Here at the Holy Ground ghosts are surely dancing inside the unignited ring of fire that could not hold back the hell-bent Mississippi Militia. The ghostly memory of the arrival of the wild Anglo-Americans and the deadly forces that broke through the invisible holy walls, burst the spiritual barriers, and ripped away the sanctity of the place must be smoldering in the deep leaf mold and creeping vegetation spilling over the ground.

I picnic inside the circle of park roads, and then cross a raised boardwalk through the woods out onto the bluff above the river. Wasps nest in the pavilion at the end of the boardwalk; I leave it to them. I hear only one bird singing. I cannot identify the song. The bluff is thick with trees. Hickory favors the cliff. Chickasaw plums grow in thick clumps up on the highland where apple trees also bloom. The apple trees escaped, or maybe just survived, domestication and cultivation generations ago and now have gone wild. A boat ramp slides into the dammed river, and a beach skirts the water to the east. The beach is closed, but two motorhome campers have staked out a claim in front of the bathhouse. There is an empty dumpster in the concession area of the bathhouse stamped US GOVERNMENT PROPERTY. The campers are setting out plants as their laundry dries on a slack clothesline.

A purple martin house stands ready, waiting for the mosquito-eaters' return. Soon the mosquitoes will find me, even in this pristine springtime. Wild unhampered woods splattered with white blossoms celebrate the season. Dogwoods bloom in the shade of sweetgum trees. Wind on the water blows strong across open space. Trailing from the trees, Spanish moss tickles the wind. The dogwoods say they do not remember. The hickories say they have not been standing that long. The pines laced with trumpet vines say nothing. Were their ancestors witnesses? Did they escape unscarred? Do they have genetic memory? Does the river know? The river flows quietly for now, holding its secrets close. Can places remember? On the highway map the only sentinels are the names of places, Big Swamp and Pintlala creeks and the Holy Ground. Back on Lowndes County Highway 40, I pass plowed red fields, red dust clouds following red tractors, rusted-red tin roofs on abandoned farm homes and buildings. Casual green expanses are united by red; green nature wraps herself in red ribbons. Palmettoes claim wild fields and swamps. Pecan orchards march in careful, erect columns across the fertile domesticated swamplands. Irrigation pipes roll out over plowed fields. The tiny communities of White Hall and St. Clair cling to the side of the road leading into Lowndesboro. Rich, opulent, antebellum mansions form a processional causeway into the town. The mansions speak volumes. They talk in Doric columns and cypress floors, filibustering with architecture and landscape, saying how quickly the town came into being after the Creek War, shouting—even now—how the rich land had just been waiting for the cotton planters, bankers, and real estate agents, how such largess had been wasted on the Indians, how the Indians had stood in the way of progress. The shouting continues all the way to Montgomery.

Well into the spring, I am still traveling to the place names on the Alabama highway map that correspond to battle and village sites from the Creek War era. Down a red dirt road, a green kudzu-sculpted landscape frames a purple concrete-block house. Riots of color rumble across a roadside garden where two quaintly dressed black women hoe weeds as if they are posing for a folk artist's brush. Always, I am listening for the thoughts of the trees, streams, and rivers to stir in the breeze. The wind touches, then scatters, all of their secrets. Buzzards eat dead armadillos by the road. At Prattville two white boys are picking wild Chickasaw plums from fencerow hedges, and a new, raw housing project is rising in the middle of a cornfield. Wetumpka, by Three Rivers, is the hillside home of wild native cane (bamboo), banana trees, the reddest of red brick, and all the romance of a titillating southern Gothic novel. Nearby, at the junction of the Tallapoosa and Coosa rivers, an even older era lingers just at the outer edges of the imagination, a place where romance, intrigue, and adventure were the stuff of everyday life for generations. Fort Toulouse, now a park, was the site of the home village of the Alabama nation for generations and was the birthplace of many of William Weatherford's ancestors. An outpost was built there by the French in 1717, and then Fort Jackson, where the treaty to end the Creek War was signed almost a hundred years later. Mounds from the Mississippian era have eroded into the rivers, but several still survive, shrouded in vines and dense woodland growth. If there is some tangible point where I can fully commune with the past, it is here.

Enter the park and enter the woods. Entrance fees, collected on the honor system, are tucked into a slotted box at the front gate. Blossoming orange trumpet vines climb trees and twist around any obstruction that falls into their path. Clumps of blackberry briars hold a bountiful crop of unripe berries. Here on the bluffs above the rivers, there is only an occasional wayward pine. Hardwoods have made their stands here—oak, ash, maple, and sweet gum. Moss lightly festoons the branches. Inside the small museum, musketballs and pots clamor for attention. The pots and bowls win out. Dated to the Mississippian era and before, their spiral designs wrap my imagination in a maze of hands shaping and molding damp clay, the smell of ancient fires, and the wistful longing to find a link that will bind people together across time.

On the woodland walks and shaded pathways in the park, cardinals, thrushes, and mockingbirds sing a variation on nature's symphony. A threatened sparrow divebombs my hat, attacking the red scarf across the crown that secures it to my head. What can I be but a threat to the peace and quiet of his home and family? I remove it. Perhaps in the shade of the tall trees I do not really need a hat. An uncommonly pleasant cool breeze blows from the river even though it is late May. The fresh fragrance of the river is reminiscent of magnolias. The forest could all too easily lull me to sleep here, entice me to doze and dream. Would the trees—persimmons, mulberries, hickories, cedars, pecans, sycamore, crepe myrtles and locusts—stand guard?

A reconstructed Fort Toulouse smells of new lumber and baked earth. I follow the path of a winding old road under a canopy of moss-draped trees further into the park. I pass the Fort Jackson site. It was built here by Andrew Jackson during the Creek War. Now willows and daylilies are sprouting around the redoubts. Across the river on the low bank, black cattle and red cattle, sleek and fat and shining in the sun, graze at a bend in the Tallapoosa just before it joins the Coosa to become the Alabama. Farther along the path, a mound rises by a meadow, a high wedge of tangled trees, wild grape vines, undergrowth, thistles, and blooming mallow making an altar where the great green god of the Alabama wilderness accepts the sacrificial remnants of the past.

Back across the brown sedge meadow just outside Fort Jackson an apple tree grows from an ancient, bent-over, snarled root. Is this my relic? I gently touch the leaves and examine the blossoms. Lachlan McGillivray, a Scots trader, planted an apple orchard here after his marriage to Billy's grandmother. Alexander McGillivray, the first overall chief of the loosely woven Creek confederacy, Billy's uncle, tended the orchard. I touch the tangled old root sprawling over the ground it has claimed. I am awed by the sprouts rising within a spiral from a few inches to a foot away. This is a touchstone. I close my eyes and see the children, Billy and his cousins, tumbling across the meadow. The work required by my long-ago vision quest has begun.

Part Two

Red Eagle's Memoirs

Three

Sehoy and the Frenchman

Wars often begin in unexpected places and ways. William Weatherford's war, the war for identity, the war I would inherit, began almost a hundred years before he led the Red Sticks in the Creek uprising of 1813–14. The war began with romance, when Sehoy, his Indian great-grandmother, my great-great-great-great-great-great-great-grandmother, met and married a dashing French officer at a frontier army post. *Grandmothers form the world, hold it together, keep the stars on course.*

The Frenchmen had come up the Alabama River from Mobile to the junction of the Tallaposa and Coosa where the rivers unite to form the Alabama and built their fort in 1717. They had held diplomatic talks with the Alabamas' tribal leaders for years, between hostilities and little wars, seeking permission to build an outpost at the rivers' junction, a place where they could monitor the activities of the British traders entering Indian country over the trails from Charleston in the Carolinas as well as establish a trading post where they could exchange guns, kettles, blankets, cloth, metal tools, glass beads, and trinkets for deerskins and pelts. But the British traders had arrived first, offering the Alabamas, a tribe related to the Choctaws but members of the Creek (Musko- gee) confederation, a chance to obtain guns, powder, balls, tools, and dry goods several years before the Frenchmen es- tablished their post along the Gulf Coast in 1699. Before the British traders had led their packhorses into the Creek towns, the Alabamas had traveled southward to trade with the Spaniards in Florida. Early on, they had developed a taste for European manufactured goods and tools. But persuading the Spanish to trade skins for guns was virtually impossible. Spanish government policy forbade the practice. The British traders' willingness to exchange guns made their business more attractive to the Creeks. With a gun, an Indian hunter could increase his bounty of skins dramatically. But soon the British wanted more than skins. In return for guns the British traders wanted slaves. The British told the Indians that they could easily obtain slaves by raiding their less aggressive and gunless neighbors. The British offered the same deal to all the members of the loose Creek confederacy, as well as to the Chickasaws to the west and north of Creek country. The French offer to trade for skins and pelts might have been pre- ferred if it had come sooner. But before the French arrived an agreement had been struck with the British and an ongoing relationship established.

The fact that the French, led by Jean-Baptiste Le Moyne, Sieur de Bienville, felt justified in declaring war on the Al- abamas in 1704 and offered bounties for Alabama scalps did not help to promote the French cause. Since the French had first come to the coast at the end of the seventeenth century, they had spread out from Mobile preaching a new economic doctrine to the Indians, especially to the members of such basically agrarian societies as the Choctaws and their small neighboring tribes. The French offered to help convert the native economies from self-sufficiency to a dependency on the skin and pelt trade. The appeal to the Indians was that the plan offered immediate relief from the slave catchers— with their own guns they could defend themselves more successfully. The Alabamas and Chickasaws harassed their Choctaw neighbors in particular. Armed with only bows and arrows, the Choctaws could do little to fend off the Chickasaws and Creeks who captured fellow Indians and then sold them to the British as slaves.

Once in British custody, the Indian slaves were marched overland to the Carolinas for shipment to the West Indies, where they were exchanged for black slaves. The black slaves were brought back to the Carolinas. Eventually this policy failed because the Indians did not make good slaves. The British said that the Indians often willed themselves to die rather than live in slavery, or they simply ceased to thrive. The Indian slave trade was discontinued after a few years. But in the meantime the Choctaws, along with small groups of neighbors and allies, agreed to the French economic plan and switched the main emphasis of their economies from farming to hunting.

Though willing to do business with the British, the Alabamas maintained an aloofness from them that often surprised the traders. After the Creeks and the Alabamas had suffered injustices in trading deals with the British and the traders, the colonial government made it clear that they would put forth no effort to police the traders' practices, and the white settlers increased their trespasses and illegal settlements on Indian lands. The Creeks living nearest to the British settlements in the Carolinas retaliated, believing, for a moment, that they could drive the British into the sea.

British traders among the Creeks were executed or driven from the villages during the conflict called the Yamasee War of 1715–16. The war and disenchantment with the British caused the Alabamas to turn to the French and offer them the post they had so long requested on the Alabama at the junction of the Tallapoosa and Coosa. The French called their new outpost at the eastern edge of their vast uncharted Louisiana Postes de Alibamons or Fort Toulouse. Even as they entered into agreement with the French, the Alabamas remained diplomatically and politically aloof, making sure the French understood that the Alabamas would not make exclusive agreements with any Europeans again. In the future the Alabamas would play European interests against each other to benefit their own people and supply their needs for trade goods. For many years afterward, the Alabamas showed their displeasure with the British for the misdeeds that led to the Yamasee War by not allowing them to build a fort or trading post in the Indians' territory despite pleas from the British who could supply more and better goods than the French. The Natchez uprising of 1729 and native perceptions of the French injustices leading to it opened the door for the British traders to return to the Creek country. In less than two decades after the Yamasee War, individual British traders had reestablished businesses in the nation.

Two Alabama villages near the junction where the French built their fort were only a "musket shot away" from the palisade to the east and west, the French reported, while several others were just a short distance away. The villages all followed the same general plan, sprawling out lazily around a town square, a town hothouse (sweat lodge) and a chunky-ball yard, then reaching out into the countryside, family compound by family compound. Four houses made up most of the compounds: a cooking house, a winter lodge, a long rectangular summer house and receiving hall for visitors, and a storage house for provisions, tools, and gear. The buildings were framed in wood, then plastered and roofed with cypress bark shingles. The storage house was usually two stories high, with several compartments for separate storage of food, provisions, and gear on the ground floor, while the top floor was opened on all sides and used as a meeting place for the men of the family and their visitors during hot weather. There was also another house, separate from the compound, a small place only for the women of the family, where they could retreat during their menses to celebrate their blood alliance with the moon or during childbirth. It was a sane and sensible world; men knew their place and women held their families together.

Sehoy, daughter of the Wind clan, lived in this world, in her mother's house. For as long as she could remember, the British traders had been coming to the villages, and the Frenchmen had always been at Mobile. In her lifetime the French and British and their activities always had an effect on the life of the people, but her mother remembered a time when the Frenchmen did not live at Mobile. Her grandmother remembered a time before the British traders came over the path from Charleston, when white men were just the stuff of stories, when many women of the villages had never seen a white man, when the very description of white men and how they lived would have been frightening if the stories had not been so unbelievable. In those times the Alabama men and a few women went to Florida to trade with the Spaniards.

But the twenty Frenchmen who came up the river in 1717 to build a post in Alabama country were so different from the Creek men, and even from the British traders who had visited the villages, that the women and children stared.

Their appearance and behavior was entertaining especially to the young girls and women. Just looking at them was a delight. At the ceremonies welcoming them to the Alabama country the Frenchmen wore costumes of vivid colors: white greatcoats lined in blue, red vests, blue pants and stockings, brass buttons, tricorn hats with black silk cockades. In their full dress uniforms, the officers displayed gleaming gorgets at their throats and swords and sashes at their waists. The sergeant's coat and vest had pewter buttons, while the drummer boy's coat was lined and trimmed with lace. Could not such beautifully dressed men be harmless, even though they had once made war on the Alabamas? They behaved so differently from the Creek men. They took an assertive role in romance, flirting and courting, a role traditionally assigned to women in Alabama culture. The young women laughed, and the older women clucked their tongues and shook their heads, smiling all the while at the Frenchmen's behavior.

The Creek men—hunters, warriors, farmers, and priests—ignored much of what they deemed silly behavior around women on the Frenchmen's part. They saw the Frenchmen's behavior as unmanly. Everyone knew women should make the first move in romantic encounters. Women pursued men. Men remained aloof. The British traders had never acted in quite this way around women, said the Creek men gossiping to each other around the village square. Any real man knew you only had to sit, behave in a dignified manner, and wait; the women would come to you. "Who would ever understand white men?" the sages of the square asked each other.

As the Frenchmen built their fort, the young unmarried Creek women and girls from the nearby villages went to survey the scene. Sehoy and her friends arose early, bathed in the river, and plaited their long hair, anticipating the day when they would be considered grown women and allowed to twist their braids into a silky crown on top of their heads. In toga-like dresses of mulberry bark linen, they darted through the woods to the edge of the clearing. The Frenchmen did not have on their fine uniforms as they worked, sweating and slapping at mosquitoes; they just wore shirts and pants, stockings and shoes, and, instead of the tricorn hats, they tied handkerchiefs around their heads in a turban fashion. Once the Frenchmen knew they were being watched, their swears turned to songs. But soon the Alabama men and boys joined the Frenchmen in erecting the fort, and the entertainment lost some of its exotic appeal.

In the months and years that followed, many of the Frenchmen married Indian women, established mixed-blood families, and stayed on in Alabama country as settlers. The Indians considered them all Alabamas—one people—and a few years later the Indians would declare that anyone born in the Alabama country was a member of their nation, even a child born of two French parents. The first French bride to arrive at the post did not stay long enough to start a family. In 1720 Marie Le Seur, accompanied by a Catholic priest, came up to the fort to marry the commandant, Lieutenant Vitral de La Tour, then left shortly afterwards when her husband was reassigned.

A new commandant, Captain François Marchand de Courselles, assumed command from Lieutenant La Tour, and, in a short period of time, his marriage to Sehoy, daughter of the Wind clan, took place at the fort. Sehoy now had her long braids intertwined with French ribbons and twisted into a crown atop her head. The marriage was a political coup for both the French and the Alabamas, despite the fact that the ceremony, a concoction of Creek and French rituals, lacked the official sanction of the French officials at Mobile.

In the matrilineal Creek culture, the Alabamas believed they had gained a position of immense influence with the French. The French at the fort saw the marriage as an alliance between French interests and the most politically influential clan of the Alabamas. Captain Marchand was *commandant aux Alibamons,* supervisor of the Alabama district with headquarters at Mobile, and detachments from his company manned Fort Toulouse, which meant that he was often away at Mobile. Sehoy continued to live in the sane, sensible world of her mother and grandmother. As if he had been married in a traditional Creek trial union, François Marchand behaved like a respectable Creek husband when he was at the fort. He was little more than an honored guest in Sehoy's home from time to time. But their union differed from a traditional Creek marriage in several ways. (Later this type of unconventional union was called a "make hasty marriage.") Normally a Creek marriage ceremony took place after a representative from the bridegroom—his mother or sister—went to the mother of the woman he wanted to marry, the woman having deliberately gone out of her way to attract his attention and possibly even seduce him. After family consultations among mothers, aunts, and uncles, the girl's family decided if they should receive gifts from the young man. The more gifts he sent, the better provider he would be, and the better provider he was, the more desirable the match. Once the gifts were accepted, the village was invited to a day of feasting during which a tribal elder formally introduced the bride to the groom's family. But the introduction ceremony and the feast were just the beginning of a possible marriage. Now the bridegroom had to plant a crop, harvest it, and make a successful hunt to prove that he was able to feed a family. During this trial period, the bride could leave the groom, and there was no marriage. She was bound only after the crop was in and a successful hunt had been made. These rules loosely interpreted made it possible for many white traders and soldiers in Indian country to have temporary marriages to Indian women that were not too far outside the traditional norm. White men intent on adultery flirted with the sharp knives of Indian justice. Both guilty parties were punished by having their ears cropped. However, if adulterers could escape punishment until the yearly Green Corn Festival (Boskita), they could claim amnesty. Divorce was a matter of mutual consent, with the woman keeping her property (the home and fields) and the children. A divorced man could remarry immediately, but a woman could not remarry for four years—measured from the Boskita—unless her husband's clan released her from her obligation.

Though Frenchmen traveling to, or stationed at, frontier posts behaved with autonomy when it came to personal matters, the colonial officials at Mobile disagreed over the policy of allowing Frenchmen to marry native women. Many of the soldiers and settlers were French-Canadian, and they preferred Indian wives to the brides imported to the colony from France. Bienville, governor of the Louisiana colony in the early years, disapproved of Indian/French marriages because the white men became Indian, due in part to the Indian matrilineal social structure, and became engaged in the Indian way of life rather than establishing European-style families. Often Frenchmen disappeared into the Indian nations rather than strengthening the colony. At least one priest at Mobile, Father Henry Roulleaux de La Vente, addressed racial concerns, noting that the Indian bloodlines could not "harm" those of the French and that the offspring of such unions appeared more French than exotic. After all the debates, in 1728 an order from Louis XV forbade the marriage of native women and Frenchmen, but it was not effective. The colonial government took the position that the Frenchmen's Indian wives were just their mistresses; however, the unions were valid marriages from the Indians' point of view.

Later, a few years after the birth of a daughter called Sehoy Marchand, Sehoy of the Wind clan was no longer considered to be married to Captain Marchand. In due time she took a Creek husband, and they had a male child who, as a grown man, gained the position of Red Shoe, or war chief, among the Alabamas.

So, Sehoy and François unwittingly started the war William Weatherford would have to fight, the war I would inherit, the war of identity, the war of the heart and soul. François and Sehoy's daughter, Sehoy Marchand, became our common matriarch. She grew up a child of the Wind clan in the house of her mother and her grandmother. Her early history is hazy. Did she marry an Alabama man and have a daughter also named Sehoy and also called Sehoy Marchand? Or was her first marriage to a British trader, a Scotsman named Malcolm McPherson, and did she have a daughter by him known as both Sehoy Marchand and Sehoy McPherson? Or did she adopt a Creek girl named Sehoy? Different members of the extended family of the Wind clan choose one of these three scenarios for William Weatherford's genealogy. The first is the most popular. It is undisputed that, in three succeeding generations of the same family, there were three Sehoy Marchands.

In time, as French trade goods became scarce and the French became preoccupied with their wars with the Chickasaws, British traders were once again allowed to do business in the Alabamas' country. In the early 1740s Sehoy Marchand II married the Scotsman Lachlan McGillivray, a British trader, when her daughter Sehoy III was a very small child. Lachlan McGillivray had made his first trading mission into the Upper Creek country with a fellow highlander named Malcolm McPherson, who was already a veteran trader. The trading company that employed both men was owned by Archibald McGillivray, a kinsman of Lachlan's who had been exiled from Scotland after the Rising of 1715. Archibald held a trading license from the legislature of South Carolina until 1744 when he returned to Scotland. His relinquished license was issued to Lachlan in that same year.

Lachlan, born at Dunmaglass, Invernesshire, in the Nairn River Valley, left the highlands of Scotland in 1736 as a tall, freckled, red-haired, sixteen-year-old boy. Recruited by an agent of James Oglethorpe's Georgia Company, he came with a group of 163 young men from the same highland clan (the Chatten clan of which the McGillivrays were a sept) with dreams of making a new home for the clan in America. His grandfather Farquhar, chief of the McGillivrays, had been a Stuart loyalist. During the uprising in support of James Stuart in 1715, his father and uncle joined the Jacobites' doomed struggle. In the aftermath more than a dozen McGillivrays were exiled to South Carolina. Though Lachlan's father, William, escaped expulsion and returned to Dunmaglass where his older brother gave him and his heirs the Dunmaglass estate, Lachlan's future did not look promising. Poor farming practices made the seventeen-thousand-acre estate unprofitable, and the British barred Jacobites from government service, one of the few areas of employment. Even though Lachlan was well educated, experienced in estate management, and the son of a landowner, he did not have the price of the fare to America. He borrowed the money from a kinsman and agreed that after he arrived in

Georgia he would work for another of his kinsman (John Mackintosh) who was making the same journey until the debt for his fare could be repaid.

Migrating with a group of young Scotsmen, the kinsmen helped establish the settlement called Darien on the Altamaha River where Creek Indians often visited. Lachlan and the other Scotsmen soon found that they had much in common with the natives. Though the Scots had patriarchal clans and the natives had matrilineal clans, the significance of clan membership and clan loyalty was very similar. Travelers to Indian country often noted in their correspondence that the living style and even dwellings of the Indians and the remote highland clans were very much the same. The emphasis in each culture on warriors, athletic games, costumes, and the importance of sacred items such as eagle feathers seemed overwhelming. The ethereal mysticism of the Indians presented no obstacle to the Scotsmen. Lachlan soon learned the Creek language and became more and more intrigued with the Creek way of life. In 1741, Lachlan left Darien, established himself in Charleston as a Creek interpreter and was often employed by official government missions. He had already made several journeys with his kinsmen into Creek territory as a trader. Each major Creek town boasted a British trader with an Indian wife and established residence. In 1736, John Tanner reported to the trustees of the Georgia Company that all the traders in Creek country had Indian wives and had fathered "more than 400" children. So when Lachlan moved into the Alabama country, married Sehoy II and established a home there, he was just one of many traders who became the progenitors of the mixed-bloods called by some the "Scots-Indians."

Lachlan prospered in the Indian trade. He built Sehoy II and their children, Sehoy III, Alexander, Sophia, and

Jeanette, a comfortable home, and planted apple orchards. Unlike many of the other traders, he had only one wife. An Indian family did not concern itself with the step-divisions Europeans designate. Lachlan saw the family as a unit and considered Sehoy III his child. He lived in the Alabamas' country for a dozen years, making several trips to Georgia and Charleston each year. Eventually he built a large house at his plantation near Augusta, and his children came to visit him and live with him there. Sehoy II preferred her home near the junction of the Tallapoosa and Coosa rivers to the mansion in Georgia and maintained her household there. The girls received a rudimentary education, being taught to read and write, while tutors were hired for Alexander in Georgia; after a while he went off to school in Charleston, then worked for an import/export firm in Savannah where his father had reinvested some of his profits in another large plantation. Sehoy III married a trader named MacFarland and went to live in the Alabamas' country. Sophia married Benjamin Durant, a French-Indian mixed-blood planter, a man of legendary strength, and for a while the couple managed Lachlan's Georgia plantations, before deciding to establish their own farm near Sophia's sister and mother. Eventually all the children, with generous gifts from Lachlan, returned to the country of their mother to establish their own homes. It was there that the youngest girl, Jeanette, would marry the Frenchman Louis Le Clerc de Milford, and Sehoy III would divorce and remarry twice. Her second husband was a British army officer named, in family memory, Tate (David Taitt in British records) with whom she had a son, David (Davy). Her third husband was the Scots trader Charles Weatherford, the father of William, Jack, Roseanna, and Elizabeth Weatherford.

Sehoy and François Marchand's grandchildren's influence in the Creek nation would spread across generations. They shaped the world into which my vision has required me to travel, the thick, damp, green world where we can hear the grandmothers of a hundred generations crooning their lulla- bies and dispensing their wisdom.

Four

Birth

Come with me. I will hold your hand as we walk inside my grandmothers' dreams, seeing the shadows of the future where we have been and the shadows of the past where they dwell, touching the reality of their songs, tasting the salt of their tears, waiting for Billy Weatherford to be born.

With each child's birth, hope is reborn. The universe becomes a world waiting to be explored. Long-established facts wait to be rediscovered. At birth, genetic memory, the soul of biology, is a sluggish dream, a dream that foreshadows the slow awakening of a newly configured spirit, the vague yearning that comes without bidding for a way of life, a method of living, a certain path. Biology shapes our dreams and suggests our paths. We are part of all that has been and all that will be. We cannot deny our biology or the universal hope that accompanies our birth.

William Weatherford was born in his mother's house to membership in his grandmother's Wind clan of the Alabama tribe. The exact date of his birth is unknown. Most family members believe that it was around 1775, more than a dozen

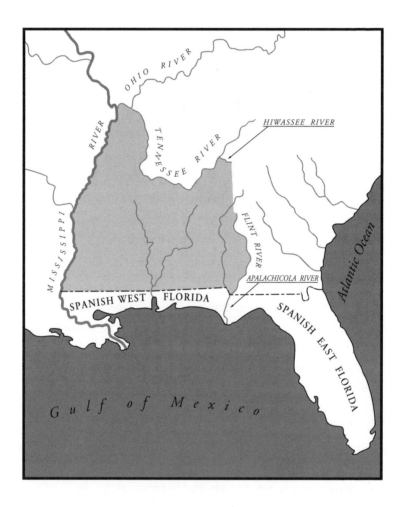

The shaded area represents land claimed by both the U.S. and Spain after the American Revolution. From the Mississippi Department of Archives and History.

years after the French had ceded claim to Louisiana east of the Mississippi River (an area that included the Alabama lands) to the British at the end of the French and Indian War. It was a time of growing political unrest in the British colonies in America. The ownership of this region would be the subject of a dispute between the United States and Spain after the American Revolution. The land north of the 31st parallel became the Mississippi Territory in 1798. Spanish West Florida lay south of the parallel.

Sehoy III's husband, Charles Weatherford, was a prosperous Scots trader who had established a trading post on a bluff above the Alabama River just below the confluence of the Coosa and Tallapoosa. The location, about three miles from the main Alabama village and the site of the old Fort Toulouse, contained several ancient mounds and the rambling collection of buildings that made up an Indian village. Contemporary colonial maps show the place marked as "Charles Weatherford's" and the main Alabama village as the "Hickory Ground." The Alabamas lived along the Alabama River from the junction of the Coosa and Tallapoosa, where their major population centers were located, to where the Alabama joined the Tombigbee to form the Mobile River, and from there to the southeast lowlands of the Tensaw (Tensas) Basin, which drained into Mobile Bay. William Weatherford's father, who often served as an interpreter and informant for the fledgling United States government, had no claim on him, just as his grandmother's French father had no claim on her. Heritage was matrilineal, and, though several generations of contact with Europeans and Euro-Americans had altered some customs and traditions, the line of descent was undisturbed. William was called Billy, a popular name among the Creeks, and his father's family name was about the only noticeable concession to European customs the

Wind clan made. A father's main duties in Creek society were to be generous with love, compassion, and material goods and to provide a constant supply of small gifts for his children. The red-haired Scotsman Charles Weatherford met those criteria.

The day he was born, Billy's grandmother, Sehoy II, dreamed. Wind clan members have passed down the memory of her dream as a mystic legacy. "Someone in the future, someone far in the future, is connected to this child. Their spirits are even now joined," she said.

I trembled as I read the vision legacy in Dr. Stout's collection of clan stories at the McCain Library for the first time. My family did not possess this story. A jolt of psychic energy riveted me to the dream. I was the one about whom she had dreamed.

A whiff of smoke from hickory cooking fires teased the air. Grandmother Sehoy emerged from the graduate library's stacks, moved out into the Mississippi Room, approached my table. Her shadow touched my arm.

"You have come," she said in the classic Creek greeting, the Alabama hello.

"I have come," I replied.

She lingered a moment beside my chair. "You have come," she whispered again before disappearing into the transparent bookdust.

Graduate students and researchers sat at their respective tables turning yellowing pages, lost in their own worlds, unaware of my visitor. Restlessness seized me. I was unable to continue shuffling papers. The librarian had placed his prized amaryllis on the window ledge near the card catalog. I was magnetically drawn to the red blossoms, which were framed by sealed windows revealing a concrete parking lot beyond the glass. I wanted to shout. The fortress of the documented past had been breached.

With the memory of Sehoy's shadow as my companion, I reached back to the place where Billy Weatherford began to hear the long chain of stories that linked the Alabamas to their past. The Alabamas had always integrated other peoples, other nations, other traditions, and other myths into their culture. Their stories of how the world began, where people first emerged, and how they migrated to the Alabama River and divided into clans contained elements of stories from the Natchez, Choctaws, and Cherokees as well as stories from the other tribes of the Creek confederacy. Uncles, aunts, and grandmothers repeated to the children of the family the stories that they had heard in their own childhoods.

A story they told from a mixture of Creek and Cherokee tradition tells how the earth came to be and how fire was first obtained. Before human beings, there was only an upper and lower world. The birds, insects, and animals who lived in the upper world decided that they needed more space. Some of them began to look for a place where they would be less crowded. Crayfish went out to explore the lower world, which was all water—an endless sea. Diving beneath the water, he finally reached the bottom. There he found soft mud. With the mud he began to build a mound which grew and grew until it became the island of Earth—the middle world. After the mud that was the Earth island dried out, the animals moved to the middle world. The Earth was in darkness, so the Sun was brought from the upper world each day to provide light.

But the Sun went home each night, leaving the nights cold and dark. So the animals asked their kinsmen in the upper world to help them. The kinsmen sent a flash of lightning which ignited a fire in a tree on another island that had risen in the great sea. Many animals swam out to the island to try and capture the fire and bring it back to the animals on

Earth. Raven, Screech Owl, and Hoot Owl all failed in their attempts and had their feathers blackened and singed by the fire. Black Snake also failed and was marked by the fire. Water Spider listened carefully to all the stories of the returning animals. She considered how their efforts had failed, then wove a basket and placed it on her back. She swam out to the island, placed glowing embers of the fire in the basket, and swam back to her friends on Earth.

Choctaw stories mixed with Creek legends tell of the coming of people. The people emerged from the Earth at the Nanih Waiya mound of the Choctaws. As soon as they had dried in the Sun, each one went off to the place where he or she would live. Only the Hitchittees of the Upper Creeks said they did not emerge from the Earth. They fell from the sky to Earth. They came from the stars. After the people arrived, Frog came to tell the people of a coming flood. A man and woman listened to Frog's warnings and got inside a hollow reed in which they floated on the flood waters until the flood was over. Then they emerged and repopulated the Earth. After the coming of human beings, the universe was divided into an upper world and a lower world representing opposites. A balance between these opposites had to be achieved in the middle world of Earth. Harmony and balance between the opposing forces had to be accomplished on Earth. This became the responsibility of the people.

Billy's family, the Wind clan of the Alabamas, was fond of the story of how the clans got their names. To the east, on the endless sea, the people and some of their animal friends drifted out on a raft and became lost in a fog. The thick fog obscured the shore for so long that when the raft touched land the people did not know where they were. They wandered in the fog across the land until a wind came and blew it slowly to the east. The first people to emerge from the fog became the Wind clan. The other people lost in the fog had held hands with the animals nearest them so they would not lose each other. As the wind continued to blow, the animal whose hand the people were holding when they emerged from the fog became the name of their clan: Bear, Crayfish, Panther, Raccoon, Squirrel, Bird, Fox. The children of the Wind clan of the Alabamas heard this story many times. The story gave an unpretentious explanation of how their clan became the first clan of the tribe. The notion of aristocracy did not exist, though as a sign of the great respect the people had for the Wind clan all adult women of the clan were addressed as "grandmother." Though they were the only clan that did not take an animal as totem, the skunk, an honorable animal whose virtues are often misunderstood, became associated with the clan.

The little people of the Choctaw—*Kwanoka'sha*—populated the secret places of the woods and dozens of the Alabamas' stories. Kwanoka'sha had been known to steal sickly children and test their spirits; those found worthy were cured, then trained to be herbal doctors and returned to their families. But such children did not use their knowledge until they were adults and always kept their training secret.

The children heard Cherokee stories of the immortals who disregarded natural laws. There was *Hanuwa*, the Great Hawk, and *Uktena*, the Great Serpent. Hanuwa built nests on heights near villages where they preyed on children, scooping them from the ground and carrying them back to the nests to feed their young. Once when a child was carried off to the Hanuwa's nest, the child's grandmother waited until the Hanuwa parents were away, then climbed the tree and rescued the child. She threw the young birds into the river where the Great Serpent, Uktena, lived. The snake ate the young birds. When the parent birds returned, they attacked the serpent, dragging it from the water and taking turns holding it aloft and slashing it into pieces. Having lost their children, the Hanuwa returned to the upper world. Among the Uktena's bones the people found a magic stone—a healing crystal. The crystal could foresee the future and cure diseases. It was surrounded with mystery. The shamans claimed that the crystal would lose its power if non-Indians learned of its location. According to some stories, the crystal had to be fed fresh blood every seventh day or it became an avenging spirit, searching in the night for the medicine man who had neglected to feed it.

Around the smokey evening fires, Billy listened to his aunts tell of how, in the very early days of human beings, animals and plants had the power of speech. Then people began to be deceitful; becoming victims of their greed and violence, animals and plants refused to talk anymore, and tried to distance themselves from humans. The animals and plants have maintained that distance to this day, though occasionally a person of pure spirit and exceptional insight is allowed to communicate through dreaming.

Hidden in the stories were the roots of Alabama philosophy, stretching back tens of thousands of years, perhaps even reaching back across a Bering Strait land bridge into Asia. A Native American philosophy parallel to the Eastern philosophy of Taoism permeated the spiritual life of the Alabamas, Creeks, and other southeastern Indians. Instinctually they followed the Way, the Path. All the mysteries of their religion and spiritualism reside in the unspeakable knowledge of the Path. The children of the Alabamas incorporated the tangibles of nature and the intangibles of spirit and saw them in the same light. One did not exist without the other. Ideally there was balance and harmony among all things, all beings. Chaos resulted when nature became unbalanced and relationships were not harmonious. Nature—the Master of Breath—the Great Spirit—God—the Universal One—meant for Earth to be a place of harmony among people, animals, plants, and every element of life and atmosphere. As the Alabama children grew older and became more sophisticated, they embraced the idea that all of life is sacred. There was no real need for religious rituals, because every act was sacred if pursued with a pure heart. The sacred could seldom be separated from the profane. All life, all elements, all of nature deserved respect.

There had to be mutual respect between men and animals. Men had to hunt and kill animals to survive. In the harmonious world, animals accepted their death if their sacrifice was acknowledged. Hunters who had slain an animal would ask forgiveness of the animal. "My family is hungry. I regret taking your life, but I must feed them," he would say, then whisper, "Thank you, brother." Stories of the hunter and the hunted stressed the bond between the two. Success was not due to the skill of the hunter but to the spirit of the animal who granted the hunter the ability to find the animal and gave permission for the kill. If a hunter failed to express gratitude and show respect to the slain animal, the animal's spirit would send sickness and death to the hunter or his family. The stories said that long ago the animals had made a pact with human beings, saying, "Our bodies will nourish you, and our souls will not die, but will return to the upper world where they will rest before being reborn and returning to Earth to give you our flesh again." Hunters needed to search their own souls and cleanse their spirits before the hunt.

Planting food crops and gathering wild food plants were no less noble or sacred pursuits. The mulberry was the ancient sacred tree of the Alabamas and the Natchez. From the bark they wove a linen-like cloth; the fruit was used for food and dye. Sometimes the Alabamas were called the Mulberry People. But the most sacred plant of the southeastern Indians was corn. Choctaw myths tell of the first corn seed being brought to the people by a crow after a great flood. Myths from some of the other Creek tribes offer several different versions of how a mysterious Corn Maiden brought the grain to the people. The Choctaw and Alabama celebrations of the Green Corn Festival (Boskita) were very similar.

When Billy Weatherford was a young child, the Green Corn Festival marked the beginning of a new year for the Creeks and was the most joyous occasion of the year for the children and adults. Billy, his mother, grandmother, and aunts traveled the short distance from their homes, villages, and outlying farms to their clan house in the main Alabama village for the annual celebration. His grandmother's brother, the Old Red Shoe, lived in the village with his wife's clan. All the relatives and tribal members who did not live in the main village came to their family homes and clan houses for the reunion.

Men and women lived in parallel intellectual and spiritual worlds. Their activities at the festival reflected this. The Boskita called for the men to purify the town and public buildings as the women with the young children met and visited with their relatives and friends and cleaned and purified the clan houses. Old pottery, utensils, and broken household furnishings were thrown out. The men performed a complex set of ritual duties. Reunions, dramas, story telling, dancing, singing, celebrating, and feasting would all be enjoyed in their proper place and time at the festival. As a young child, Billy joined the other youngsters peeking through the fence into the main square ground to catch a glimpse of the men's ceremonies. During the three-to-eight-day ceremony, debts and quarrels had to be settled. The men had to purge their bodies, purify themselves for the new fire and give thanks for the new corn crop. They were responsible for achieving purification for the entire group. Those who had achieved honor for the group would be recognized, and those who had brought shame would be forgiven. In the world of the Alabamas, each person was responsible for his own ethical behavior. The great majority of people behaved honorably and adhered to a code that valued generosity and compassion above all other virtues.

All males past puberty went to the Boskita ground. Those absent from the yearly celebration faced a fine which had to be paid in animal skins. Each man had specific duties. Younger men cleared the square ground, sweeping it clean and surrounding its four buildings with a fence with openings at the four cardinal corners. The buildings were open on the side fronting the square and contained tiers of wide benches forming galleries for viewing events taking place on the square. Likenesses of rattlesnakes twisted up the posts at the open front of the council house, and a partition sealed off the rear of the building, which contained a sacred space— a shrine—with three evenly spaced arched openings. To enter or exit the small openings, a grown man had to crawl on his hands and knees. The other three buildings around the main square were constructed in much the same manner, except that they had no partitioned sacred space. All the buildings on the main square were reserved for public functions. The frame buildings had walls filled with clay mortar and were plastered; they were much like the regular houses of the people except that the front was open. A two-foot gap between the walls and the roof allowed for extra ventilation in many buildings. The tiered seats in each building, covered with woven cane mats, were broad enough to sleep on. Each year at the Boskita new coverings were laid over the old to make a thick padding. The center section in the east house was reserved for beloved men and called the beloved seat. (Beloved was a title of respect for older men and women who had led exemplary lives.) A pictograph of an animal on each section signified the clan to which it belonged. On the rafters under the roofs, trophies were displayed—eagle's feathers, swan wings, wooden knives, war clubs, and baskets containing herbs. Paintings and hieroglyph-like drawings covered the walls. These pictographs told stories of men and animals and depicted myths that the children had heard their uncles tell. The main avenues of the village ran out from the four cardinal corners of the square.

Near the northwest corner of the main square stood a hothouse. At the southwest corner was the large circular yard where the game of chunky required the control and rolling of a stone with a stick, a battle to be carried out between opposing players. A tall pole at the chunky yard was used for the striking-the-post ritual and was also a popular spot for dances. Built on a circular base, the hothouse differed in shape from the other buildings of the village. The walls were plastered with clay, and, inside, a broad circular seat made of canes was attached to the wall around the building. A fire was made in the center, and there was no ventilation. In the winter the hothouse was a snug, smokey retreat. At other times it was used as a sweat lodge. Each home in the village was erected on a plan similar to that of the main square with its four rectangular, plastered frame buildings of equal size, roofed with cypress bark shingles, forming a square around a courtyard with exits at the four cardinal corners.

The square area with buildings encompassed about a half acre and crowned the most elevated spot in the town. From the square, youths were sent to the four directions to gather logs for the new fire at the Boskita. They also gathered herbs for emetics—each herb had to be taken from the east side of a tree or bush. Men stayed at the square ground until the ceremony was over. At the appropriate times women and children brought them food and messages.

The older men prepared the shed-like public houses around the square for the ceremony by cleaning, repairing, painting, and decorating the tiered galleries, then installing new woven cane mats on the benches. The men would sit and sleep in the shelters for the duration of the festival. Creek class organization was built on merit, not inheritance. By noting where a man sat and looking at his paint, tattoos, and feathers, one could tell his rank and history.

Little Billy Weatherford and the other boys peeking through the fences paid little attention to the abstractions. They saw the ceremony and ritual, an entertaining drama in which one day they would play a part. For the first two days of Boskita, men on the square ground fasted, but the women and young children in the town did not. The first day of the Boskita was Peace Day, a time when all debts were settled and quarrels ended. All fires in the town were extinguished. Any matter that was not settled had to be forgotten so that the new year with its new fire could start clean. Oaths sworn to the Sun and Sky, since they could see everything, insured that witnesses did not stretch the truth when tribal officials judged any disputed case between tribal members. To prepare themselves to judge, the officials not only fasted but also took a ten-herb-brew emetic. When not settling disputes, the same officials lectured the assembly on moral and ethical matters. There was much time for personal reflection.

The second day of the ceremony was the Day of Purification. On this day, the new fire was made with a wooden drill by a priest, known as the firemaker, who dressed in white buckskin. The four logs gathered from the cardinal directions were laid for the new fire, each pointing in the direction from which it had come. When the fire became strong, youths lighted torches and ran to the corners of the square, where women representing each clan house waited with torches of their own. When their torches were ablaze, the women ran to their houses to light the household fires for the new year.

The black drink made from leaves and tender shoots of the yaupon, a variety of holly, was brewed and drunk for personal purification. The leaves and shoots were pounded on a ceremonial stone, parched in a pot, mixed with water from a running stream, and cooked on the fire by a priest. The priest chosen to make the drink was required to have visions that gave him the ability to put "power" into the brew. Before removing the black drink from the fire, he breathed into it through a tube, repeating an ancient thanksgiving incantation in a language the Alabamas no longer understood. Youths took pots of the black drink as the brew came off the fire, and served them to the men around the square ground, first to the chiefs, then to the others in order of their rank. After each man had received a conch shell of liquid, an official gave the Boskita cry "*Yahola.*" After the cry, the men drank. They repeated the drinking ceremony at least three times throughout the day. Black drink consumed in such quantities caused nausea and vomiting, which proved to the men that they were purified.

By the third day, the purification and peace of the town were strong enough so that the bounty of corn could be celebrated. This day was for feasting. Corn was prepared in stews, soups, breads, and all the classical Creek dishes, especially *sofke,* a type of hominy, which the Indians called a "heavenly" food. The young children's favorite was "roasting ears"—whole ears of sweet corn roasted over the fire in their husks. The women cooked the food and brought the first cooked corn of the new harvest to the men on the square. The men's two-day fast for the purification of the town resulted in eager appetites. The women and young children, who had been eating all along, waited until the men had consumed their fill before dining on the new corn.

Now the square ground was no longer off-limits. Women and children joined the men for the yearly ceremonies bestowing new titles and names. Also, the right to wear any decorations or tattoos was awarded to those who had earned them. Young boys were scratched with a garfish spine to release bad spirits in the blood, then lectured on morals by a town or clan leader. At night there were dances by groups of men or women. Usually the evening's festivities ended with the "stomp dance." Men and women joined forces for this dance, forming a line and putting their hands on each other's shoulders. The leader called out a phrase as he stomped around, winding the line into a tight spiral. The dancers followed, laughing and shouting responses to the leader's calls. The winding and unwinding dance was delightfully hypnotic and left the participants in a joyous mood.

In the years when the Boskita lasted more than three days, mock battles, which were really large outdoor dramas, were performed. Ballgames were often played at the Boskita just for fun, in the same spirit as the mock battles. Sometimes men opposed women in these games. Serious ballgames were played against rival towns and were so furious that they were called "little brother of war." A day might be given to "striking the post"—a ceremony in which all adult men and women who desired to do so could strike the post at the edge of the chunky court with a war club and claim the attention of the assembly for the recounting of their personal exploits and adventures. Any adult present could challenge the story—a measure that worked to keep imaginations within the bounds of reality.

To conclude the Boskita, the entire group of men, women, and children "went to water," a common southeastern custom at the end of ceremonies. The group, led by the firemaker, went to a nearby stream. There the priest recited another incantation in words from the language no one could remember. After the words, the people splashed themselves with water, or jumped into the stream and immersed themselves.

Five

Childhood

The grandmothers' web of love spans the ethereal distances between their hearts and mine, the gleaming threads weaving the fabric of my soul. The grandmothers speak in dreams of genetic memory. Their teachings are written in the heart: Love unconditionally. Do good. Be kind. Share everything generously. Be loyal. Stand by your friends no matter what. Be true. Do not commit adultery. Do not wantonly destroy anything. Respect animals, plants, and the land. Do not waste water or food. Be at one with Nature. Be at peace with the universe. Do not separate your mind and body from your soul. Do not antagonize anyone. Maintain your dignity. Stay aloof from quarrelsome behavior. Do not hate; if you do, you will become whom and what you hate. Do not compete in egocentric activities. Be faithful to your pledged word. Remain calm. Promote the common good. Nurture all children as if they were your own.

A thick insulating layer of love surrounded young Billy Weatherford. Excessively cared for and nurtured, he was a spoiled child by European and Euro-American standards of the time, as were all American Indian children of the Southeast. Adults entertained and indulged him. Aunt Sophia, Aunt Jeanette, Grandmother Sehoy, and other older female relatives took great delight in telling him and the other children ghost stories in the evening when the light of the moon waned and the fire on the hearth shrank to embers. Fathers showered their young children with presents and kind words. Maternal uncles and mothers meted out meager amounts of punishment when absolutely necessary. Letters and journals of visitors to Indian country from the eighteenth and nineteenth century report that Indian children concocted mischief at about the same rate as children subjected to harsh discipline and punishment, but that their overall demeanor was one of carefree happiness, a state seldom seen in Euro-American children on the frontier.

Adventures beckoned all the children, Billy included. All of life was to be explored—even those areas normally off-limits—like the mysteries housed in the sacred precinct of the council building on the town's main square. Bold youngsters dared each other to peek inside. Who would be so bold as to enter? A scratching with a gar tooth to release the ill-tempered blood that inspired such a trespass would await a captured intruder. (Most childhood transgressions were punished with ridicule, scratchings being saved for the worst offenses.) But how many children can totally resist the forbidden? The council house was closed on three sides with its front open to the square; the rattlesnake likenesses carved into the front posts warned of the serious nature of business transacted in the house. The partition behind the tiered benches with the three evenly spaced arched openings enticed the children. Behind the partition, a sanctuary dedicated to the most precious talismans of the village held pottery, stones, crystals, calumets, the strands of beads from

which the tribe's history could be read, and the village's standard—a staff festooned with painted feathers called the
eagle's tail. Only the initiated were allowed to crawl beyond
the partition and participate in the rituals that took place
there. Each day people who had business to discuss with the
chiefs and leaders of the village met in the front part of the
building. Conferences with warriors and visitors also took
place there. Children played around the council house on the
main square, lingering far enough out of the way of serious
business so that they did not draw undue attention to themselves, absorbing the methods and means of conducting government and learning the art of oration by listening. On
quiet or slow days, children ventured closer; then, when the
assembly was gone, they staged their own conferences and
hearings. And, when no one was looking, the most daring
slipped down and crawled through the arched openings of
the partition into the forbidden sanctuary.

Once inside, they were overwhelmed by darkness. The
only light came from the three openings. Slowly, as their eyes
adjusted to the darkness, they saw shadows and vague outlines of the talismans before they escaped quickly back into
the light. They could only imagine the rites the priests celebrated there in the dark. The secret of their covert visit could
not be shared with anyone but the brave souls who had accompanied them on the foray.

The children watched with mundane curiosity as the
chiefs, warriors, visitors, and elders—the beloved men and
women—came and went up the avenues to the main square.
Awe was reserved for the town's priest and spiritual leader,
the firemaker. This shaman, or medicine man, knew the secrets of life and death and how to maintain the delicate balance of all things and beings in harmonious coexistence. His
apprentices, wearing white robes and headdresses made from

stuffed owl skins, strolled through the town each day, intoning spiritual chants in a low voice.

In each village, children were called out by an elder early in the morning and went in a group to the river to bathe, even in the coldest weather. Adults were compelled to join the bathing ritual also. Games and chores were opportunities for learning. The tumult and chaos of war was learned in the mimic ball games the children played. Little boys learned to use the bow and arrow early and gained expertise out in the fields, which they were charged with protecting from birds and animals during the daylight hours. The birds and small animals that fell prey to their arrows were added to the community larder. In the evening, men guarded the fields from the deer who relished the sweet potato vines and the bears and raccoons who lusted for the tender green corn.

As a youngster, Billy Weatherford often visited with his Wind clan relatives and family in the villages clustered near the confluence of the Coosa and Tallapoosa. His mother's sisters and her brother, Alexander McGillivray, the leader of the Creek confederacy, all lived nearby and played important roles in his upbringing. In 1787 his father was in a Spanish jail in Pensacola, after which the elder Weatherford was often in conflict with McGillivray, politically and philosophically. The ever-diplomatic McGillivray did eventually try to smooth over much of the squabble, which grew in large part out of a debt the British trading firm of Panton, Leslie and Company, operating out of Pensacola, said Weatherford owed them, a debt he refused to satisfy. McGillivray enjoyed a close relationship with the firm as had his father, Lachlan McGillivray, and often seemed more closely allied with the trading company than any government outside the Creek nation.

The Creeks supported the British in the American Revolution, and wealthy traders and trading companies doing business with the Indians suffered financial losses when the Americans emerged victorious in the struggle. Much of Alexander's and his father's property and wealth were confiscated by the Americans at the end of the war, and the elder McGillivray returned to Scotland, where eventually the British government compensated him for some of his American property losses. Despite personal losses, Alexander attempted to work out fair agreements with the Americans for the treatment of the Creek nation. In 1789 he refused to sign a treaty with the Americans because they were asking concessions of land in Georgia. But the next year he traveled to New York City, was feted with a parade down Wall Street, met with George Washington, who gave him a gift of gold epaulets that had been Lafayette's, was entertained by and given membership in the St. Andrew's Society, and signed the Treaty of New York (1790). It was virtually the same treaty he had turned down the year before, except that the Creeks were allowed to continue their trading with the British company of Panton, Leslie, which had moved to Pensacola, once again Spanish territory as a result of the American Revolution. The Creek nation dealt with the United States government under this treaty. The Creeks saw themselves as a separate and sovereign nation, a position that the Spanish recognized. Much of the trouble that would arise among the United States government, the Creeks, and the white American frontiersmen positioned near the boundaries of Creek country would be over different interpretations of this sovereignty. The Creeks for their part made special efforts to honor all the provisions of the treaty and expected the United States government to act with an even hand. The Creek country fell between boundaries that were being disputed by Spain, the United States, and the state of Georgia.

George Washington and the United States government denied Georgian claims, but on the frontier there was constant tension as white settlers continuously encroached on Indian lands. When Spain and the United States settled the boundary at the 31st parallel in a dispute growing out of the Revolutionary War, the portion of the Creek country from the Chattahoochee westward was included in the new Mississippi Territory. This was the country of the Upper Creeks. The Lower Creeks found themselves in the state of Georgia.

Shortly after Charles Weatherford's sojourn in the Spanish jail, he became a spy for the United States, working as a double agent against the Spaniards. In 1792 he testified before Congress on the political situation in the Creek nation—the encroaching Georgians, relations regarding trade with the British firm of Panton, Leslie operating out of Spanish territory, and the relationship between the Creeks and Spain. Alexander McGillivray practiced high expertise as a diplomat and had a working relationship with the United States after the American Revolution, but he remained independent from loyalties to foreign powers.

Uncle Alexander enjoyed such a high position in the community and nation that he doubtlessly influenced Billy. If he taught the boy only one lesson through example, it was that his duty lay with the well being of his people. Billy often overheard the intriguing gossip of international politics as he was growing up, none of which stopped him from joining his contemporaries in unself-consciously exploring the culture, customs, and natural world of the Alabamas. He did share one passion with his Scots father—a love of horses. Most of the Creek nation was likewise infatuated. Many Alabamas and other Creeks congregated at the racetrack Charles Weatherford built near his trading post. Gambling was a favorite recreation, so much so that Weatherford's racetrack became a landmark in the area. At a very early age, Billy learned to ride. He was still a boy when he began to break horses for his father. The Alabamas broke horses for riding by taking them into the muck of the swamps where the horses could not lift their feet easily or buck as vigorously as they might on dry land. Knowledgeable horsebreeders often commented on the particularly flat feet possessed by the horses bred on Charles Weatherford's farm. The popularity of the horses and the racetrack are still remembered in the Alabama country of the old Mississippi Territory.

Billy's grandmother, Sehoy Marchand McGillivray, watched over him from a distance. She kept vigil as he galloped on his pony across the fields or sat in quietness at the edge of the yard. She pondered the depth of the peace that emanated from his presence. Was there anything to mark as unusual the qualities Billy displayed? Grandmother Sehoy gauged the reactions of people, animals, and the spirits—the elements—to Billy's presence and also Billy's reaction to the world. At an age when his half-brother and cousins had been sent to Savannah and Charleston to learn to read and write, Billy was said by her to have a special spiritual quality. She voiced what was obvious to the community. Billy had entered this middle world of earthly existence without having lost touch with the spirit worlds. This child was a special trust, a real and true human being. He could, in time, with lessons from the priests and beloveds, help maintain the balance and harmony that was needed for the people in their relationships with all the spirits of the upper and lower worlds. Virtue would be his destiny, pure spiritual simplicity his goal. Grandmother Sehoy's brother, the Old Red Shoe, joined in the soulful care of his grandnephew. They nurtured Billy's spirit in the shadow of a half-assimilated, half-acculturated world. His half-brother, his younger brother, and his cousins learned to read and write, so as to be able to deal with the Europeans from their own perspective, but that was not the kind of education his spirit guardians wanted for Billy. His spirit must be kept pure, his soul uncorrupted. He must learn the old ways and continue on the path. Grandmother Sehoy had dreamed of quill pens and ink before his uncle Alexander was born. She gave up Alexander to the tutors of Savannah and Charleston. Dreams must be heeded. Grandmother Sehoy's birth dream for Billy was mystic and not readily decipherable beyond the fact that his spirit was linked irrevocably to someone in the distant future. But the will of the spirit realms seemed obvious. Billy's mother and the clan agreed. His father, who could read and write and was often in correspondence with American and Spanish officials, was not consulted. Billy Weatherford's spirit was pure, and would not be diluted. He would not be taught to read and write. He would not learn in the white man's schools. He eagerly entered into agreement with the family decision.

There were songs to be learned for all the occasions of life, songs that must be sung for the ill to aid the work of the medicines, the making of the medicines, the preparation of herbs, the gathering of the wild plants. There were songs that must be learned for power and to cleanse the soul, songs of joy, songs of sorrow. For every act of life there was a song— some that followed ritual and others that must be composed as the occasion demanded. There was all the lore of the people, the length and depth of the beloveds' knowledge that must be explored, the beads of history to be touched and deciphered. There were days and months to be spent with the firemaker.

Along with several other boys who wished to learn the old ways, Billy followed the firemaker to a thickly wooded area near a branch of the river. As they began the day with solemn words and fasting, the priest instructed them to erect a shelter of green boughs to which they could retreat, where no one would be able to see or hear them. The boys were sent to gather the red willow root (*miko hoyanidja*). Back at the shelter the firemaker taught them how to pound the root into a pulp. Then he put the pulp in a pot of water and simmered it over a fire as he blew air through a hollow reed into the pot and chanted over the concoction. The firemaker presented the brew to each boy in turn and they drank. In the green bough shelter they listened to the priest's words and at intervals again sipped the *miko hoyanidja* until they had vomited and purified their systems and made themselves ready for the serious lessons that would follow. By rote they learned chants, songs, and rituals as well as plant and herb lore that offered cures and solace. After four days they erected a sweat lodge. Fires were made to heat stones, which were then placed inside the lodge, and, as the boys huddled together, the firemaker threw water on the stones. From the steamy heat of the lodge the priest ordered the boys into the cold waters of the creek. After this session they returned to the community to contemplate what they had learned, to practice the chants, to gather the plants and herbs, and to test the medicines. After several months they asked for another lesson and returned with the firemaker to the forest. These lessons continued at intervals over a period of several years and climaxed with a symbolic rebirth. For this graduation ceremony, each of the boys was placed in a shallow grave and given a hollow reed through which he could breathe. He was then covered with a thick layer of soil. On top of this mound, dry leaves were scattered and then ritualistically set ablaze.

When the fire had subsided, the boys had entered the brotherhood of the firemaker and were called forth from their graves. They arose from the Earth and accepted a horned owl's feather to be worn as a badge of honor in their headdresses. Some of the young men eventually became priests themselves; others used the knowledge and experience to enhance their diverse paths, to aid their individual journeys on the road to enlightenment.

Simpler rites of passage marked the division of time from boyhood to young adulthood. Billy, along with all the other boys, was isolated from the community; then they were purified as they fasted, although they were allowed to have the three scoops of corn meal gruel which formed a ceremonial meal each day. At the end of four days, each boy received a new pair of moccasins, and, following this period, the boys were not allowed to eat venison, turkey, fowls, peas, or salt for four months. During this time each boy had to cook his own meals. For one year the four-day fast was repeated at each new moon. At the end of a year the boys burned corncobs, rubbed themselves with the ashes, purged themselves in a sweat lodge, and then plunged into a river, emerging free of boyhood, though they were still not recognized as fullgrown adults and would not be until they had undergone the warrior's initiation. The crux of that initiation was an invitation to join a war party which succeeded in taking an enemy scalp. Returning to their home village, the leaders of the expedition reported on the behavior and demeanor of the young person, and from those actions a war name was given which would be assigned at the next Boskita.

After all of this, there was still the way of the warrior to be learned. In the quiet of his own shelter, Billy Weatherford painted his body black, made zigzags of vermillion lightning bolts up and down his arms and legs, strapped swan wings to his arms, and danced around the fire of his own hearth, preparing for the confrontations and wars that could engulf the soul. The duty of the warrior was to fiercely protect the people and to promote good. Most important, there was the walk on the spirit road, a journey on the path that Billy Weatherford had to make alone until a spirit guide appeared to him. It was a journey that the warrior had to continue all his life.

He grew to young manhood hunting the forests, farming the land, and disappearing into the world of the Indians. He received the name Red Eagle (Lamochattee) at a Boskita. In the games the Alabamas played, Billy gained fame for his speed and skill. Many years afterwards, elderly Creek women would recall him fondly. They spoke of his beauty and vowed that there was no more wistful memory from their youth than the sight of Billy Weatherford-Red Eagle-Lamochattee racing across the fields on horseback with the sun glinting on his reddish hair. They remembered taking breaks from their chores to watch him pass. He easily assumed two names which did not seem inherently in conflict and which did not interfere with his identity. Indians, kinsmen, and white frontiersmen called him both Red Eagle and Billy Weatherford, and he responded to either name. His mother and immediate family called him Billy.

At gatherings on the square, Billy spoke on the moral and ethical issues confronting the people and how they should strive at all times to keep in balance and harmony with nature, with the universe. He became renowned as an orator, pleading the case for the good path so eloquently that he soon earned a title, which was awarded at a Boskita. He became *Hoponika Futsahia*—the Truth Speaker (or Truth

Maker). He spoke English as fluently as he spoke Muskogee, the language of the Creek confederacy, and white men delighted in his oratory as entertainment when they were visiting the Indian town squares and had a chance to hear him speak. His gift to each listener was a reminder of the teachings of the grandmothers.

Six

Uncles and the Would-be Director General

Saturday comes and the graduate library closes, funding cuts at the university having limited the hours of operation, so I move downtown to the Hattiesburg Public Library, which proclaims itself THE LIBRARY. In the steamy stillness of early morning, I sit waiting on the concrete steps of the arched stairs leading to the entrance. At the top of the stairs, two small black girls play a hand-clapping, word-chanting game. Their mother stands nearby leaning against the brick wall. We all wait as best we can. I am searching for the uncles, looking for the documented pieces of their world, the details of their lives so I can reconstruct Billy's. Fill in the blanks. Is my clock fast? My wristwatch wrong? Why isn't the library open? Finally the shade over the door is raised; a clerk on the other side turns the "closed" sign to "open" and unlocks the door. There is no Mississippi Room here, only a Mississippi corner, and that is overcrowded with a table-top model of the new library being constructed a few blocks away, but the librarians are nothing short of miraculous. They borrow books and microfilm for me from all over the country.

(The university's libraries brook no such coddling.) Microfilm is the modern researcher's salvation, making the most private collections in remote locations accessible. The public librarians keep telling me that their facility is not a research library, but they never turn down a request for material and will spend up to a year locating microfilm and books they can borrow for me. Sometimes, when I have long since given up and forgotten about a source that I had desperately wanted to see, after months have passed one day the telephone rings. "We have that book you wanted," they say, or "Your microfilm is in." I am stunned. I have to ask, "What film? What book?" They remind me. In the library they smile at me—an inscrutable smile. We are coconspirators in the war to access knowledge.

Now, I walk down the stacks of heroes and villains, the biographies and memoirs. The lessons of the uncles come in the hunt, stalking the game, following the trail, providing for the family, seeking peace, stabilizing, neutralizing the outside forces so that harmony and balance can be achieved. And I want all of that from a biography, a book with all the words written down, or a government document, or a frame of microfilm of some record long since forgotten in British, French, or Spanish archives. Billy is doubtlessly somewhere suppressing a laugh.

While the firemaker oversaw Billy's education in the spiritual and mystical realm, his uncle Alexander McGillivray, chief of the Creek confederacy, was his mentor for military tactics and diplomatic liaisons. Alexander McGillivray, considered one of the most skilled diplomats on the frontier, was also a successful military tactician and leader. Despite his Scots father's wealth and social standing in the white world, Alexander chose to be an Indian. Lachlan McGillivray had given the family the material wealth valued in the white world and with it the acceptance that only money can buy as it erases racial and cultural barriers. But after living in his father's world and being schooled in Charleston and Savannah, Alexander returned to his mother's home when he was about seventeen years old, at the outbreak of the Revolutionary War. In addition to having studied the classics, Alexander had learned to run a business smoothly and confidently. He took this skill and expertise and in time creatively transposed it to the operation of a government—the largely informal confederacy of the Creek nation.

The confederacy had always been a very loose collection of towns, villages, and remnants of tribes, with an estimated population of "about 20,000" who banded together when their common interests or security were threatened. They called their collective nationality Muskogee, but the British traders dubbed them Creeks, supposedly because of the many small streams in their country. As is often the case in American history, the name by which the people became known was conferred by outsiders. Though many of the towns, villages, and tribal remnants spoke their own languages in individual groups, they adopted Muskogee as the national language of the confederacy. Alexander relied heavily on his sister Sophia Durant to act as an interpreter and translator for him. She accompanied him to council meetings and addressed the gatherings as his "speaker." Chiefs often chose a particularly eloquent person to present their positions before councils, but his sister was more than his speaker; she was his confidant and advisor. The Alabamas said that Sophia had been born beloved—she had always possessed a timeless wisdom.

When Alexander came home to his mother's people, he built himself a log house with dormers at Little Tallassee, also called the Hickory Ground, near Sophia's home, cultivated the apple orchards his father had planted years earlier when he had lived at his trading post in the area, and began to raise cattle across the Coosa from his home. To work his plantation he had brought sixty black slaves from Georgia. His frontier home was charmingly rustic, incorporating comforts from both his heritages. White frontiersmen considered it luxurious. Because of his mother's membership in the Wind clan, Alexander enjoyed an automatic acceptance into the society of the Alabamas and Creeks. His steady manner and good business sense won him increasing amounts of prestige and influence, and, in 1783, he was elected chief of the Creek nation. Up until that time there had not been one main chief for the nation, only a collection of representatives of leading men from each of the Upper and Lower Creek divisions. Alexander offered a new way of conducting national government business under the direction of one leader chosen by all the representatives. The representatives, or chiefs, met for a national council every year at Tuckabatchee on the Coosa above Little Tallassee. These councils were not an innovation; what was new was the amount of business they accomplished and the efficient manner in which the confederacy now dealt with external matters.

The skin trade continued to be the major industry for the Indians, and the young mixed-bloods, like Alexander and the numerous Scots traders' sons and daughters, were developing plantations and raising cattle while developing a lifestyle that incorporated the elements which they considered to be the best from both worlds—taking the traditions that appealed to them from their Indian mothers and grandmothers and melding them with their fathers' customs.

Driven by the European market for leather, the skin trade flourished throughout the eighteenth century. Leather served the same myriad of applications in that time as plastic does in our own. The Indians of the Southeast had enjoyed self-sufficient economies before the French and British convinced them to hunt deer full-time and then sell the hides in return for items the Indians would no longer have time to manufacture. This change in economy profoundly affected the culture of the Indians and in time tied them to an industry that virtually enslaved them. Their governments and wars became the tools of traders wrangling for bigger and better markets. By the time of the American Revolution, the Southeast had become vastly overhunted and the game depleted. The Choctaws and Creeks began a series of skirmishes over hunting rights. Some Creeks as well as Choctaws were eventually forced to go west of the Mississippi to hunt in an effort to satisfy the debts they had run up with the traders.

The traders also brought rum into the Indian country and, to an alarming degree, corrupted the spirit and the health of the people with liquor. Many Indians considered alcohol, usually in the form of rum, to be the greatest ill ever introduced into their country by the white men. The evil could be seen in every village: men, women, and children were destroyed. Though representatives from the tribes pleaded with the English and French authorities to stop the traders from bringing liquor into Indian country, they did not. The traders, the skin-trade-based economy, and rum weakened the fabric of tribal life. The skin trade continued to drive politics in Indian country even after the American Revolution. One of the largest British trading companies, Panton, Leslie and Company, arranged to continue to operate in Indian country after the American victory by working out a deal with the Spaniards in Florida. (A reconstructed Panton, Leslie and Company building is on Seville Square in Pensacola, part of a historical corner of the city which visitors can experience firsthand.) The company's ledgers and correspondence form a detailed record of the Creek economy during this era.

The Spaniards, having allied with the Americans and fielded armies against the British in the Southeast during the conflict, regained East and West Florida. But the Spaniards were very sensitive to the Indians within and near their borders. There was no market for deerskins in Spain (the vast Spanish empire's cattle industry supplied all the leather the market needed), but the Indians, having abandoned their native manufactures so they could hunt, were now dependent on the skin trade, so the Spaniards allowed Panton, Leslie and other British trading companies to operate out of Pensacola, Mobile, and even New Orleans for a while.

Intrigues played out in the confederacy brought the influences of Britain, Spain, and the American British colonies into conflict. White squatters kept pressing the eastern and northern frontiers of Indian country. To the west, disputes with Choctaws over hunting grounds occupied the attention of warriors as game became more and more scarce; all the Indians of the region found themselves deeply in debt to traders whom they had traditionally paid in deerskins. Trading companies began asking to be paid in land since the overhunting had made the possibility of paying entire debts in skins nearly impossible.

Young Billy Weatherford heard the discussions and debates in his uncle's house. He listened as possible solutions were formulated, as retaliation for intrusions into Creek territory were plotted, as the motives of the United States were questioned. Uncle Alexander had allied with the British in the Revolutionary War, serving on the frontier with the rank of colonel. The confiscation of his father's vast estate in

Georgia had fueled a particularly strong dislike and disrespect for the state and the citizens of Georgia. When Billy heard his uncle Alexander speak of "Georgians," the word resonated with disgust. Often in private, Alexander lamented the fact that the British had made no strong provisions in the Treaty of Paris (which ended the Revolutionary War) for firm boundaries of the Creek nation. Once Billy had heard discussions of the possibility of making a treaty that would give the Georgians some of the lands they were demanding if in return the United States would allow the Muskogee nation to come into the Union as the fourteenth state. Any plan that might deter the Georgians on the east and the Tennesseans on the north had to be considered. When he listened to his uncle lead a planning session for a raid against the illegal white settlements being made on Creek lands, he heard the flawless details and strategies presented by a natural military genius. Unobtrusively, Billy was being trained as a military leader and tactician. When the men at his uncle's house talked of their trips to New Orleans, Mobile, and Pensacola to visit the Spanish dignitaries, they were teaching Billy the importance of alliances for a small nation bordered by a land-ravenous country such as the United States. When his uncle accepted a colonel's commission and a yearly pension of fifty dollars from the Spaniards and a few years later accepted a commission as a United States general with a yearly payment of two thousand dollars, with the Spaniards then upping his commission and payments to match that of the Americans, Billy learned that the Creeks' alliance was a valued commodity, that the Muskogees could play a leading role in determining the international presences in the region. When Uncle Alexander adamantly refused to go to St. Mary's in Georgia to negotiate a treaty with the U.S. Commissioners in

1785 after the Revolutionary War, Billy learned that, united, the Creek nation had strength that would not be broken even by the Americans.

Billy always enjoyed the special prestige of being a favored nephew in his uncle's house. He made trips to Mobile and Pensacola with both his uncle and his father on separate occasions, learning through observation the delicate art of trading commodities and alliances. He also assisted the fire-maker and the female herbal doctors who came to sing for his uncle Alexander, make medicine, and administer poultices to the frail chief's swollen arthritic joints and to ease the pain of the deep depression he suffered. Despite his choice to live as an Indian, his success in uniting the towns under his leadership, and the support of his sister Sophia, this chronic depression often left Alexander feeling lonely and friendless. He established several plantations near the Hickory Ground, as well as one at the Tensaw, and these were operated by black slaves who were treated more like tenant farmers. This was a common practice among the slave-owning Creeks. Left to their own devices, the slaves ran the plantations as they pleased and paid a fee in goods to the Indian owners each year. Black slaves in Georgia often ran away from their white masters and crossed into Indian country, where they were immediately "claimed" by an Indian who set them up on a farm or plantation. One of the greatest attractions to the slaves was that their children were born free under the Indians' system of laws, and usually the Indians had no desire to harass the runaway slaves or treat them in a demeaning manner.

In keeping with an ancient custom that was beginning to lose favor at the time with the Indians but that was very popular with the white men, Alexander had two wives—one at the Hickory Ground and one at the Tensaw. His wife at the

Tensaw, Vicey Cornells, sister of Alexander Cornells (also children of a Scots father and Creek mother) remained childless throughout their marriage. His wife at the Hickory Ground, the daughter of William Moniac (a Dutch trader) and an Indian mother, had three children.

Lurking near Alexander's biography on the library's shelves are the memoirs of another uncle by marriage, Louis Le Clerc de Milford, an adventurer attracted to the Indian country for the sheer romance of being there. Even with the weakened fabric of tribal life in the latter half of the eighteenth century, the Indians' lifestyle, their compassion and open manners, seemed preferable to the society of the Euro-Americans. Le Clerc wrote that he thought these white men, the Euro-Americans, were the most wicked and evil of any human beings. While he gallantly excluded their wives and daughters from the condemnation, he marvelled at how men had reached such an uncivilized state as the white men on the Georgia frontier. He said that after listening to their tales of the Indians, he had decided that anybody such men disliked so much and considered the opposite of themselves needed investigation.

Even though he had the means, he chose not to hire a guide and simply set off into the wilderness to the west of Augusta, Georgia. Having no knowledge of the Upper or Lower Paths (the long-established Indian trails) to the Creek country, he wandered in the wilderness for several months. A kindly Indian eventually found him and brought him to Coweta in the Lower Creek country. He wrote a fanciful account of his brief sojourn at Coweta: how he met the young Alexander McGillivray during a council there and how McGillivray was so delighted to find someone who spoke English that he invited the Frenchman to Little Tallassee. Of course, Le Clerc is the hero of his own memoirs and claims responsibility for innovations and progressive movements within the Creek nation that are disputed by other documentary evidence. The Spanish and American officials with whom McGillivray and the Creeks had dealings considered Milford incompetent and a nuisance, but he did become a close personal friend of McGillivray. For Billy he added another dimension and perspective to the lessons a boy must learn. The romantic Frenchman, in love with the wilderness and the very idea of Indians, offered a lesson in the philosophical realm, teaching that the freedom of the forest and the identity of an Indian were highly valued intangible commodities that should be retained.

Uncle Louis claimed that he gained the position of overall chief of the Creeks for McGillivray and that he himself was so loved by the Indians that at the same time (1783) he was named overall war chief. His claims are in serious doubt since there is no mention of him in Creek documents until 1788. He did marry Uncle Alexander's sister Jeanette and establish a home with her near the Hickory Ground, living in much the same manner as the Indians and mixed-bloods at the junction of the Coosa and Tallapoosa.

Le Clerc's *Memoirs* offer valuable insight into Creek society but were written in France after Uncle Alexander's death with the intent of gaining the French government's support in sponsoring Uncle Louis's ambition to become the supreme leader of the Creek confederacy and to sever Creek country from United States dominion. The French government declined the sponsorship. Where the memoirs leave off, family stories pick up. Aunt Jeanette accompanied her husband back to France, where he hoped to gain support for his plans. Good-byes spread over months as plans were laid for the long and serpentine journey. The couple left the Mississippi Territory with Alexander, Jr., and traveled to Philadelphia, where they picked up David Tate, who was attending school there, so he could act as a companion to the young Alexander. Then they escorted both young men to Britain, where Lachlan McGillivray put the boys in school in Scotland, and Aunt Jeanette and Uncle Louis continued on to France. (Alexander, Jr., died within a year of arriving in Scotland.)

Nearly lost in a crevice of the Mississippi corner at the public library is a thin, faded volume, the Authentic Memoirs of William Augustus Bowles. *The tiny biography is packed full of the adventures of one of the most dynamic men ever to enter Creek country and the most relentless foe Uncle Alexander ever faced. Without Bowles, even the family stories lose their depth and width. He played out the drama of his life in broad strokes and bold colors.*

Augustus Bowles came into the Creek country after the American Revolution. The son of a Maryland planter, he had at the age of fifteen enlisted in the British army to fight the American rebels, but in 1778 resigned his commission. When circumstances stranded him in West Florida with no money or companions, he quickly adapted to life on the frontier, making friends with the Indians, mainly Lower Creeks, and entering the deerskin trading business. Bowles, a self-taught artist and actor, gained considerable influence with the Lower Creeks through his expanding trading operations and challenged McGillivray for leadership of the nation. In 1791 he declared himself "director-general" of the Creek nation. He opposed McGillivray's compromise with the Americans that had resulted in the Treaty of New York and sought to oust him from his paramount position. He had a particularly loyal following among the Seminoles, Creeks who had wandered into the wilds of Florida where they were freer to pursue their traditional lifestyles than they were in the old Indian country of Georgia and the land that would become the Mississippi Territory. But the interests of large trading companies such as Panton, Leslie were so far-reaching that they were able to rally official Spanish protests against Bowles, whose enterprises were being underwritten by the firm of Miller, Bonnamy and Company operating out of the Bahamas. Both Panton, Leslie and Company and the Spaniards considered Bowles a troublemaker, not good for business or politics. Panton, Leslie and Company saw him instigating a trading war; the Spaniards saw him as a front man for British efforts to gain control of the area. Bowles spent the time from 1792 to 1798 as a prisoner of the Spanish at Luzon in the Philippines. When he managed to escape, he made his way back to London, where he proclaimed himself the ambassador from the Creek nation. While in Britain with a troupe of Indians, he often performed "rituals" and plays depicting Native American themes. By 1799 he was back in Creek country, with an expedition underwritten by political activists in the Bahamas, trying to set up a pro-British Creek state with himself as director-general. He established headquarters at Wekiwa, Florida, and invited Creeks and Seminoles to a conference at which he said that no more Indian lands would be ceded and that all people holding commissions from or working for the United States government would be expelled from Creek territory, a position which gained him support among many Indians. In early April of 1800 the Spaniards burned his headquarters at Wekiwa. Bowles declared a state of war between the Creeks and Spain. On April 9 he led about three hundred Creek and Seminole Indians in an attack on Fort St. Marks, and the fort surrendered. Governor Vicente Folch promptly offered a bounty of forty-five hundred dollars for Bowles's capture. Bowles continued his activities among the Lower Creeks, promising all who would listen that British aid would be available to those who rose up against the Spaniards and Americans.

For as long as he could remember, Billy had heard stories about Bowles, the wild white man who agitated the people and demanded that they reclaim all the land that had been ceded to the United States. Once when Uncle Alexander was away from the nation, Bowles had called a meeting at Tuckabatchee for the purpose of replacing McGillivray with himself as the overall chief of the Creeks. Aunt Sophia, residing at the Tensaw in an advanced stage of pregnancy, heard of the dastardly plan. She called a slave woman for assistance, and the two of them mounted horses and rode alone overland to Tuckabatchee, stopping only briefly along the way. Aunt Sophia, with her massive swollen belly, made her way into the warriors' council and in her most eloquent and persuasive speech retained the warriors' allegiance to her brother. When she believed that the warriors were once again in firm support of her brother, she left the council house and, with her slave companion, retired to a woman's hut at the edge of the village, where she gave birth to twins. If Aunt Sophia was on your side, how could you lose? (*Billy's aunt Sophia is my grandmother's grandmother's grandmother. She is on my side.*)

Uncle Alexander had died while Bowles was imprisoned in the Philippines in 1793. Had he been able to escape capture by the Spaniards until 1793, Bowles could easily have stepped into a leadership vacuum that would have given him the power and position he sought. After Alexander's death, the leadership of the nation reverted to multiple chieftains, without any one man being able to represent the entire nation.

    I make my notes and return the Authentic Memoirs *to its resting place. The public library closes early on Saturdays. I go home to paint my word pictures of Billy's world.*

Seven

Half Made Whole

Billy's world is forest green, dense, rampant, matted, semi-tropical. Occasionally there is a smear of earth that is literally red. The sky is white, faded from blue by haze and humidity, except on those rare days when a cold front has moved through, wrung out the dampness, and re-dyed the sky azure. This is the backdrop for all the actions of Billy's life. Across this stage we can watch the unfolding drama move.

Billy gallops across the open meadows and prairies, through woodland groves and into the swamps on sleek black horses from his father's racing stables, exercising the animals, testing their endurance, training them for the races they must run. At the water's edge along the river, rider and mount move among herds of cattle grazing on the tender mosses, then up the bank to the edge of the canebrakes where the horse prances nervously around and through the beloved bear ground, the sacred place preserved for bears who are ritually hunted in season. A horse with heart and a determined spirit, one with which the rider has established a rapport and which has been treated with compassion by human beings will do whatever is asked.

As Billy trained horses in the close places of the forests, he would become uneasy, his eyes searching the leafy green tangles for another presence. Was someone hiding there, watching him? As he and the other young men rode into the villages from the hunts, the fact that young women were watching from less and less secret places became obvious not only to Billy but to all the hunters with him. Young women watched for a young man who would make a good husband as well as a young warrior who excited their imagination. More naive than coy, the young men riding with Billy's party self-consciously ignored the appraising gazes of the women, knowing that the married men would tease them at the first opportunity. More than several of the young women had made it plain that Billy was the object of their desire. With each passing season the young women became more bold in their flirting. They followed him to the ballgames and wildly cheered each of his plays on the chunky field. At the dances they jostled each other for the opportunity to put their hands on his shoulders and squeeze in tightly next to him in the spiral of the stomp dance. Some tried to persuade him that none of the other young women would be as pleasant a companion on a walk by the river in the moonlight when he had tired of dancing. Embarrassed, Billy hid behind a facade of silence, a straight face, and an aloof manner. Haughtiness only made him more attractive. On feast days when the young warriors struck the post in the town square and told of their exploits against the outlaw white men who invaded Indian country and committed atrocities, the young women formed large appreciative audiences for Billy's stories. As he spoke on the town square about the moral and ethical issues confronting the people, saying that they should strive at all times to keep in balance and harmony with nature, his most appreciative audiences were always the young women. Even when he spoke at the council in the debates and discussions of national policy, a crowd of young women hovered nearby. His was the fate of a young Alabama warrior who had entered manhood, who had the ability to plant and harvest a crop, make successful hunts, and build a house: he was now ready for marriage.

In time, embarrassment gave way to good-natured acceptance of the admiring young women and the teasing of the men. Though as a proper young man he never flirted back, at least not too vigorously, the young women's flirting and attention became more serious. His mother reminded him that he should think of selecting a wife. A man was not complete without a wife. The grandmothers taught that a single human being is incomplete, only half of a whole. He promised his mother that he understood. At ballgames and horse races, during hunts, on trade missions to Mobile and Pensacola, and at council meetings, he pondered the choice he must make. There were many attractive young women with many attributes, but choosing a person who would be his other half, without whom he would be incomplete, was intimidating. Then, through the green tangles of the forest, Billy caught a glimpse of a familiar figure, a familiar set of eyes. "Mary," he said, as he reined his horse to a halt.

Mary (Polly) Moniac and her sisters and brothers—especially her brother Sam—had been constant childhood playmates of Billy, his brother Jack and his sisters Roseanna and Elizabeth. Throughout his life, he counted Sam as his friend; theirs was a bond sealed in the sacred time of childhood innocence that would not be broken by diverging philosophies as they grew older. Sam married his sister Elizabeth. His uncle Alexander had married Sam's aunt. Like the Weatherfords and McGillivrays, the Moniacs were mixed-bloods. Their grandfather had come into the nation from Holland as a trader, and had married and stayed. Billy's mother, Sehoy, had spent much of her early childhood at the Moniac household in the town of Tuskegee, and, after Alexander McGillivray's death, his two daughters made their home with the Moniacs. The Weatherford and Moniac children played together and raced their ponies back and forth between the villages at the confluence of the Alabama where the clan houses stood. Above the river where the old French fort lay in ruins, the youngsters, sometimes alone, sometimes in the company of Billy's brothers and sisters and other children, scrambled across the five disabled French cannons (rendered useless by the French when they turned Fort Toulouse over to the British) in the yard of the town house, ran through the McGillivray apple orchards, climbed the mulberry trees, and slid down the steep riverbanks on a thick carpet of fallen leaves to the water's edge.

Now Billy spoke to his mother and his aunt Sophia. They spoke to Mary's mother and aunts. They agreed that Billy could present gifts to Mary and her family. Several horseloads of apparel, deerskins and pelts from his hunts, scissors and bright cloth from the trading house, silver brooches from Mobile, carved shell combs from Pensacola, earbobs, glass beads, pigs, turkeys, corn, and everything else his mother and aunts thought appropriate were left at Mary's door. The gifts were accepted and a day chosen for a feast and the formal presentation of Billy to Mary's family. The firemaker came to perform the ritual introduction; his solemn apprentices came to sing. After a feast of venison, turkey, roast beef, sweet potatoes, sofke, corn bread, corn pudding, dried persimmons, hickory nut oil, berries, and cider, the wedding party listened to a black slave's fiddle music, and danced the night away while Billy and Mary disappeared into their marriage bower and from there into their lives as Indians.

Unobtrusively and quietly, writing no journals, keeping no records (except the wordless ones of the heart), they balanced the acculturated world and evolving society around them and created a harmonious lifestyle. In that time and place they believed that they were Indians, that they had a choice of how they would think and live. They chose the way that seemed natural, taking their native souls and spirits into a social and political world that was demanding material changes.

All Creek and Alabama lands were owned in common, but individual plots were allotted as needed or requested by tribal members. Billy was allotted plantations along the Alabama and in the Tensaw district. Technically the fields belonged to his wife, but in the evolving culture under white dominance the Indian agent declared the fields the property of the men. Billy had acquired black slaves from his mother, father, and Uncle Alexander over the years and then placed them in charge of the various plots he farmed and planted. The black slaves had the responsibility of running the places while being free to live as they personally saw fit. Billy, like many other Creek owners of black slaves, only asked that they offer him a share of produce or livestock at the end of the season. Billy traveled from plantation to plantation as needed, but he and Mary particularly enjoyed their home on the bluff of the Alabama in the Tensaw district. They built a boat landing below the bluff, and furnished their house with the necessities and comforts that appealed to them, whether the items were native or European. Billy's and Mary's relatives had neighboring plantation plots and farms up and down the Alabama and in the Tensaw district, so there was opportunity for regular visiting.

The American government had made a wholesale assault on the Indians' traditional way of life, and, unwittingly, the plantation assignees and the mixed-blood residents of the Tensaw aided their antagonists by moving out of the towns and villages onto separate farmsteads and plantations. More and more the mixed-bloods saw the villages and towns as places with a clan house, to which they would return for an occasional traditional festival, ceremony, or council meeting, but where they would not take up permanent residence. The American government saw the dissolution of these towns as a first and vital step in the destruction of the Indians' communal way of life.

Mary, her kinswomen, and all the other Alabama and Creek women were directly targeted by the government in an attempt to "Americanize" the Indians. The women laughed and joked as they agreed to the dubious plan the American agents proposed to them as a way to "civilize their men." The Indian agent enthusiastically reported his success in gaining the women's agreement to "civilize their men" without taking into account their sense of humor. Women enjoyed honored places in their native societies. They considered themselves essential to the order of all things. They were indispensable. Creek women, with an air of tolerance and patience often reserved for children, indulged men by admitting them to their own company and consenting to the rituals, ceremonies, and talks that marked the men's days. European and Euro-American men saw Native American women through a veil of European perception that cast males as superior to females, thus blinding themselves to the native women's true condition and place in society.

American government officials from the president to the local Indian agent spoke of the United States's plan for the Indians as a "civilization program," while rallying against what journalists of the day labeled "native communism," claiming that the Indian was doomed if he could not be taught the values and virtues of capitalism. Though the white male authorities of the time negated the roll of Native American women at every opportunity, when Benjamin Hawkins, a U.S. senator from North Carolina who had served as a commissioner at Indian treaties in the region since the revolution, was chosen to fill the position of Indian agent, women were the major target of his program. Hawkins came to Creek country in 1796, calling himself the "temporary" southern Indian agent. He served in the position until 1816. At first he established his agency headquarters at Tuckabatchee, the recognized "national" capital of the Creeks, but a short time later moved to a site on the Flint River. Hawkins spent much energy persuading Creek women to take up cottage industries such as weaving, truck farming, and raising livestock to support their families. Several devastating droughts in the 1790s made wild game and farm produce even more scarce and brought the southeastern Indians into dire economic times. Mary and most of her relatives fared better than many. The wealth of the Moniacs, Weatherfords, McGillivrays, and other mixed-blood families, who had long since begun the acculturation progress Hawkins was calling civilization, made cultural transitions easier for them than for many of the traditional and full-blood Indians.

Hawkins brought white women to his agency to teach Creek women weaving and domestic chores as they were performed in Euro-America. He shared Thomas Jefferson's dreams of a stronghold of yeoman farmers on the southern frontier that could be called upon to reinforce the militia against foreign intrusions. He went about trying to change the Indians into Americans and make them over as yeoman farmers who could form a militia. He had some success with acculturated mixed-bloods. Some American Christians, such as the Quakers and Moravians, thought these goals admirable and earnestly believed that by becoming "Americanized" the Indians could save themselves. If they could live on small, individually owned, self-sufficient farms they could not be seen as a menace or a burden to anyone. The Quakers sent blacksmithing and farming tools as gifts to hasten the progress. Hawkins lamented that these tools lay for more than twenty months untouched by the Indians, who could not be convinced to readily embrace the white-yeoman-farmer way of life. Hunters still struggled to meet their obligations to traders with hides and pelts, while women relied on the skills they had half-retained from the days before the white men came, when their societies were self-sufficient. Women still made clay pottery, though the quality had deteriorated since the French had come and introduced European glassware and pottery as trade goods. Dried gourds served as dippers, ladles, and containers with just a minimum amount of carving. Most women did beadwork, and all sewed for their families. Some women still wove baskets, while almost all could weave cane sifters and cane fans. Women had always spun the wool of bison and other animals into thread and woven the wool into cloth on small looms or on their fingers. Now Hawkins introduced the European spinning wheel and loom along with cotton planting as an economical way for the women to clothe themselves and their families. With much pressure from the agent, the full-blood Indians gradually began to accept some parts of his program.

Hawkins was convinced that the only way to run a household was in the white Euro-American mode. He recognized Billy's aunt Sophia Durant as one of the most energetic and best organized of the Creek women, but marveled that she often did not bake enough bread to last the day. Why could she not just figure out how many people she had to feed and bake the corresponding amount? Never in all his years in Indian country did he seem to grasp the fact that Aunt Sophia fed everybody who showed up at her door and never knew on a given day how many hungry visitors might arrive. He also faulted her for not demanding more of her black slaves, writing that if she would just be stricter with them and require more work they could be productive. She had eleven children, of whom eight survived infancy, and owned eighty black slaves (of whom, he said, only fourteen were "working negroes") yet lived "poorly" because she "shared all in common" with her slaves. He declared her house on the Alabama near the Hickory Ground "less comfortable than any Indian hut no matter how poor." Slaves throughout the Creek nation traveled to Aunt Sophia's at Christmas for an annual frolic and feast, as well as for gifts—a custom both Aunt Sophia and the slaves had acquired on the white plantations of Georgia. The holiday had no special religious significance. Hawkins was appalled that both Sophia and her sister Sehoy had "complete and absolute command" over the affairs of their families and husbands. He declared that the handsome French-Indian mixed-blood Benjamin Durant, Sophia's husband, was "a man of good figure, dull and stupid, a little mixed with African blood." (*Thus history documents my grandfather seven generations back.*) From Hawkins's viewpoint, Sophia Durant's faults paled beside her sister Sehoy Weatherford's. Both sisters had been traders running businesses with Panton, Leslie and Company independent of their husbands. Acting as middlemen between the trading company and the hunters, the women in the course of their business traveled to Mobile and Pensacola as well as throughout the nation. Sophia diplomatically told Hawkins that she no longer did business with Panton, Leslie because of a misunderstanding. Sehoy no longer did business with Panton, Leslie because she had run up a large debt, and the company would no longer extend her credit. According to Hawkins, Sehoy lived well, was given to pleasure and extravagance, exercised absolutely no control over her thirty slaves, and allowed them to do as they pleased. He said much of the "mischief" in the nation was initiated at the Weatherfords'. Questionable characters often traveled to and from the place. Travelers from outside the nation stopped there without clearing their visits with Hawkins. In May 1798 at the national meeting at Tuckabatchee, Hawkins had the Creeks banish Charles Weatherford from the nation as an "unworthy character," but the Creeks softened the decree by saying that, in consideration of his Indian family and a promise from the Indian leader Opoie Hutke that Weatherford's conduct would improve, he would be allowed to stay.

Hawkins considered Creek women to be less than desirable as wives because, he said, every white man he had known who had married an Indian woman had been enslaved by her and her family. (This statement was at odds with remarks he frequently made in official letters in which he called the Creek women "drudges" of their husbands.) Though he wrote that he had thought of taking an Indian wife and was even tempted to do so, he overcame the temptation. Instead he began an illicit relationship with one of the white women who came as a weaving and domestic arts teacher to the agency. They lived together for many years and had numerous children; only when Hawkins thought he was dying did he legalize the union and seek the blessings of the clergy.

Several Moravian missionaries worked at the agency in the fence-enclosed compound of model fields and the farm Hawkins established along the Flint River so he could teach the Creeks modern agriculture. They made no overtly aggressive efforts to convert the Indians, though they often took the opportunity to discuss spirituality with visitors to the Flint River Agency. The Indians listened politely to the talk about Jesus of Nazareth, the Almighty God, and the Holy Bible, and then, under questioning, assured the Moravians that they understood and just as politely turned away. When the Moravians brought up the subject with Alexander Cornells (Ouche Haujo), the mixed-blood interpreter from Tuckabatchee employed by Hawkins as a deputy agent, Cornells explained, "I have heard the same word of God which you speak . . . from the old chiefs. The Indians know it without a book; they dream much of God, therefore they know it."

Most of the mixed-bloods shared the Indians' view of spirituality. They had no need for Christianity. They lived with God daily, communed and prayed with him in every breath. They were at peace with God. For the wild Euro-American frontiersmen, a religion had to be vigorous, assertive, loud, and authoritative just to get their attention. Spawned by this need, frontier evangelists held carnival-like revivals that filled a deep social void. Brush arbor tabernacles were erected in the wilderness where throngs would gather, camping out for a week or so, singing, performing river baptisms, listening to sermons, and pursuing fellowship rituals. Whiskey usually flowed freely nearby if not on the campgrounds. Under the hypnotic spell of charismatic evangelists, frontiersmen and their families would renounce their sins and vow to live by the biblical commandments, leave the campgrounds, and return to their former ways untainted by the experience. But at the turn of the nineteenth century, these brush arbor and camp meetings on the borders of Creek country were rare, and the most common ecumenical term that could be applied to the frontiersmen was "unchurched." The frontiersmen called the Indians "Godless heathens," while the Indians remained respectful of multiple interpretations of spirituality and walked their own path.

Aunt Sophia became the spiritual head of the family after her mother's death. She advised young and old. She counseled the wise. She spoke for the sage. Declared beloved by the nation, addressed as grandmother by the traditionalists, she calmly went about her duties, keeping track of her own eight living children as well as those of the family and clan, whom she also considered to be hers. When people despaired, they visited Aunt Sophia to be comforted and cheered. In times of need, spiritual or physical, Aunt Sophia would stand with a person. To proceed without her blessing was unthinkable. Mary's world meshed perfectly with Aunt Sophia's. The world of women supported the world of men, just as the world of men supported the world of women. One would collapse without the other.

Now that the wild game was less abundant, the wealthy mixed-bloods depended more and more on their livestock, instead of the trading houses, for a living. Men divided their time between hunting and raising cattle, hogs, and horses. Along the Alabama River their plantations grew cotton and corn. The nation was ever aware of the white men and squatters who were violating their boundaries. The young warriors spent much time and effort encouraging the whites to leave if not forcefully expelling them from the nation. Each action called for councils and deliberations. The Georgians, the Tennesseans, and other white Americans along the western bank of the Tombigbee, in the Bigbee settlements across from the Tensaw in the Mississippi Territory, violated Indian space at will. They illegally ranged their livestock on Indian land, and, when the Indians confiscated the stock, dubbed them "horse thieves."

As Indian men became more vigilant, the women followed the pattern of chores the seasons dictated. The deerskins and pelts used in trade had to be processed and aired regularly, families fed and clothed, gardens planted, crops gathered. The women appreciated any restful moments they could pass stirring a breeze with a turkey-wing fan in the shade of a mulberry tree. The wild bounty of the forest was gathered communally. In the spring, children scampered through blackberry patches and Chickasaw plum and mulberry groves with their mothers, cousins, aunts, and black slave women, filling baskets, buckets, and vats, gathering fruit for immediate consumption as well as drying and preserving for later. In the fall after the first hint of frost, the lush, ripe persimmons were gathered and pressed into multiple use, persimmon flour and persimmon bread being favorites. The wild nuts—chinkapin, walnut, pecan, and hickory— were gathered in the late fall and were eaten straight from the shell, shelled and pounded into flour, or made into "milk" or oil. The nuts offered protein and fat. (Hawkins himself declared hickory oil the equal of olive oil and promised the women a lucrative market for it if they would make it and bring it to the trading post.) For the boldest gatherers, honey could be had from the hives made by bees descended from the European imports that had escaped domestication. Each expedition proceeded with the excitement of a holiday. The abundance of the forest spoke of nature's embrace in an uncomplicated manner that the Indian heart never failed to hear.

The Creeks continued to travel to Mobile and Pensacola to do business with the British merchants operating out of Spanish territory and to accept gifts from the Spanish colonial government—the "dons," as the Americans called them. As Hawkins worked with the Spanish and American surveyors drawing the line between their territory at the 31st parallel in 1798–99, the Indians watched and protested the white men's continuing encroachment of Indian territory. After 1798, when Hawkins declared that all Creek country north of the 31st parallel was definitely American territory, he brought even more pressure on the Creeks to cease trading in Mobile and Pensacola. Accepting gifts from the Spaniards was disloyal to the American government, he insisted, but the Creeks had a different view. Hawkins marveled that the Indians acted as if they were doing the white men a great honor by accepting their gifts. In fact, that is exactly what the Indians thought. In the Native American societies of the Southeast, the presenting of generous gifts to everyone brought prestige and honor to a person or a nation. The more generous the gift, the more honor and prestige the presenter received. No one accepted gifts automatically. The motives of the givers had to be considered. Therefore, it was indeed generous of the Indians to willingly accept gifts from people who did not have a coherent policy toward their nation. Unfortunately, in the years of severe drought and scant game, the gifts from the white governments were nearly the only succor a desperate people received. In the early nineteenth century, Hawkins introduced the U.S. government-owned trading houses and enforced a strict policy of no credit. Credit was still available in Mobile and Pensacola. Indian traders crossed the 31st parallel into Spanish territory without hesitation. Convinced that the continued exposure to the Spanish dons and the British merchants operating from their territory would cause the Indians to be unduly influenced in their favor against the United States, Hawkins discouraged the commerce at every opportunity, while at the same time working out a deal with the British merchants to pay cash for Indian lands ceded to those companies in payment of Indian debts.

There had not been a strong, overall leader of the Creeks since Alexander McGillivray's death. The United States had hoped Hawkins would fill the leadership vacuum. When Augustus Bowles escaped from Luzon and made his way back to Creek country in 1799 still determined to claim the position for himself, Hawkins asked the Creek National Council at Tuckabatchee to go on record as opposing Bowles, which the council did. But as the United States and the Georgians brought increased pressure for the cessions agreed to in the Treaty of New York as well as for new cessions and for a formidable river boundary between the Indians and Georgians, Bowles found a receptive native audience for his anti-cession messages. He consolidated his forces, still strongest among the Lower Creeks and Seminoles, over the next few years.

Billy spent these years in Hawkins's sphere of influence, working to preserve the national entity his uncle had shaped and honoring the commitments his uncle had made at the Treaty of New York. He traveled to Tuckabatchee with his father, Charles Weatherford, and his friend Sam Moniac in May 1803 for a council called by Hawkins. The announced purpose of the council, which had been ordered by Secretary of War Henry Dearborn, was to work out a boundary that would be acceptable to the Georgians, the Indians, and the Americans. But the real purpose of the meeting was the capture of Bowles by subterfuge. Upper Creeks, Lower Creeks, and Seminoles, as well as Choctaws, Chickasaws, and Cherokees, were invited. Tuckabatchee was a sanctuary (white) peace town, which, according to Creek tradition, precluded a capture of Bowles in the town. But two men—John Forbes, representing Panton, Leslie and Company, and Estaban Folch, son of the Spanish governor of Florida—traveled to Tuckabatchee for that purpose.

Bowles had confidence in his own presence and speaking ability. He believed that just by talking he could sway the Indians and have them join his side. He showed up at the council with a personal guard of sixty Seminole warriors. The Bowles group had set up their camp just outside the town and had settled in for the evening when Hawkins led Sam Moniac, Bob Walton, Efau Haujo (Mad Dog), Charles Weatherford, and Billy Weatherford into the camp, walked up to Bowles and announced that he was under arrest. The Indians with Bowles grabbed their guns, hastily raised their sights, and prepared to fire as Sam and Billy stepped forward and seized Bowles. The two subdued the self-appointed director-general as Estaban Folch put manacles on his wrists and fastened them.

Many Indians were upset that Bowles had been taken captive at a peace town, but they made no active protest. Billy and Sam rationalized that the arrest took place at the Bowles camp outside the town, but knew it was a shaky argument. Billy, Sam, Forbes, and Folch put Bowles in a boat and started down the Alabama River to Mobile, where he was to be handed over to the Spaniards. As the boats passed the Indian towns, the inhabitants came out to catch a glimpse of the infamous Bowles and the warriors who had captured him. On the fourth day of the trip, as the party camped for the night on an island in the river well south of present-day Selma, Bowles escaped. When his captors slept he managed to free himself, steal a boat, and row to the mainland. The men tracked him through the river marshes, and, after a few hours of excitement, Bowles was recaptured and the journey to Mobile continued. Governor Folch met them as they landed at Mobile, accepted custody of the prisoner, and presented Billy and Sam with the forty-five-hundred-dollar reward, which they returned to the council. Bowles died about eighteen months later while in Spanish custody at Havana.

Mary, busy with her household and children, waited for her husband's return. At her house on the bluff in the Tensaw, provisions were shared with any Indian who came to the door. Despite the uncertain politics of the time, the spiritual life of the family rested in the certainty of nature. Mary and Billy named their first child, a son, Charles Weatherford. Then in short order came a daughter named Polly. The idyllic episode came to an end when Mary died in 1804. The firemaker sang Mary's spirit across the divide. Grief pummeled Billy's spirit. Mary's female relatives came to claim the children as Billy wandered in and out of Mary's house, through the woods, up the river to the other plantations, and through the spirit journey of separation. *Never separated from nature, we change form, moving from dimension to dimension. Death is part of the cycle we must travel. In the quiet of the deep woods by the river beside the red dirt plantations, a vista of flat swampland covered with palmettos could be seen on the other side. Here one could enter the center of nothingness. The Path, Billy's path, led deeper and deeper into the unobtrusive thought-world of the Indian, the thoughtless-world of nature.* In the same time period his mother, Sehoy Weatherford, died, and Billy was drawn ever closer to Aunt Sophia.

The young unmarried mixed-blood women of the Tensaw calmly waited for the mourning period to end. Then they courted the well-to-do widower, Billy Weatherford, aggressively. On his trips to the towns, the Creek women entertained Red Eagle and made their availability known. To make themselves more attractive, they dug the root of the *talewau,* mixed it with bear oil, and applied it to redden their hair. The songs of Sapoth Thlaine (Kaney), a Creek woman renowned both for her great physical beauty and for her sweet voice, penetrated the no-thought world. Sapoth Thlaine knew the spirit world and sang the songs that illuminated the path. She became Billy's wife.

Eight

Promise of the
White Sapling

*I take the visions from my grandmothers' dreams with me as I
enter the poorly ventilated world of the libraries and archive
stacks. Universes of nearly invisible dust float, suspended in air,
illuminated in stray shafts of thin sunlight coming through the
rare glass windows in the back corners of these places. I travel to
distant archives and collections, visiting Indian tribes and
communities, playing detective, searching for the remnants of
thoughts and perceptions that have survived. I wait for the
recorded facts to tell me their story. I wait for the scattered details to draw themselves into the magnetic field of my story-
teller's mind. Billy Weatherford sits across the table from me in
the archives watching me, waiting.*

The gossip at Weatherford's racetrack vibrated with the
pulse of the Creek nation. There around the paddocks and
stables, all the news and opinions of the Indians spilled out in
torrents of words that stopped for the running of the horses.
Patience was the essential ingredient in raising and training
horses. Beyond the racetrack, patience became a virtue Billy

practiced as he listened, and, in turn, spoke, as the warriors argued in the council houses throughout the nation, debating what action they should take, what was prudent and reasonable conduct in reaction to the continuous violations of treaties and agreements by the Americans and their government. Action by the entire nation could not be taken until after the council debates ended with all members attending in agreement. Such agreement tended to elude the council.

The other southeastern Indian nations had gone to Hopewell, South Carolina, and signed treaties with the United States after the American Revolution, but for years Uncle Alexander steadfastly refused to treat with the Americans. Benjamin Hawkins, as one of the American commissioners at the treaties, had reduced the problems with the entire Creek nation to the simple issue of the chief being upset over the confiscation of his father's estates in Georgia. The United States government at the time had no coherent or cohesive Indian policy, and the treaties and negotiation reflected the indecisiveness within the government. Secretary of War Henry Knox, who oversaw the Indian Department, offered his opinion that the Indians could not be "civilized," though he recommended that every effort be made to do so. If nothing else, Knox stressed, the Americans must teach the Indians the concept of exclusive ownership of property. Alexander doubtlessly saw the irony of the situation. Though George Washington had supported the Americanization program, when John Adams became president he said that he believed Indians could not be "civilized" and withdrew his "confidence" from the program. Thomas Jefferson, becoming president before the program was completely dismantled, decided to continue it.

I read the messages from George Washington, who frequently spoke of the "critical nature" of the southern frontier. If the southeastern tribes allied with a foreign power such as Spain on their southern boundary or with Britain, through the British trading companies operating out of Spanish territory and the Bahamas, they could do considerable damage to the new union if not destroy it. No matter what Washington or anyone else said, the Georgians in particular rallied against any fair treatment of the Indians on their state's frontiers. The land speculators throughout the South had long been sharpening their knives in preparation for the day when they could carve up Indian lands among themselves.

Among the ongoing questions the Treaty of New York of 1790 was designed to solve was that of the boundary lines of Creek country within Georgia. Also, the treaty called for the return to their owners of all runaway slaves in the nation. The Creeks believed that those slaves who had fled their white masters and deliberately sought the protection of the nation should be offered refuge and not returned. Seminoles protested this provision of the treaty for years and continued to openly offer refuge in Spanish Florida to runaway black slaves, while the Americans believed that all the Creeks were granting refuge to runaways. In fact, many individual Creeks did continue to embrace the ancient philosophy of refuge. Traditionalists believed it to be a fundamental law that could not be revoked. In the treaty, the Indians received, at least on paper, the same rights of commerce as United States citizens. Because of Alexander's strong, unified leadership of the Creek nation in the beginning years of the republic, the United States spent more time on the Creek question than on that of the other southeastern Indians who generated records reflecting their concerns.

I amass a ledger of indictments. In 1793, the year of Uncle Alexander's death, the White Birdtail King of the Cussetahs, Tuskatchee Mico, and several hunters, all Indians friendly to the United States, hunted by permission of the Indian agent James Seagrove in territory some Georgians were illegally claiming. In the evening, as the Indians prepared supper in their camp, some white men appeared, feigning friendship, and the Indians welcomed and fed them. The white men returned later and murdered all the Indians in the camp. Were the white men testing the United States's willingness to act for justice on behalf of Indians? Were they testing the Creek nation's state of unity after the death of the overall chief? Or were they just white Georgians who needed no excuse to murder Indians? On February 19, 1794, the Creeks complained to the government that the deaths had still not been avenged and demanded to know if they could ever expect any justice from the United States. These murders formed part of a continuous pattern of harassment and provocation committed by Georgians against which the Indians were forbidden to retaliate in their traditional manner and about which the state and national government did nothing to protect them and their rights. After many such insults, even the patient and long-suffering among the Indians were not interested in merely debating the issues in the council houses, and occasionally exacted their own justice, which in turn whipped the Georgians into an emotional frenzy over the "hostile acts" for which they demanded the government punish the Indians.

The American State Papers (congressional documents) from the period record the ongoing atrocities and injustices being committed against the Indians and the failure of the United States government to take action on their behalf, along with its excuses. *My portfolio grows.* The War Department considered establishing a line of military posts to enforce treaties. Meanwhile, with no provocation, the Georgia Militia fired at Indians on sight. The Dog King of the Cussetahs complained that "Georgians everywhere are shooting Indians." At the same time, the Georgians complained that the Indians were not returning runaway black slaves and were stealing horses. Young warriors said that they had not been paid for returning black slaves in the past and that now they were taking horses in lieu of the long-overdue payments.

On June 29, 1796, a treaty between the Creeks and the United States was signed by Creek leaders at Colerain, Georgia. Article VII stated: "The Creek Nation shall deliver, as soon as practicable, to the Superintendent of Indian Affairs, at such place as he may direct, all citizens of the United States, white inhabitants and negroes, who are now prisoners in any part of the said Nation, agreeable to the treaty of New York, and also all citizens, white inhabitants, negroes and property taken since the signing of that treaty. And if any such prisoners, negroes or property should not be delivered, on or before the first day of January next, the Governor of Georgia may empower three persons to repair to the said Nation, in order to claim and receive such prisoners, negroes, and property, under the direction of the president of the United States." The Georgians gave themselves more authority and latitude than the treaty allowed. They acted under the guise of law to penetrate Indian country at will and remove anyone or anything that they decided had been "stolen."

In May 1798, Creek ownership of a tract of land between the Oconee and Oakmulgee rivers in Georgia was still being disputed. This tract had been ceded by two maverick chiefs who had attended a St. Mary's treaty meeting in 1783 with the Georgians. Neither the Creek nation or the United States recognized the cession. The United States held the position that only the national government could make treaties with the Indian nations, but the Georgians claimed that their states' rights superseded national rights. The United States government hoped the naming of Benjamin Hawkins as the overall southern Indian agent to the Creeks, Cherokees, Chickasaws, and Choctaws would help to formulate a cohesive overall Indian policy in the region instead of the "impulsive, spur-of-the-moment" reactions of which the government had been guilty, according to officials in the War Department.

The government trading houses were to be continued, even though the Indians found few of the goods they wanted or needed in stock. Often the yearly hunts were delayed for weeks or even months due to a lack of ammunition for their guns at the trading houses. The government tried to restrict commerce among the Indians by licensing traders and undercutting the prices being offered by the British firms in Pensacola and Mobile, but desperation as much as need drove many Indians to trade in Spanish Florida at least occasionally. In the time of Alexander McGillivray, the Spaniards sent an agent, Juan Pilar, to live among the Creeks near the Hickory Ground, and the traders, licensed by the Spanish, working for the British companies and operating out of Mobile and Pensacola, never failed to encourage the Indians to distrust the Americans. The traders often joined the warriors, leading men, and beloveds in the councils, hoping to shape local public opinion in their own favor. To publicly proclaim American policy at the turn of the century, Hawkins established the tradition of a yearly national council each May at Tuckabatchee. Here Billy heard him preach the American government's civilization program, the benefits to be gained from modern American agriculture, and the necessity of moving out from the communal towns and villages onto individual homesteads and renouncing communism for capitalism. He stoked the fires of town council debates for months to come with just one speech at the yearly council. Those were the times when Billy recommended caution. The old ways should not be abandoned in favor of American innovations. Perhaps experimentation would lead to a mixture of methods that would benefit the Creeks. The Creeks should choose what would work best for them, not what would work best for the Americans. It is easy to imagine Billy's position, even his words. His talks echoed those of the Tattooed Serpent speaking in Natchez to Le Page Du Pratz a hundred years earlier and foreshadowed that of Sitting Bull and Crazy Horse of the Lakota many decades later.

Listen to the beloveds, to the sages. Do they not tell us that before the white man came we had no need of his manufactures? We had no need of his methods or his science. We made what we needed, farmed our land, raised our corn, hunted the wild game, fished the streams, and enjoyed the abundance of the Master of Breath's blessings. Only when the white man came and offered us the ease of his guns over the bow and arrow did we begin to falter. Only when we gave up our way of life, the ways of our fathers and grandfathers and of our mothers, our grandmothers, and the ancient beloveds—the communal caring and living—did we decline into poverty and despair. Little by little the white man has dripped his tar-like greed and senseless laws onto our councils, into the hearts of our people; now he sticks a fire to pine tar and we become aflame with greed and want. Perhaps it is not possible to turn back, but it is possible to preserve what we have. It is possible to be prudent, to be careful and accept customs and manufactures and machines from the white man only after long and careful investigation. It is possible for us to remember that the earth is sacred and that we must honor the sacred. It is possible for us to remember who we are. As long as we remember who we are, there is hope.

Billy adopted from his Scots-trader father and his uncle

Alexander the practice of raising livestock and keeping cattle. Many Creeks accepted the practice of raising cattle on a large scale. The mixed-bloods were among the first to develop herds, which were in place before the arrival of Hawkins and his program. Hawkins did bring in some sheep and a few goats, making gifts of them to selected chiefs and their wives. He hoped to introduce wool manufacture, but the sheep and goats never rivaled cattle and hogs as favored domesticated livestock among the Creeks. The Indians' idea of domestication was basically to give the animals free range within a given area, in much the same manner as the British settlers on the frontier. Hawkins preached the virtue of fences.

At his Flint River Agency, Hawkins set up a peach tree nursery and distributed more than five thousand peach trees throughout the nation. In many households, peaches—fresh, dried, and/or processed—began to replace persimmons in traditional recipes. Hawkins introduced Green cotton into the upper towns and Sea Island cotton into the lower towns. He believed that flax was also a promising crop. He planted experimental crops of wheat, barley, rye, and oats. He reported that the oats failed due to dry weather in the spring, but that the early white and brown wheat ripened by the middle of May. He invited Indians to come see his agency farm, where he grew apple trees, grape vines, raspberries, and "the roots, herbs and vegetables usual [*sic*] found in a good garden." His deputy, Alexander Cornells, established a model farm and fields at Tuckabatchee. In his correspondence to friends and officials in Washington, he often repeated his belief that much more could be done if the Indians could be convinced to erect fences and leave their communal towns for individual farms.

The town councils and the national meetings bristled with talk of Hawkins's plans. In 1801 he brought in a hundred pairs of cotton cards, eighty spinning wheels, eight looms and a "young Englishman" who could build more. His plans always revolved around the women of the nation rather than the men. He wanted the women to plant the cotton, spin the yarn, weave the thread, sell the cloth, and make the profit, as well as take over most of the other crops. Billy and the Creek men were taken aback that so much energy was being expended by the agency to "civilize" and "Americanize" the women without any thought given to the traditional roles in a Creek family. Hawkins behaved as if he believed only the women could be trusted to care for their families. He showed no sensitivity regarding the spiritual importance to the men of planting (especially corn) and of growing crops, an activity that determined their identity. Reports in the American State Papers say, "The chiefs were apprehensive that their own women would become independent." In the new order Hawkins wished to establish, the men did not understand what he expected their role to be. A man supported his family largely by farming and hunting. He always had. A marriage was not binding until the man proved that he was successful both as a hunter and as a planter. After the Europeans had introduced the skin trade, the economy and traditional work of men and women had gone somewhat out of balance, but the Indians still perceived their traditional way to be the correct way.

The American State Papers confirm all the rumors I have ever heard about the callous and insensitive nature of Euro-American commerce in Indian country. The French and English Provincial Archives of Mississippi offer even more confirmation. The most destructive element the white men brought into the nation was alcohol. Usually in the form of taffia or rum, alcohol eroded the very core of Indian morality. In treaty meeting after treaty meeting, beginning in colonial times, the Indians begged the colonial authorities and then the Americans not to allow the traders to bring alcohol into their country. Though the treaty negotiators and white government officials lamented the destructive nature of the drink, they maintained that the traders had a right to bring a certain amount into the nation and sell or trade it there. Many chiefs and leading men accepted alcohol in much the same fashion as they did tobacco—it was for ceremonial use only and was never used to the point of addiction. But the addictive qualities of alcohol were such that even ceremonial use was eventually condemned. The traders often used alcohol as a way to put the Indians at a disadvantage in trading deals.

In addition to relating the atrocities and insensitivities suffered by the natives, the American State Papers offer surprising in-depth glimpses into Indian thought and beliefs through the ritual of ceremony as performed at treaty meetings with the Americans. Within the hard cold facts of the Americans, the poetry of the Indians' earnest intentions resides. In the late spring of 1802, when Jefferson was president and Henry Dearborn secretary of war, United States commissioners once again met with the Creeks, hoping to work out a cession that would include the land between the Oconee and Oakmuglee and make the Oakmuglee a strong recognizable border of Indian country that could not be mistaken. This meeting was typical of treaty gatherings and offers insight into the mindsets of the two sides. Even as they began the negotiations, the U.S. commissioners—General James Wilkinson (arguably the most notorious military leader on the southwestern frontier), Andrew Pickens, and Hawkins—knew that the Georgians would never be satisfied until they possessed all the Indian lands within their state. At the chosen treaty site on the opening day of the talks, chiefs and representatives from the upper and lower towns paraded in a grand processional into the town square and proceeded to perform the eagle-tail dance, accompanied by a singing chorus of men and women, which, they explained to the Americans, was their ancient custom. As the procession of these representatives moved into the square, the American commissioners walked to a place prepared for them on the square. Each commissioner was touched by the eagle wings in the hands of the dancers. General Wilkinson stood in front of a small pit with a white staff (the color of peace) beside it. Warriors brought bows and arrows painted red (the color of war), showed them to Wilkinson, broke them and threw them into the pit, covered them with earth, and then placed a white deerskin on the mound. Three chiefs from the upper and lower towns wiped the faces of the commissioners with white deerskins, spread the skins on a log beside the buried arrows, and led the commissioners to the log, where they were seated. General Wilkinson was then directed to place one foot on the deerskin covering the pit. With three other white deerskins, the chiefs covered the commissioners, greeting each one as a friend and embracing them.

Efau Haujo spoke for the Upper Creeks, saying, "We this day, a fine one for the occasion, a clear sun and sky, meet our friends, brothers and fathers, to take them by the hand according to the custom of our forefathers, as old as time itself. We have at the foot of the general buried the sharp weapons of war, which were used in old times, and such as we have. Our white deer skins we place on the seats of our friends, and cover them with same: we add one other emblem, a pipe."

Coweta Micco spoke for the Lower Creeks, saying, "I am going to talk to our friends, brothers and fathers. The day is clear and bright, emblematic of our intentions. Our friends will look upon us, as we are a poor people, and we receive them with such things and such ways as come to us from our forefathers. We are old, but what we do will serve as a lesson to our children, who may, both red and white, follow our example, and grow up in peace and friendship. We shall take our friends by the hand, sit down with them, and close out our ceremonies with the (black drink)."

Eutau Haujo then addressed the commissioners for the entire nation: "I am speaking for my young kings, warriors and nation, to the commissioners that all may know we wish them well. I have a white staff [sapling] now in my hand for the new great general, which I will plant: it will grow and have a shade fanned with cool breezes. When this tree is put there to grow, it will have a shade for our friends. . . . I have but a short talk today and I deliver it along with the staff to the commissioners. You commissioners called the Creek nation to meet you here. We have treated you with our ceremonies and a short talk, and hope you will begin tomorrow and let us progress until we have finished."

On behalf of the commissioners, General Wilkinson replied, "Chiefs, headmen, and brothers of the Creek Nation, I have received from your chief this white staff: it is an emblem of peace; I shall lean upon it and I trust no event will wrest it from my hand."

The opening day ceremonies came to a close and the council adjourned until the next day, when General Wilkinson again addressed the Indians: "When honest men meet on business, no concealments are necessary, nor are they practiced: for our parts our hearts are pure, and our intentions good: We are here to remove the grievances of the red people, and their white brethren. We feel the trust a solemn one: and standing as we do in the face of Heaven, before white men and red men, we shall endeavor to promote the interests of both without fear, favor or affection. With such principles and such motives for our guidance, we can have no hesitation to say to you, that having waited for the ceremonials of your ancestors, which you yesterday exhibited to us, and having been received in form by the nation, we are ready to proceed to the important business confided to us by your father, the President of the United States, but as your brethren beyond the Oconee may feel themselves interested in what we have to say, we are desirous that the governor of that state or some agent from it, may be present to hear us."

The U.S. commissioners continued their delaying tactics from May 24 to May 30, when the Creeks demanded that the negotiations get under way. The Georgians had not appeared at the site or sent representatives or any word of what they intended to do.

In the days that followed, Eutau Haujo brought up the Tombigbee problems. Americans came across the river grazing their cattle on Creek (Alabama) lands, especially on the hunting grounds. The whites contended that the Indians did not use or manage the land, while in fact hunting lands were well tended and managed, especially with seasonal burning, which kept the undergrowth controlled without damage to the large trees and offered refuge and new growth for wildlife. So many vows and oaths had been broken, and the Creeks were patiently waiting for redress. Georgians squatted on Creek lands and continued to disregard all the laws and treaties of the United States. As for the complaints against Indians who might be perceived to be breaking the laws and treaties, the nation would appoint Tussekiah Micco to cooperate with Hawkins in "suppressing disorders." The speaker assured the commissioners that tools the Quakers had sent were receiving a fair trial and that the women remained interested in weaving. Game was scarce, but the hunters wanted the option of continuing the hunt when the opportunity arose even though they were not being given fair measure by the traders. He said that the men of the nation deeply regretted the suffering and poverty of the women and children who were now out in the fields with their hoes, as the Americans wished.

Hawkins gave details of murders Indians were accused of committing and listed the keeping of runaway black slaves and white prisoners as a point of contention between them and the Americans that had to be resolved. The Creeks said that the "white prisoners" were in fact free and could do as they pleased. The truth was that though their white relatives wanted them "returned," the former prisoners did not want to go. Many were married and had Indian families. White women, especially, rejected the opportunity to return to the Euro-American male-dominated world.

The commissioners warned that the Seminoles "acted as spunk to a fire" in their dealings with the Americans and had to be controlled. They accused the Creeks of having European loyalties, declared that most of their land was of little value to the Creeks, especially that between the Oconee and Oakmuglee, which could be ceded to satisfy debts, and said that "you can not exist much longer without government" (completely disallowing the Indians' concept of self-government, which the Americans viewed as anarchy). At the end of the conference, the Creeks agreed to send a "talk" to the Seminoles to advise them to accept American policy and asked in turn that if Indians quarreled whites would remain neutral. Even as the treaty was signed on June 26, 1802, in the basic fashion dictated by the Americans, Tustinugge Thlucco (Big Warrior), Hopoie Yauholo, and Yaufkee Emautlau Haujo reminded the assembly that the provisions of previous treaties had not been fulfilled by the Americans.

Over this undercurrent of dissatisfaction, the commissioners praised the Indians particularly for the fields they had fenced and then proceeded to tell them again that white men would not accept the Indians' idea of communal ownership of tribal lands and towns. After signing the treaty, the Indians said they had to go home and to report to their individual towns on the treaty and have additional councils to see how they would go about implementing the changes, if their towns agreed, and would report back to Hawkins. Though the American Congress would have to ratify the treaty, the Americans were not sensitive to the fact that the Indians had their own ratification process. When asked to clarify the overall picture to the American people, the commissioners said they felt satisfied that they were helping to protect an exposed frontier by keeping the Indians under control.

In 1803 the Choctaws ceded a buffer zone between themselves and the Creeks, in the Tombigbee and Alabama rivers' watersheds, to the United States government. This area, known as the Bigbee district, was opened for white settlement, and settlers crowded the Creek nation's borders. The population in the district centered around Fort Stoddert (present-day Mount Vernon) near where the Tombigbee and Alabama came together to form the Mobile River. Fort Stoddert was the port of entry for the United States above the 31st parallel that separated the Mississippi Territory from Spanish West Florida. (The area from the east of the Mississippi to the Perdido River below the 31st parallel was still claimed by the United States through the American interpretation of the 1803 Louisiana Purchase agreement with France, but Spain occupied the space.) A U.S. customs collector resided at Fort Stoddert and levied tariffs on imports and exports that enraged the citizens of the Bigbee district, who were "double-taxed," once by the Spaniards at Mobile and then by the Americans at Fort Stoddert.

Captain Edmund P. Gaines commanded the soldiers stationed at the fort and pursued a very conservative policy in his relations with the Spanish authorities at Mobile. The United States did not press the claim of ownership of West Florida at this time because of Spain's alliance with Napoleon. The American government did not wish to risk arousing the rancor of a powerful French military.

Rather than resenting the Americans breathing down their necks at the outpost, the Spanish authorities at Mobile considered Fort Stoddert protection against the "firebrands of the Bigbee"—the American settlers—who would like nothing better than to take Mobile by force if for no other reason than to free themselves of the steep, double tariffs and ad valorem duties they had to pay on imports and exports. The Bigbee settlers had neither interest in international diplomacy nor the sophistication to understand that their actions on the local front could have international repercussions. The American military at Fort Stoddert literally offered protection to the Spaniards from the Americans.

Mississippi Territory organized the Bigbee district into Washington County in 1804; McIntosh Bluff, the home of the Tohomé Indians and the residence of the colorful Scotsman Rory McIntosh (who traveled the Creek nation attired in Highland kilts and tartans) was made the county seat. Since the area was so far from the territorial capital at Washington (a village near Natchez), a territorial judge, Ephraim Kirby, was appointed for the area. He was soon replaced by Harry Toulmin. A sheriff, six lawyers, county judges, and justices of the peace appeared in the Bigbee district. The county seat moved to Wakefield, a site which the English-born Toulmin, a Unitarian minister, named after Oliver Goldsmith's novel *The Vicar of Wakefield*. The Washington County courthouse and jail stood on opposite sides of the St. Stephens-to-Mobile road at Wakefield. While most of the American settlers located mainly west of the Tombigbee and to the east at Bassett's Creek in the Choctaw cession, some joined the mixed-blood community in the Tensaw district. The establishment of American legal and legislative institutions so near the Creeks' homes threatened their borders even more directly than did the settlers.

Judge Toulmin described the citizens of his jurisdiction as "better Republicans than Jeffersonians," but, despite their politics and aspirations, the everyday lifestyles of the white settlers did not appear on the surface to be very different from those of the mixed-bloods. Both groups of people had adapted what they could best use from the Indian and the Euro-American world into their homes. Ironically, many of the "white" settlers were mixed-bloods who had rejected or were rejecting their Indian heritage and disappearing into the white world. Galleries (long, deep porches) ran across the fronts and sometimes the backs of their houses. The front gallery was the social center. Often a "dogtrot," or a hallway open at both ends, ran down the center of the house. The open hallway was a dining room in warm weather. The kitchen was a separate building where, in cool weather, meals were both cooked and eaten. Smokehouses for preserving meat and cribs for storing corn, along with barns and chicken coops, made up most homesteads. Rough, homemade, primitive furniture in sparse utilitarian amounts could be found inside. Woven cane formed the seats of chairs, and beds were large wooden boxes, the mattresses stuffed with corn shucks or Spanish moss. Clothing was "homespun," except for a rare jacket or dress imported through the Spanish and American ports. Moccasins made sensible everyday footwear, while bear and buffalo hides added more warmth to a cold bed than a cotton quilt. The whites preferred whiskey to the rum and taffia they sold to the Indians. The "Bigbee firebrands," the Spaniards feared, consumed such enormous quantities of whiskey that they acquired reputations as heavy drinkers. They shared a passion for horse racing and gambling with the Indians. Barbeques and public speaking entertained the settlers. No public schools had been established in the district, making education and religion rare commodities. Lorenzo Dow, the frontier evangelist, visited the Tensaw in 1803 and bought land there but established no permanent congregation.

Samuel Mims, an Indian countryman (a Euro-American married to an Indian woman) settled at Tensaw Lake on the lower Alabama near a channel called the Cut-off, which served as a route (across Nannahubba Island) to the Tombigbee and Mobile rivers. Mims operated a ferry there, and his home became a favorite gathering place for settlers and mixed-bloods. Mims often entertained the neighborhood with frolics, dances, and barbeques.

When treaties in the early 1800s called for federal post roads to be built through Indian country, even more rum poured into the nation, as well as unwanted and unwelcome immigrants from Georgia and the Carolinas. The government promised that the roads would be well regulated, that passports from the Indian agent in each nation would be necessary for travelers using the roads, and that only Indians would be allowed to keep stands (inns) on the roads and operate ferries over streams in their own country.

Billy's friend and brother-in-law, Sam Moniac, was one of several Indians who opened stands offering overnight lodging, food, and refreshment on the Federal Post Road between the Flint River Agency and Fort St. Stephens. Hospitality to travelers now provided a livelihood for some Indians. But even as this economic opportunity arose for a few, the tribe was being lured unwittingly into a financial trap by the government and by such national leaders as Thomas Jefferson and other champions of American equality and justice. The government trading posts, called factories, were permitting individual Indians to run up debts which were tallied against the whole tribe. When the debts became insurmountable, the government planned to demand payment in land cessions from the entire tribe. The cessions, usually granted, pushed the boundaries of the Indian country inward to smaller and smaller territories.

In 1807 a federal road from Natchez to Fort St. Stephens, with a link to Fort Stoddert and on to Georgia and Washington, D. C., was completed. Though in spots it was little more than a rough trail, the road boasted a ferry across the Tombigbee and one across the Alabama at the Tensaw boatyard, the latter operated by Mims; both ferries had been in place since 1797. The ferries were luxuries travelers in the Mississippi Territory did not often encounter. Causeways rose over some bogs and branches, but most rivers, creeks, and streams had to be forded or swum. The road builders marked the entire route at intervals by carving three lashes, or "chops," on trees, which caused many travelers to call the road the Three-Chop-Way, while others called it the Creek Road. The traffic along the road brought a steady flow of travelers, mostly immigrants, across the Creek nation into the Bigbee district. By 1809 the area had a population of six thousand.

Sawmills and cotton gins drew customers as timber and cotton became important crops. Gins were hauled by horseback over the trail from Georgia to the Bigbee settlers, and Abram Mordecai, a Jewish trader, brought one into the nation itself and established it near Weatherford's racetrack. The wealthier mixed-bloods embraced the profit potential of cotton as readily as did the Bigbee settlers. Gins were established at Tensaw Lake near the boatyard and at McIntosh Bluff. The two latter operations had become successful by 1802, the year Mordecai's ginhouse was burned in punishment for an act of adultery with a Creek woman. The avenging clan sliced off one of his ears and beat him severely before he was able to escape.

Soon a printing press was brought by packhorse across the Creek nation to the Bigbee district, but it was potentially more dangerous to the Spaniards at Mobile than to the Creeks. The *Mobile Centinel* was established and first printed at Fort Stoddert on May 23, 1811. The paper's editorials were concerned with the acquisition of West Florida, while its very name announced the publisher's intent to be the voice of Mobile. The idea that Indians could be dealt with easily enough and removed from their lands once the Spaniards were expelled from West Florida dominated the Americans' talk of the Indians in the territory, especially the Creeks. The settlers often said that the Spaniards plotted with the Indians against the Americans.

Congress's diplomatic attitude towards Spanish West Florida shifted dramatically after a civil war broke out in Spain when Napoleon had his brother Joseph crowned king. Spain did not have the resources to stop the United States from taking Florida by force. Napoleon had engaged France, England, and much of Europe in a catastrophic war. But the Americans who had settled in West Florida were far more anxious to live in the United States than the United States was to have them. An uprising in 1810 at Baton Rouge declared West Florida free. Reuben Kemper, calling himself a commissioner from the new state of West Florida, arrived in the Bigbee district, where his cause gained much support. Folch, the Spanish governor, offered to abolish duties on

Americans goods to discourage the Bigbee citizens from taking hostile action along with Kemper against Mobile. But the offer did not stop the white men of the Bigbee from joining forces with Kemper and making their way down the Tensaw River toward Mobile. They sent an emissary to demand the surrender of Mobile before stopping to camp and to celebrate a premature victory twelve miles above Mobile at the site of the Apalachee Indian settlement made in the French period. Fiddles played all night as the men danced with each other and drank whiskey from Baton Rouge. As they dallied, an Indian countryman reached Governor Folch and warned him of the rebels' approach. Two hundred Spanish soldiers came up the river in boats, captured the entire group, and sent them to prison at Morro Castle in Havana, Cuba. The United States disavowed the operation.

In fact, the United States dealt with the entire situation in a curious manner. President Madison refused to recognize the new state of West Florida or annex it. Troops from the U.S. 2nd Infantry were dispatched to the 31st parallel (Orange Grove) above Mobile to protect the Spanish from any other possible revolutionaries or filibusters. When the crisis passed, the troops moved to the highland in the vicinity of Fort Stoddert and built the Mount Vernon Barracks. Then on October 27, 1810, President Madison issued a proclamation taking possession of West Florida from the Perdido River west to the Mississippi below the 31st parallel. United States troops from New Orleans seized Baton Rouge, and the Spanish governor, Folch (east of the Perdido at Pensacola), offered to surrender Mobile peacefully if he received no relief from Europe by January 1, 1811. The civil war still occupied Spanish resources and resolve in Europe. Folch did not expect relief to arrive. Madison sent Folch's offer to Congress, and a joint resolution from both houses authorized the

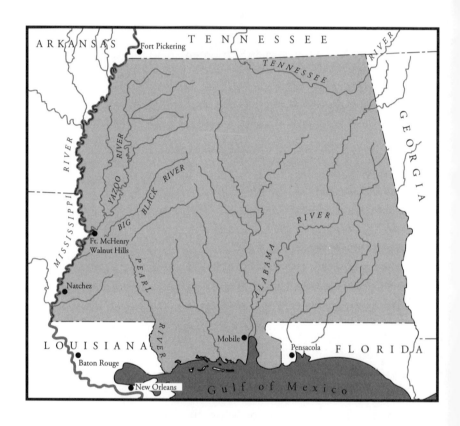

Mississippi Territory, c. 1816. Courtesy of Mississippi Department of Archives and History and the Mississippi Historical Society.

president to take full possession of Florida (not only West Florida), but Congress instructed the president to wait for one year before implementing the action. On May 14, 1812, Madison annexed West Florida to the Mississippi Territory, delaying the possession of East Florida temporarily. But the Americans made no attempt to occupy Mobile.

In 1812 Mobile was a town of ninety wooden houses, mostly one story high, and a well-built brick fort erected by the French at the southern end of town. Called Fort Condé by the French, it became Fort Charlotte to the British and Fort Carlotta to the Spanish. The Spanish governor lived next door to the fort in a house built by the British army major Robert Farmer. A town of lively commerce and mainly French and creole inhabitants, Mobile had taverns and plazas which offered spectacles for the visiting Indians. But the most delightful sights could be seen at the Catholic Church, where the locals practiced their religious rituals in mists of incense, accompanied by ancient chants and other intriguing bits of pageantry. Billy often wandered through the town's sandy, oyster-shell-paved streets, sat in the shade of the ancient oaks, and watched the traffic move back and forth on the government wharf as he talked with the Choctaws who frequented the town.

Part Three

Lessons of the Spirit

Nine

The Spirit Speaks

Billy sits across the table from me in the McCain Library. The pages pile up between us. The list of indictments seems endless. The Americans transgress all the laws of human decency, claiming justifications for their actions by virtue of their civilization. One action leads to another; a chain of never-ending atrocities is created. This pile of events is history—a stack of hard cold facts dictated by military victors, words written by men who eliminate people with philosophies that offend them.

I ask Billy what I will accomplish if I compile one more book listing all the wrongs people commit against other people. How many books have already been written? What light can I bring to this darkness?

Billy sits quietly, waiting.

"Why don't you just tell me what you want me to say, what you want me to write, what you want me to understand?" I ask. I collect my papers and go home. Reading about events leading up to the inevitable—the war, the destruction—has wearied my mind. I do not want to be a part of this war.

Billy and I move back and forth in space and time. In the sacrament of the dream, the divinity of the vision, Billy begins to answer my questions: "Because you are the wind, like me you are the wind. Because our souls are of the wind. Because you can cross the barrier. Because I am your vision. You are my soul. Because if I am a murderer, you are a murderer. Because only if my heart remained pure is there any hope that yours will. Because the past is the future. Where I have been is where you are going. Time is a circle, a spiral loop, closing in on itself. Because the good dies and you are powerless to stop the destruction that you must mourn. Because from death comes rebirth, regeneration. Because everyone needs hope."

Waking, I tell myself that I must reclaim Billy Weatherford's life from the nonrecords so I can reclaim my own soul, my native soul, which lies half hidden and takes cover at the slightest provocation, the primitive natural soul whose existence I am all too willing to deny in the company of strangers and scholars just to protect my fragile ego. I have been given the vision that is a beacon on the spirit road. I must tend the fire.

Time is the place where I travel. This is the deep wilderness of was, what has been. Time, like the circle, the spiral loop, exists without beginning or end. Time cannot isolate us just as we cannot isolate ourselves from the universe. We are all part of the one. We are united with the whole. We trick ourselves into believing that we are separate. The ephemeral visions and the tangible are yin and yang; without one there is not the other.

I have built a fortress of the American State Papers, an impenetrable wall of documents. I am armed with an arsenal of records, letters, and memoirs. I am safe in this fortress. I am well armed behind this wall. Attackers can be easily repelled. But this is not where the war must be waged. This will not even be the scene of a battle. Billy Weatherford cannot be redeemed behind this wall, in this fortress. I must give up my intellectual safety, the neutrality of the academic and scholarly world to enter the world of the spirit. I must fight my inherited war in the quicksand of the intellect, the dreamscape, the dimensions beyond the physical, a place where Pierre Teilhard de Chardin, William James, and Carl Jung may be my only white allies.

While I am in fitful sleep, the dream claims me. I am lost in the deep fog. I cannot find the way. Billy guides me. Together we wander through the dream back to the pine forest where I am sleeping.

I awake to see the path more clearly. I cannot avoid the battles, the blood, the war, the deaths, the madness. I can no longer be a spiritual coward, a neutral scholar. I can no longer pretend that other dimensions are closed to me. I must walk Billy's path with him. Immersed in incense of cedar and sage, we must travel the spiral loop of time. I must remember the taste of dirt in my mouth as I wait in the shallow grave with him for the fire that will announce our rebirth. Doubt must die.

I travel with Billy into his segment of time. We enter the dimension along the Alabama River. About half a mile upriver from his father Charles Weatherford's racetrack, a large sandbar forms a beach where each evening swarms of black crows fill the sky, and then, in swirling spirals, descend onto the beach. The deafening roar of their calls makes conversation or thinking impossible. Some birds swoop up and dive-bomb the water for a drink, while others wade out to drink, then fly off to roost in a nearby canebrake, a place the naturalist William Bartram described so vividly in his journals. *This place is my introduction to the chaotic noise that is erupting in the council debates throughout the nation.*

The town meetings begin with the same sort of momentary frenzy of gathering and greeting, then climax in the attendees' sipping the black drink to purify their bodies and minds until darkness comes. Preparing for sleep around the council fires, the warriors dance, chant, and breathe in rhythm to the music of drums, hoping to lure messages from the spirit world into their dreams and visions. *I am here in this place, an unseen spirit with Billy Weatherford, an unformed shadow of the Truth Speaker.*

At times madness seems to grip the council participants as their words swirl in black clouds of frustration over the continued indignities suffered by the people at the hands of the Americans. Billy speaks as Red Eagle, Lamochattee, at the councils in the town houses on the town squares. He advises caution infused with hope that the Americans can be turned back, that an accommodation can be made allowing the frontiersmen to pursue their interests while not violating the boundaries of the Indian nation, that the Creek nation can be freed by negotiation of the continuous assaults and infringements from Georgia, Tennessee, and the western settlements along the Tombigbee. He says that the people must keep their minds steady and still and their spirits quiet, that they must listen for the Master of Breath to speak to their hearts. Yet he is the first to point out that the people must be ever aware that the Americans will enslave the red men just as they have the black men if they have the opportunity. A person had only to look at how the white Americans treated their black slaves for a preview of how the Indians would be treated if the Americans had their way, if they continued with their "civilization" program and completely eroded the Indians' moral value system. The only salvation for the Indian lay in rejecting the white Americans' tainted civilization and confused morals. A return to traditional beliefs and ways would result in such a wide gap between white and red cultures that the very distance could be the Indians' salvation. Members of the white men's religious sects who actually practiced the religion they espoused, such as the Moravian missionaries the Creeks had met, survived by separating themselves from the rest of white society. Perhaps red men could learn from these sects how to survive surrounded by corrupt white men without succumbing to their society.

Hawkins declares that the town meetings, the endless round of talks within the nation, the incessant taking of the black drink, and the dancing are worrisome, while advising federal government officials that, left alone, the Creeks can solve their own problems, which are internal. Perhaps more to humor Hawkins than to honor him, the Indians declare him the "beloved man of the four nations"—Choctaws, Cherokees, Chickasaws, and Creeks—for which he is the United States Indian agent. He delights in the title and often tells his correspondents of it. The title lulls the agent into believing he is utmost in the Indians' affection and attention. He has hired a white farmer to come into the nation, to visit the different towns and teach the Indians how to plow in the Euro-American manner which he calls scientific. At Tuckabatchee, Alexander Cornells, Hawkins's deputy, sets up a model farm. *In less than two hundred years scientists will say that the traditional Indian method of planting without plowing was a better method—that it did less damage to the soil and the environment, required less water, and produced abundant crops.*

Hawkins expresses delight that Billy's older half-brother, Sehoy Weatherford's eldest son, David "Davy" Tate, has attended school in Philadelphia and Scotland and learned the latest scientific theories. Now, he offers to send Aunt Sophia's son Alexander Durant and a neighbor's son, Richard Bailey, to Philadelphia to be "trained" by the Quakers. Aunt Sophia agrees on the condition that her son stay with the Quakers and study for at least six years.

Hawkins's messengers come to the councils, and he

attends a few himself. When he appears, he constantly scolds the Indians for their methods of horse and slave dealing. Another son of Aunt Sophia, Lachlan Durant, is often mentioned in Hawkins's records and letters as a culprit in both. The sweet dream of freedom has lured runaway black slaves into the Creek country. As soon as a runaway slave arrived, an Indian would appear, claiming that he was the slave's owner; then the "ownership" would immediately change hands back and forth many times among other Indians, in a scramble of paperwork or a lack of it, making the situation so confused that it became highly improbable if not impossible for white men to reclaim the runaways. In the meantime, the runaways were moved around the nation so frequently that no one could really keep up with them. After a while, they were allotted a spot to farm, for which they gave a share of their produce to their "owner" as rent, and were left to their own devices in much the same manner as individual Indians' legally owned slaves. Sometimes the white slaveowners declared the runaways stolen and demanded that the government force the Indians to return the stolen property. In many such cases the Indians kept moving the runaway blacks through the nation until they reached the wilds of Florida, deep in the Seminole country.

The runaway slave problem and Lachlan Durant's major role in it frustrates Hawkins, but he is even more aggravated by the Creek horse-trading industry. Various young men of the tribe take horses from the white plantations and farms bordering Indian country but do not consider it stealing. Warriors using vigilante methods merely take what they believe is owed to the nation as the result of various treaties and transactions with the whites. They view ownership as a communal situation and consider themselves to be collecting long-overdue debts. The horses enter a trading maze not unlike the one created for the runaway black slaves. Because of the large number of horses dealt with in this way and the fact that so many whites have lost property, Hawkins writes, "Trading in horses . . . [creates] endless mischief that will ruin all the government's plans." He institutes a system of special licenses for selling and trading horses that he hopes will force the young warriors to give up their vigilante activities. Accusations fly back and forth across the boundaries of the Indian nations. The Creeks avow that horses stolen in the Cumberland region of Tennessee are taken by the Chickasaws, not the Creeks. The Chickasaws say that the Creeks have been stealing their horses, too, while across the Creek border with Georgia a white frontiersman accuses the Creeks of stealing his dog and makes an official complaint.

Horses, slaves, and a dog divert no one from the real issue. The white men want the Indians' country, their land. They hide their desires so poorly that Willie Blount, the governor of Tennessee, becomes Fusse Micco, the Dirt King, to the Creeks.

The national councils at Tuckabatchee become so exclusively a platform for Hawkins to chastise the Creeks and to make demands forcing them to betray their culture and sacred beliefs that they hold an opposition council at Coweta. Hawkins protests that he has not consented to the Coweta talks attended by the chiefs of the upper towns. Just as Hawkins read the long list of grievances against the Indians at the annual national councils, an account of the crimes they had allegedly committed against white people, now the Indian leaders at the unsanctioned council speak aloud the names of the Indian victims of white crimes that were never mentioned in the American records. The roster of Indians wantonly murdered grows. But the greatest crime of all is the hunger and poverty that has been inflicted on the nation by the transition to the American civilization process. Two little girls of the nation have died of hunger, a heinous crime for which the spiritual leaders indict the whole nation. Any Creek child is the responsibility of all the Creek people. How can you let your own child starve? the firemakers ask. No one should go hungry if there is food anywhere in the nation. Children are suffering hunger and want because the ancient laws of sharing are not being practiced as the result of the Americans' attempt to dissolve the native communal bonds of concern, care, ownership, and matrilineal descent and to replace them with capitalism and patriarchy. The time has come for the people to return to their traditional value system and communal lifestyle or lose them forever.

The cry for the return to the old ways is nowhere greater than at the Shawnee village of Souvanoga (located southeast of the Hickory Ground), which belongs to the Creek confederacy but still retains links with the larger Shawnee communities in the Northwest Territory along the Wabash. Shawnee bands often settled among other tribal groups, where the warriors were employed as mercenaries by their host nations. The Shawnee war chief Tecumseh's mother, Methoataske, had grown up in the Creek band of Shawnees. Tecumseh had visited the village in 1787 and was well known in the Creek nation. News of the native religious revival among the Shawnees along the Wabash traveled swiftly. A prophet, Tecumseh's own brother Laulewasika, had appeared among the Shawnee there. The prophet brought a message of hope, of the possibility of deliverance from the spiritual enslavement in which the white men and their culture had ensnared the Indians. The Master of Breath spoke to the prophet: "Reject the white man, reject his culture, reject his government, reject his ways, return to the path of the spirit, the path of Nature." Laulewasika became the prophet

Tenskwautawa (the Open Door); the spirit's teachings and directions came through his visions and dreams. His guidance reopened the door to the Path for the red men to follow.

Blinded in one eye in a childhood accident and an alcoholic at the age of nine, Tenskwautawa led a desolate and forlorn life until he happened onto Shaker missionaries in the northwest territories in modern-day Indiana and western Ohio. He listened to their teachings and watched their dancing, movements of trance-like communion with their god. The Master of Breath spoke to him as he observed the Shakers: "Salvage your soul, your culture and your people. Reject the whiskey and rum that devour the mind, that block the vision and cripple the nation." Tenskwautawa never drank alcohol again. The prohibition of alcohol became the most important tenet of the new religion. It was no coincidence that the Creeks and the Shawnees were suffering from the same spiritual malaise and had reached a crisis in their cultures at the same time. The Americanization of the Indians was under way in the Northwest Territory just as it was in the Southeast.

Tecumesh found his brother's new insight to be the spiritual twin of his own political views. His dreams and plans for a pan-Indian confederacy now had a philosophical and spiritual platform as well as the appeal of native sovereignty. Like an evangelist, Tecumesh took the message to other tribes. With an entourage of thirty warriors and spiritualists, he traveled to other nations, preaching the native gospel, initiating converts into the philosophy of the Open Door, and enlisting allies for his confederacy.

He and his entourage of warriors stopped in the Chickasaw and Choctaw nations on their journey to the Alabama River. The Chickasaw leaders had embraced the Americanization program and believed that it was the best policy for their small nation. The Choctaws, as always, were divided in their opinions. There were as many individual opinions of Tecumesh and his message among the Choctaws as there were Choctaws. The Shawnees visited with Mushalatubbee, one of the three principal chiefs of the Choctaws, before traveling on into the southern, or Six Towns, district of the nation and the village of Hoentubbee, a well-known Choctaw warrior, where Tecumseh was to speak and where warriors and leading men from the western, eastern, and southern districts were invited to come and listen. All of his life Hoentubbee would remember the appearance of the Shawnees, their great physical beauty and the favorable impression they made on everyone who saw them. The men of Tecumseh's party were all dressed alike, in buckskin hunting shirts, a cloth flap with buckskin leggings, and moccasins profusely fringed and beaded. All wore beaded garters below the knees. Their hair was plaited in long cues of three braids hanging down between the shoulders, and their temples were closely shaven. Everyone except Tecumseh adorned his hair with hawk and eagle feathers. Tecumseh wore two long crane feathers, one white for peace and one dyed red for war. They wore silver bands on each arm, one around the wrist, one above and below the elbow; a few wore silver gorgets suspended from their necks. Around the forehead of each, encircling the head, was a red flannel band about three inches wide, and over this a silver band. They adorned their bodies with paint. Red semicircles drawn under each eye extended outward on the cheekbone; a small red spot on each temple and a large red spot on the center of each breast unified the individually applied body paint. They carried rifles and had tomahawks and knives stuck in their belts.

The Shawnees performed their pantomime ballet-like

drama, dubbed the dance of the lakes, for the Choctaws in a traditional three-day ritual, with the calumet being passed from hand to hand. Choctaw and Shawnee orators entertained the gathering. The climax of the affair was Tecumseh's speech, warning, then pleading, with the Choctaws and a few of their Chickasaw neighbors in attendance to return to the traditional teachings of their people and reject the "civilization" program of the Americans. He reminded everyone of the long list of grievances the red man had against the white man, of how the red man's kindness and compassion were continually rewarded with murder and robbery. He named the many Indian nations that had disappeared in the wake of white men's arrival on Indian lands.

He said: If we are forced to war, we must restrain ourselves and use the least amount of violence necessary to insure victory. We must all adopt the ancient Choctaw and Creek custom of never killing women and children. A warrior has no need to kill women and children. A true warrior will seek the road to peace if he is given a choice; if he is not, then he must take the route open. A true warrior is the guardian of the people, the nation. If the Americans force Indian people into a war, then we must seek the aid of the British. Our complaints against the Americans are just. We can honestly accuse the Americans of injustice. We must stand together. All red people are bound by consanguinity to a common cause.

Some of the Choctaws answered Tecumseh's talk by saying they were comfortable in their relationship with the white Americans. Others who were more receptive to the message were silenced by Pushmataha, a chief of one of the three divisions of the nation. (Puckshenubbee was chief of the third district.) Pushmataha declared himself an American ally and friend and told the Shawnees they were not welcome in his nation. The Shawnees moved on to Yazoo Old Town (about eleven miles east of present-day Philadelphia, Mississippi) and repeated their performance and speech with Pushmataha again giving the major response. After making several more stops in the Choctaw country, the Shawnees had few converts. Pushmataha might not have spoken for all the Choctaws, but the entire nation was so slow to anger and so eager for peace that Tecumseh considered them unlikely allies and soon continued his journey, accompanied by an escort of Choctaw warriors led by the mixed-blood David Folsom, to the Tombigbee River, the boundary of Creek country.

In the Creek nation along the Alabama, Billy and the unformed-shadow-that-I-am watch the horizon and wait for Tecumseh, the panther in the sky, the man born under the light of a comet coming to us, as a comet begins to rise in our evening sky in October 1811. How many signs will the Master of Breath offer us before we know Tecumseh's words should be heeded? This message coming to us by the comet's rising light may cause the people to see the ways of American civilization in a true light and turn them back to traditional values.

Tecumseh stops at Autauga and makes his first appeal to the Creeks for his pan-Indian movement. The people there clearly hear the call to brotherhood. They unite in purpose with the Shawnee. More than the call to brotherhood and unity, Billy hears the call of the spirit. Seekaboo, originally of the Creek band of Shawnees, a traditional medicine man of the Shawnee and a prophet of the revived-reinterpreted native spirituality, speaks Choctaw, Creek, and English, as well as Shawnee, and is traveling with Tecumseh as a translator. He plans to stay among the Creeks as an evangelist and teacher. During shared meals and around the campfires, Billy listens to the prophet as a warrior-priest.

Seekaboo answers questions about the Open Door's conversion, telling how the prophet met and watched the Shaker missionaries, how he saw them enter trances where they heard the voices of their leaders who had died, where they heard the advice to repent and to return to the correct path, and where they learned what would be in store for people who do not heed the warnings of the spirit world. He heard the admonition to lead a good and decent life, far from the influence of the worldly Americans and the evils they practiced. He realized that the Great Spirit, the Master of Breath, was using the Shakers to teach him a lesson, to point him on his own true Path. The Shakers opened the door, and the prophet saw the possibilities translated into Indian thought. The mystic realm was not forbidden territory for Tenskwautawa's imagination or for his everyday consciousness. His society and culture encouraged him to wander there.

Billy and I follow the Shawnee entourage as it moves on to Coweta. The spirit speaks in his heart. He is Billy Weatherford-Lamochattee-Hoponika Futshia, a man of multiple identities, a man of two fires and one heart, the firemaker-farmer, the warrior-priest, the mystic who has found his own path and now must rescue his people, people of the one heart, from the depravity of the American civilization process, which prohibits sharing wealth or owning property and land in common and which denies the importance of a mother to the clan, replacing her with the father. To those who broach the topic of the civilization process, he says that if the wild American frontiersmen are civilized, then he prefers to remain savage. The dances at Coweta, the talks, and the people's responses convince us that he is not alone in his belief.

Watching the dying embers of the council fire at night while the visitors sleep in the hothouse after the hosts have gone home, I listen to the thoughts inside Billy's head. One man must see himself in all other men. In the collective group there is unity, spiritual support, the strengthened awareness of common purpose. Survival. A way of life gives an individual strength and personal courage, individual commitment to beliefs. People must share a common consciousness, a common spirituality, a collective soul. How do you gain an acceptable perspective on war, one which makes it acceptable? Not a war of individuals, but a war of right and wrong. War demands that you think only in terms of right and wrong. People striving to rise to a higher level of being must overcome forces that threaten to stop the move toward that goal. In the struggle, what can be done about a deviant group that does not share the desire, conscious or unconscious, to reach a higher level as individuals, as a race, a people? How do sane men justify war to themselves? We are each part of the collective, whether we want to be or not. It matters little how far one person journeys unless that journey marks the way. One person alone may not be able to mark a path wide enough, make a war fierce enough, or reach a goal inclusive enough.

The councils at Coweta are small. Most of the leading men have gone to the national council at Tuckabatchee, where Hawkins plans to address the nation. *Billy and I travel there with Tecumseh.* At Tuckabatchee, five thousand Creeks will have a chance to hear his message. Tecumseh stops outside the town. His horses are turned over to Creek warriors to be cared for and pastured. Runners are sent ahead to announce his party's arrival to the council on the town square. Ritual endures, and a welcoming committee comes from the town square to greet the regal Shawnees and escort them on the walk back there. Most of the people have moved out from the town onto individual isolated farms as part of the Americanization program, and now they have returned to their traditional homes in a festive mood of reunion for the duration of the council.

The Shawnees' silver ornaments glisten in the sun as they walk toward the square. The tall, beautiful men, with their painted faces and purposeful stride, turn the ritual greetings of respected visitors to the council into awesome ceremony. As they approach the square, a Creek warrior at the entrance blows a call on a conch shell. At the four cardinal corners of the square, the visitors stop and make offerings of tobacco. The tiered galleries of the open houses around the square shelter Creeks in their ceremonial dress. Big Warrior (Tustinuggee Thlucco), chief speaker of the Upper Creeks, acts as master of ceremonies for the gathering. Tuscenea, chief of Cusita; William McIntosh, chief of Coweta (nephew of the colorful Rory McIntosh of McIntosh Bluff [Alabama]); Timpoochee Barnard, chief of Yuchess; Captain Sam Isaacs (Tourculla), chief of Coosawda and son-in-law of Alexander McGillivray; and the ancient warrior Efua Haujo keep their seats in the council house as Big Warrior steps forth to greet the Shawnees.

"I am Tecumseh," the Shawnee says, as he presents Big Warrior with a wampum belt of different-colored strands. The Creek speaker, a giant of a man splattered with freckles, closely examines the belt and passes it on for each of the other warriors on the square to inspect. The Shawnees have brought a large, elaborate, ceremonial sandstone pipe decorated with shells, quills, beads, and eagle feathers; it is lighted from Tuckabatchee's continuously burning sacred fire and passed from warrior to warrior. Politeness dictates that those gathered smoke, but there are white men present—Hawkins himself, the traders, and a band of American frontiersmen like Sam Dale, a frequent guide or "pilot" across Indian country for immigrants and settlers from Georgia. The latter group will give a completely false report of Tecumseh's visit. One or two warriors who know the Americans' dislike of the Shawnee and do not wish to incur their wrath refuse the pipe. The Indian greeting ceremonies remain circumspect. Despite many years of living in proximity to the Indians, most of the white men present still misunderstand and misinterpret Indian manners and protocol as readily as newcomers do.

Tecumseh says he would like to speak to the council but he has disrupted the proceedings enough for one day. He speaks in the American Indian's universal tone of self-effacement. This is proscribed behavior, good manners. Big Warrior conducts the Shawnee party to the town hothouse, which serves as a lodge for honored guests, and encourages them to rest from their journey. Then he returns to the square and the council house and the speeches of the assembled, where the admonitions and directives of Hawkins continue. Hawkins demands that the Indians agree to a new federal road across their land to run from Tennessee to Fort Stoddert. The Indians say no. The Federal Road from Georgia across the nation to the Tombigbee and Tensaw settlements has brought nothing but trouble. The presence of so many misbehaving white people on the road drives the young men wild, the chiefs explain. Hawkins says the new road from Tennessee will be built, that the Indians cannot disagree. At night the Shawnees dance around the small fire they have made outside the hothouse. Filled with introspection, they dance themselves into hypnotic trances where their spirits are embraced by the Master of Breath. Their souls move through the Open Door to the spirit world as their bodies wither and twitch and collapse on the ground around the fire. This is their private worship, apart and separate from the council meeting.

In keeping with the Indian customs of self-effacement

and modesty, each day at the council Tecumseh says he would like to speak but the business of the council should proceed without him interrupting. The same statement is made for three days in a row, the proscribed length of time for any well-mannered visiting American native. The business of Hawkins and the white men with the Indians is concluded. The council is adjourned. Tecumseh's visit coincides with its conclusion. The white men are expected to leave Tucka-batchee. Later they will say they were banned from the speeches of Tecumseh there, that the Shawnee came to talk war, to ally the Creeks with the Shawnee and British in a war against the white Americans. But Hawkins says that was not the case. Tecumseh has been traveling among many nations preaching his new gospel. The agent sees it as a type of harmless drama, a performance for entertainment. He has heard the words and read the speeches; there is nothing to be concerned about. Only the Americans with greed-blackened hearts can interpret the call for a spiritual revival as a call to a bloody war.

Sam Moniac and Billy take their respective places in the tiered galleries of their clans at the council. *I am the phantom that hovers nearby.* The Creeks will listen to any message of hope, will seek any route to the salvation of their nation. Now on this October night with the council fire crackling and the flares of the flambeaus—the cane torches—lighting the square, the tustinuggees, the warriors, gather.

The conch shell sounds and Big Warrior stands and speaks. These are the words tradition recalls: "From somewhere in the outer darkness, where spirits live beyond the moon, a comet torch is racing toward us—a thing of wonder, a sword of fire! To those of us whose hearts are downcast, whose breath is stabbing pain, it puts into our hands a tool, a weapon, it gives us hope for our salvation, it gives us hope to avenge the wrongs committed against us. It gives to us the yellow wildfire which leaps across from pine to pine, a mighty, reeking, roaring furnace! Tecumseh, springing like a panther, whose eyes are coals of deadly fire, gives words of hope to all who listen. Look now, Tecumseh comes!"

Led by Tecumseh, the Shawnees come from the guest lodge into the square, dressed only in breechcloths, moccasins, and paint. Their bodies are painted black with semicircles of red beneath the eyes, jagged red zigzag lightning streaks down their legs and arms, and a round red circle like a target on their chests. Their steps are carefully choreographed as they move to the center of the square, where Tecumseh announces, "I am Tecumseh," and his entourage shouts. The ceremonial pipe is brought out, lighted, and passed through the gathering. Then Tecumseh speaks. He makes a plea for brotherhood, for unity, for the honor of the consanguinity that binds all Indians. He asks that the Creeks renounce the corrupting practices of the Americans and return to the spiritual teachings of their ancestors. His message is the same as it has been throughout his travels. If Indians unite and regain the moral standards of their ancestors, they can enjoy a good life. Having a good life means strengthening the tribal communalism that the Americans feel they must eradicate at any cost. The Americans will not retreat from their goals of destroying the Indians and possessing all their lands unless the Indians are united. No Indian should be allowed to sell any piece of land; in fact, none can because the land is owned in common by all Indians. In unity there is strength. If the Indians speak with one voice, it will be so strong and resounding that the Americans will have to listen.

Tecumseh speaks the truth the Creeks are living and shares the same heartache. What might happen? If war comes—if the Americans cannot be reasoned with and resort to war—then the British will ally with the Indians, Tecumseh says. Hostilities already jostle American and British relations, and the Shawnee foresees war between the two. Perhaps this is the time to forge an agreement with the Americans in which the Indians will be treated honorably; if not, then the united Indians can join forces with the British.

Some of the warriors grow restless with this aspect of the talk. Indians should not side with white men on either side in a conflict between two white nations. Let white men fight each other without Indian involvement. War should not be the answer—a strong alliance, perhaps, but not war. Sane men did not seek war. Creek warriors must remain sane. Yet warriors must be prepared to wage war for the salvation of their nation. Warriors are not always offered a choice.

Seekaboo speaks of the spirit. Tecumseh's entourage begins their dance of the lakes. It is a pantomime of an Indian raid that portrays an ambush—warriors creeping up on the enemy, the attack, the enemy overcome, flashing knives, hands thrust high in victory. The dancers pound out a cadence with their feet on the hard ground of the square and end the performance with cries of victory and shouts of joy.

Big Warrior rises and promises to respond to Tecumseh's talk tomorrow. Then his words reiterate that Indians must not become engaged in a war between two white nations, that returning to the ancient ways requires seeking peace and contentment for the people. Tecumseh's talk of the spirit is taken. The prophet Seekaboo is accepted as a resident mentor of the new religion, but Big Warrior will assure Hawkins that the war talk was rejected by the council, that the possibility of an alliance between the Indians and the British in the British war against the Americans was not the proper course for the Creeks. No one wants war. There must be more deliberations, more talks, more communication with the spirit and with the hard-headed Americans who claim Indian lands and violate treaties.

Tecumseh leaves for the Wabash. Little Warrior and a party of Creeks travel with him. All lines of communication must be kept open. Some of the Upper Creeks have long thought that the American frontiersmen are incapable of reason, that killing them is the only way to stop them. But other Creeks hope that reason will prevail and a middle way found, that some harmony and balance can be reached.

The lessons learned in the shallow grave come back to Billy and whisper inside his head: hope is not irresponsible; it can slow your heartbeat, ease the burden of breath, soothe the troubled spirit. Hope can exist buried beneath the raging fire that destroys all that has been. Hope and reason.

Visitors attend the regular daily gatherings on the town square at Tuckabatchee. Big Warrior speaks in private to some of these mysterious strangers. A Scotsman from Pensacola, rumored to be a British operative, talks with Big Warrior. *We don't know what he says.* Emissaries from Indian towns throughout the South come for closed talks and private meetings with Big Warrior, recognized by the Americans as chief of the Creeks and by the Indians as speaker for the Upper Creeks.

Creek towns and communities experience their own version of frontier revivals as prophets are trained and directed by Seekaboo. Josiah Francis, the mixed-blood son of the silversmith David Francis, is among the first. Josiah's father and grandfather were Scottish mystics. He has inborn knowledge of the spirit. Under Seekaboo's guidance, he cloisters himself in darkness for several weeks in a circular hut guarded by the Shawnees, who periodically dance around the enclosure to keep the place sacred and to ensure that the spirits are in attendance. In the darkness, Josiah Francis (Hillis Haujo) seeks his vision, his message, which will come through the Open Door to guide him. He and the Spirit, closeted in the isolation and darkness, in time commune in a sacred dance that ripples through the apprentice prophet's body, making his calves tremble and his whole body shake with the fervor of his growing devotion. When he finally emerges from the darkness, he is blind. Seekaboo leads him into the circle of Shawnee prophets and warriors, announcing that Josiah Francis can no longer see the world as he had before, that the Spirit has taken that vision of the world away. Now, after the time alone with the Spirit, Josiah is emerging without sight and will be led by the Spirit to see again with a new vision. Slowly, over the space of a day or so, Josiah Francis regains his sight. Now he is a priest of the Open Door, a prophet, a light maker (*coole-jir*). He joins Seekaboo in seeking new converts. In the forests and deep woods, in circles under the tall trees and beside the rivers, the prophets call people together and preach a return to traditional ways, to communal living. The gatherings have the fervor of Euro-American frontier revivals, with chanting, dancing, and vision-seeking. But December comes before the prophets make any significant number of converts. Then, on December 16, an earthquake of great magnitude ripples the surface of the earth throughout Creek country. Devastating aftershocks are felt for months. Rivers temporarily flow backwards, acres of land collapse into rivers and lakes, new lakes appear, streams change their courses, and the earth continues to tremble. Captain Isaacs dreams that the great serpent of the underworld is restless and ready to wreak havoc on the earth. Others dream that the Master of Breath has tired of the chaos in the middle world and of mankind's refusal to accept responsibility for maintaining balance and harmony and is now in the process of destroying the earth. Thousands of converts make their way to the Open Door and embrace the vows that call for the renunciation of the evils of the white world and the return to the traditions of the ancestors. In white communities throughout the South, Christian churches experience similar conversions and rededications as the earth continues to tremble at intervals from December 1811 through February 1812 in the New Madrid quake. Some of the young naive Creek prophets, caught in the trance of their own dance during which aftershocks occur, begin to believe that they can cause the earth to tremble with their spiritual power.

Tensions within families grow. Those of two fires, two bloods, red and white, often find themselves choosing opposing sides. Some choose the Americanized lifestyle mainly because they believe that by doing so they will avert war, that they can somehow stop the American onslaught, or that they will at least be unscathed by it, perhaps able to hide in their own shallow grave while the wildfire of war sweeps over the land and emerge unsinged when it has ended. Many others who choose that life do so because they have become very wealthy practicing capitalism and paternalism, and the resulting wealth has bred greed.

Billy Weatherford talks with his friend Sam Moniac and his brothers Jack and Davy Tate. The conversations swirl through the smoke of the fire. Who said what? The words have no owner in the darkness beyond the fire's edge.

"Philosophy is one thing, but the possibility of war and ruin another."

"Differing philosophies cannot break the bond of brotherhood."

"We can choose to be white men or red men."

"Your heart knows that there is no choice."

"Are you so in love with ideas that you will make the sacri-fices that those ideas demand?"

"Can't you see the ruin that will pour in on the nation?"

"An even more wretched state of affairs for the people?"

"A man must follow his heart."

"A man must search his heart."

"A man must walk with the spirit."

"A man must seek the path."

"His own path."

"If it is just ideas then it is easy enough to choose."

"Your heart is good but you also have a head—use your head in this. You are a sacred human being. You talk with the spirit. The spirit talks to you. You must follow the spirit path."

"Is life worth living if it is not honorable? If a person can-not follow his own path? When there is no harmony in the order of the world, when the balance of nature is upset, how can people who dream of god and know good not make a stand? If we plan, if we purify our hearts and beings, if we return to the way things were, if we reclaim the ancient teachings, the words of the Mas-ter of Breath, the giver of the ancient word, might we not find what was lost? Build a new nation?"

"The British will not come to our aid."

"They have long since forgotten us."

"The Spanish are as near as Pensacola and Mobile. We can barter for aid. They find the Americans as frightening as we do."

"The Spanish at Pensacola and Mobile are hard-pressed to feed themselves. They can barely fend off the Americans in peace. How could they succeed in war?"

"They have resources that we could gain. We can call on the French. They are champions of freedom."

"Talk. Words. There are no viable options. We must make

our peace with the Americans. Make it in our hearts as well as our heads and become Americans with them."

"They are the scourge of the earth."

"Yes, and if we are to survive we must unite with them."

"I cannot."

"Brother, you are lost."

"Time. If we have time we can build alliances. Musha-latubbee does not see the world so differently from how we do. If we can ally with the Choctaws, we will be strong enough to earn the respect of the Americans. Strong enough to be left to our own devices."

"There is no time. There are only unrational men. Reasonable men always move too slowly. Hotheads on both sides dictate the timing with their wild impulses."

The smokey talk reaches no resolutions.

The prophets and converts decide that, in order to rebuild their lives and restructure their culture free of the Americanizing influences, they must build new towns, move from the scattered farms the Americanization process has forced on them, and return to their communal lifestyles. New towns arise at several different locations in the Upper Creek country and are made sacred by the prophets' appeals to the Great Spirit. Ekon Achaka (Eccanachaca), the Holy Ground, eventually contains several interconnected villages along the Alabama River above Big Swamp at Pintlala Creek. Billy's children move to the Holy Ground with their surrogate mother (Sam Moniac's sister), followed by Sapoth Thlaine and her sisters. Billy's own sister, Sam Moniac's wife, moves to the Holy Ground with her children. Aunt Sophia chooses to move there, as do some, but not all, of her children and their families. Her sons Lachlan, Alexander, Peter, and John are major leaders of the new community. The new homes are consecrated. Women and men burn their Americanized clothing, slaughter their cattle, and smoke the meat as they prepare for their new life, the life of their ancestors. Men such as Billy and Sam Moniac continue to move about the nation without making their intentions clear to the Americans.

The white settlers and Americanized mixed-bloods see the retreat to the Holy Ground and the other new towns as hostile acts. The prophets call for a moral and spiritual war against white influences. The whites cannot imagine that it means anything but a bloody war. They retaliate by building stockades and demanding that martial actions be taken against the prophet-led Indians. The rhetoric frightens whites, Americanized Indians, and mixed-bloods, who must choose who they will be, driving them into forts or into the consecrated precincts of the new towns.

Ten

Friends and Allies

I am the shadow of grief, dwelling in the raw wound of the heart. Distractions cannot turn me from this appointed time. Billy says that people must believe and obey the voice of their own dreams, and my own dreams have brought me here. The Spirit will triumph. The Spirit leads us to a sacred place, a beloved space, holy ground. What must we suffer to reach the sanctuary of the sacrament, the communion of the sacred?

Little Warrior and the thirty of his countrymen who went north with Tecumseh start toward home after a lengthy visit on the Wabash. On the homeward journey in February of 1813, they encounter a group of Chickasaws who tell them that war has begun between the Americans and the Creeks. The traveling Creeks have attacked an American settlement near the mouth of the Ohio, allegedly killing members of the seven families living there. This was the second attack by Creek warriors on white settlements north of their homeland in a matter of months. Another group of Creeks traveling in the Chickasaw country along the Duck River, acting independently and allegedly without direct provocation, attacked the home of an American settler, and kidnapped Mrs. Martha Crawley during the raid. They forced Mrs. Crawley to come with them as a servant and cook until they reached the Tuscaloosa Falls, where they traded her to an Indian living there.

Tandy Walker, a mixed-blood blacksmith in the employ of the U.S. government at Fort St. Stephens, took a trip up the Black Warrior River to visit his old friend Oceeochee Emathla, chief of the town where Mrs. Crawley was living in servitude, and managed to purchase her from the Indians and bring her back to the fort. Mrs. Crawley testifies that the Indians harmed her person in no one way though they burned her home and killed several of her grown boys. She says that they required nothing more of her as their prisoner than that she cook for them on the trail. Her testimony is never used for or against the raiding party at a trial. There is no trial.

After receiving a message from his deputy in the Chickasaw nation, Hawkins declares the kidnappers guilty and sentences them to death. William McIntosh, the mixed-blood chief from Coweta in the lower nation, accepts the position as head of Hawkins's execution team, a group that is so adept at carrying out Hawkins's orders in direct contradiction to established Creek law and tradition that they become a death squad.

Hawkins also finds Little Warrior and his warriors guilty without a trial or a hearing to determine the circumstances of their actions. He demands that they be executed by their own people. Such an action is against the Indian moral code, *lex talionis*, the law of retaliation. If the families of Mrs. Crawley and the other murdered settlers had declared their intent, then tracked down the murderers and kidnappers and killed them, the Indians would have seen it as justice, but for the U.S. government to order the Indians to kill their own people, who had caused neither them nor their families any harm, sets off an endless round of internal tribal strife. Much to the distress of Big Warrior, the father of Little Warrior, a secret council at Tuckabatchee in April 1813 dispatches a group of warriors appointed by Hawkins and led by McIntosh and mixed-blood James Cornells, who has a plantation on Burnt Corn Creek on the road to Spanish Florida, to kill Little Warrior and those who were with him on the Ohio. McIntosh divides his warriors into several small groups. One of these units goes to the Red Warrior's Bluff on the Tallapoosa, surrounds a house where five of the accused are staying, and opens fire. The trapped warriors defend themselves as best they can, but, when all seems lost, they begin the dance of the lakes. The executioners kill all the occupants of the house and then torch it. Captain Sam Isaacs leads the unit that pursues Little Warrior into a swamp above Wetumpka and kills him. After the men of Little Warrior's raiding party have been executed, Hawkins's death squad is targeted by traditionalists for their betrayal of Indian justice. Now the unjust murders have to be avenged on the men who performed the executions. Captain Isaacs, son-in-law of the late Alexander McGillivray, has, with his much-publicized dreams of the great serpent, aligned himself with the lower world and mocked the prophets with his talk of personal visions. He especially incurs the traditionalists' ire.

In 1812, Mormouth, an ancient chief, accidentally shot and killed Thomas Meredith, an American settler passing through from Georgia, on the Federal Road to the Bigbee district of the Mississippi Territory. Sam Moniac buried Meredith near his stand on the road. Sam assured Hawkins that the death of Meredith was an accident, but Hawkins did not believe him and proceeded to charge Mormouth with murder. The death squad executed the aged Indian on July 19, 1812. But when Meredith was scarcely buried, another white man, William Lott, was murdered along the road near the Tensaw settlements. One of the accused murderers sought sanctuary in the white (peace) town of the chief Hopoithle Micco, also known as the Tallassee King. The alleged murderer entered the town and claimed the ancient and irrevocable right of sanctuary by sitting on the peace seat. McIntosh shot him dead on the spot. Hawkins's death squad, led by McIntosh, becomes in the eyes of the traditionalists the symbol of all that is wrong with the Americanization of the Indians.

As the murderous events that will set the stage for a civil war begin to unfold, Billy collapses into a world deprived of the music of Sapoth Thlaine. Her songs end. The birth of her son exacts the toll of her own life. Her sisters take the baby into their homes at Ekon Achaka (the Holy Ground), and Billy mourns. *The gnawing ache that philosophy cannot soothe foreshadows his actions. Life is so precious, so sacred, so rare that it should not be lived carelessly. A human being unattuned to nature, unconnected with the vital pulse of the universe might never find his way through the wilderness of grief. To sit quietly and empty one's heart into the nothingness of no-thinking will consume days and weeks the Creeks do not have.* Sam Moniac leaves his house on the Federal Road in the charge of servants and goes to be with his mourning friend, to rescue him should the grief try to claim more than a small space of time. *We sit with Billy through the dark days and endless nights, the time when pain must be endured.*

Sam suggests a diversion. A cattle drive demands that the drovers surrender their minds, that they become intellectual drones, supervising the movement of animals across the prairies and hills, fording streams, growing physically numb in the saddle. A cattle drive can serve a number of purposes. Sam suggests that a herd can be sold in Choctaw country. Billy agrees. What is more American than a business transaction while the war rhetoric reverberates throughout the nation? The Americans will applaud such an action. Men seeking to do business, to make a profit, are always admired by the Americans. With their herd dogs and African cowboys, the two friends round up cattle from Billy's plantations and drive them into the cowpens. When several hundred cattle are collected from the open range, the men drive the herd northwest into the Choctaw nation. Should any American ask, should Hawkins himself ask, it is only coincidental that Mushalatubbee will be waiting at the end of the trail. The Choctaw chief is a well-known entrepreneur himself.

Selling the Choctaws a herd of cattle is easier than selling them an idea. Billy presses for an alliance with the Choctaws. Mushalatubbee is not without followers and influence, and he is open to talk. An alliance of the Choctaws and Creeks would be such a powerful force, of such numbers, that war with the Americans will not be necessary. The numbers alone will convince the Americans to back off and leave the Indian nations to live their own lives and solve their own problems. *I listen as Billy makes an eloquent argument for the alliance.* The Choctaws listen just as carefully. Their well-reasoned answer is no answer. They will consider, but they will not commit themselves. No one chief can speak for all the Choctaws. There will have to be a consensus. Slow to anger and eager for peace, the Choctaws often find that the best route is no action. But Billy's arguments merit at least a full consideration. Mushalatubbee will assemble a meeting of the three main chiefs and the leading men of the nation, and the leaders of the dissident Creek faction can make their presentation.

If Billy and Sam could gain a positive commitment from the Spaniards, would that sway the Choctaws? With strength, with enough warriors, there could still be a way around war. He and Sam round up another herd of cattle grazing on the open range of the nation and set a drive towards Pensacola. *I am the phantom rider unseen by cowboys and dogs.* The Spanish dons politely listen. Governor Mattio Gonzales-Manrique grants *us* an audience, but the Spaniards are in no position to offer *us* any assistance beyond moral support. Their outposts are poorly supplied and as threatened by the Americans as are the Creeks. War was officially declared between the United States and Great Britain on June 18, 1812. The Spaniards are nervous.

The United States annexed West Florida below the 31st parallel between the Perdido and Mississippi rivers, and Congress passed an act on February 12, 1813, authorizing General James Wilkinson to take possession of Mobile from the Spanish. By March 8, Wilkinson and his troops aboard U.S. naval ships from New Orleans had reached Dauphin Island at the mouth of Mobile Bay and sent the following message to Cayetano Perez, the Spanish commandant at Mobile: "The troops of the United States do not approach you as the enemies of Spain, but by order of the President they come to relieve the brave garrison which you so worthily command, from the occupancy of a post within the legitimate limits of the United States. I hope that you will peacefully retire from Fort Charlotte, and from the Mississippi Territory, to the eastern side of the Perdido River."

After a few days, Perez, knowing that his garrison of about sixty men and sixty-two cannons were in a perilous position, with no reinforcements and no supplies, agreed to the American demands. The Americans provided transports and provisions for the Spaniards from Mobile to Pensacola. The grave insult to Spanish honor and sovereignty had to be endured. Spain's resources had shrunk to such meager portions that she could no longer readily supply her outposts or even rigorously defend her American possessions as the mother country revolted against the forcibly imposed reign of Napoleon Bonaparte's brother. In Europe, Britain was aiding in the Spanish struggle against Napoleon. On the southern United States frontier, Spanish outposts struggled to survive as best they could in a diplomatic limbo. They could hardly risk antagonizing the United States with the American territorial ambitions so evident.

Manrique listens to Billy and Sam but can offer little more than empathy. However, if they were to proceed with their plans, and those plans should result in a war with the United States which ended in failure, Spain would evacuate the Indian leaders and their families to the safety of Havana, providing they could reach Pensacola in a timely manner. If the Indians sent their women and children south of the 31st parallel, along with their old men and young boys (who could hunt for them), while the warriors sought solutions to their quarrels with the United States north of the parallel, the Spaniards would consider them diplomatic refugees and offer the Indians what protection they could.

The Spanish dons do not foresee a scenario in which the Indians will be victorious, but, ever gracious, they write out their evacuation proposal and give it to Billy in the form of a letter which he as graciously accepts. *We must fight and die or surrender our identity without a struggle. There is no one we can rely on or ally with except the Spirit and the visions of the prophets.* The closest the Creeks come to viable British aid is in the imaginations of the Americans. Are the Creeks to wait as pitiful victims for the white frontiersmen while the Mississippi, Georgia, and Tennessee militias invade their homes and evict them? The people dare to hope, dare to believe that in the battle to bring harmony to their world, to return balance, the spirits who proclaim the necessity of balance and harmony will align with the Creeks.

How can a logical person be anything but cynical? The people will be helpless and defenseless, sheltered only by the Holy Ground's promise. Traveling back into the nation, Billy and Sam pass on the result of the trip to Pensacola to High-headed Jim and Peter McQueen, then round up more cattle from their plantations and send them with the African drovers into the Holy Ground for a commissary herd. Billy and Sam now turn their attention to a traveler passing through the nation.

After securing Mobile, expelling the hapless Spaniards, and bragging that the "Mississippi Territory now reached the Gulf," the notorious General Wilkinson was ordered to Canada. With twenty armed men in a procession of forty persons, including his wife and several of the other officers' wives, in carriages and on horseback, the general's entourage has been traveling over the Federal Road headed for Washington. The group has stopped for a respite at Sam Moniac's stand. Billy Weatherford and Sam Moniac assume the roles of genteel Indian mixed-blood plantation owners and solicit the comfort and ease of the general, patiently listening to his stories, his news from Mobile, his opinion on why he is being posted to the north, and his outlook on the unstable politics and growing tensions in the region. Who could imagine two such well-to-do, highly civilized planters having Indian sympathies? Even if they were mixed-bloods? Over dinner, Wilkinson gossips with the innkeeper and his charismatic friend Billy Weatherford.

The presence of the ladies is an added factor. The charming and handsome Billy sends for his favorite fiddler, a black slave, and provides the officers' wives with music and an opportunity for dancing. When the ladies press Billy to join them in their sets, he demurs. He is in mourning. His own dear wife has passed away recently. His deference to his departed beloved wins their admiration and increases their estimation of his charm. They will form a loyal faction of defenders if their husbands ever question his character or motivations.

Major General Thomas Flournoy of Georgia has been ordered to Mobile to replace Wilkinson as head of the U.S. Seventh Military Division. As soon as he arrives, Flournoy orders Brigadier General Ferdinand L. Claiborne, with his six hundred Mississippi Militia volunteers, to Mount Vernon to be in position "to protect the Mississippi Territory from any invasion from Spanish, British or Indian forces." The growing tensions between the Tombigbee and Tensaw settlers, the mixed-bloods, and the Indians is the true reason. Wilkinson himself offers overblown justifications, while at Mobile calling the situation "perilous . . . with the Creeks at my back, Seminoles to my left, Choctaws to my right and the ocean to my front" and saying that he "can only be offered help from Georgia and Tennessee." Of course, the only immediate peril is directed toward the Creeks, and the help from Georgia and Tennessee of which Wilkinson spoke was an invading army bent on plundering the Indian nation of its land. Claiborne's orders also call for him to oversee the construction and manning of the stockades the settlers in the region believe they need to protect themselves from the Indians.

Wilkinson's stay in the nation is prolonged as Big Warrior asks for a meeting with his old friend of the White Sapling Conference. Big Warrior has sent urgent messages to Wilkinson saying that the dissidents, or "war party," as they have been dubbed by the Americans, in his nation are making more converts daily and that he is beginning to fear for his own safety. The dissidents have been threatening the life of Big Warrior since the execution of the warriors involved in the Duck Creek incident. Now Wilkinson writes to Judge Harry Toulmin, one of the three U.S. judges of the Mississippi Territory at Fort Stoddert, Mount Vernon, dating his letter June 25, 1813, Sam Moniac's, Creek Nation. Big Warrior has informed him that the dissidents expect to "intimidate" the rest of the nation into joining them and then to make war on the whites. He writes Judge Toulmin that it seems to be the general impression in the nation that the majority will join the dissidents and make war, but no one seems to know where the first blow will be struck. Josiah Francis, who lives on the Federal Road, the same road where Sam Moniac has his inn, is claiming to have had "a visit from the Lord" and, along with more than three hundred fellow believers of the Open Door faith, is at a camp on the Alabama about sixteen miles above the Big Swamp near Pintlala Creek (the Holy Ground); Wilkinson has heard rumors that Francis's party is "about to move down the river to break up the half-breed settlements and those of the citizens in the forks of the river." He writes that the agent, Colonel Hawkins, is "profoundly silent," and that Alexander Cornells, the interpreter and deputy agent of the Upper Creeks, has fled the nation.

The general writes, "I know not what stress to lay on these wild reports, but the whole road is deserted—the Indians are all assembled, and their villages ahead of me, many towns on the Alabama and Tallapoosa and Coosa are deserted, and consternation and terror are in every countenance

I meet." He says that if he were in the judge's place he would call up the volunteers immediately. He asks Jack Weatherford, Billy's brother, to deliver the message to Toulmin.

Billy and Sam begin to wander in and out of documented time, assigning many of their activities to tradition and the imagination. Their movements up to this point have been unquestioned. Now their plan calls for Billy to rejoin the people at the Holy Ground and do what he can to prevent a catastrophe there, as he searches for a way to maneuver the people through the madness that has overtaken the nation, brought down by the Americans, the Americanized mixed-bloods, and the settlers in the Tombigbee district and at the Tensaw.

The chiefs, the traditionalists, the prophets, the converts to the Open Door, the moderates, and the dissidents in the villages on the Holy Ground respect Billy Weatherford and seek his advice, but he is not a chief. As in all American Indian politics, the government at the Holy Ground breeds a certain amount of anarchy. Billy offers Manrique's suggestion that the women and children be sent to Florida, but it is rejected. In his cabin at the newly constructed village on the Holy Ground, he stores his letter from the Spanish governor. There is peace in the simplicity of his new home, in its stripped-down circumstances, which pushes the thought of impending danger temporarily out of his mind. Without the clutter of materialism, Americanization, a man can see his place in the world more clearly.

Sam travels to Fort St. Stephens and meets with Judge Toulmin to give his deposition on the situation in the nation and along the Federal Road. He will appear to be friendly to the Americans and not a member of the group they now call the war party. From such a trusted position he will be able to keep Billy informed of the Americans' activities. His deposition will say what the Americans want to hear and offer an explanation of Billy's behavior that will fit the Americans' moral code. The Americans cannot be expected to understand the Indian code of honor.

In Judge Toulmin's chambers, in the presence of Lieutenant Colonel George Ross of the Mississippi volunteers and a stenographer, on August 2, 1813, Sam begins his story with the arrival of Tecumseh and thirty northern Indians in October 1811, answering questions and offering insights. "Tecumseh said he had been sent by his brother, the prophet, but it was not until Christmas that any of our people began to perform the dance of the lakes. Seekaboo, a prophet, stayed and taught the people the religion and the dance after Tecumseh went back north. The dance of the lakes is a sort of war dance, though it is danced as part of the religion of the Open Door. The Muskogees have a similar dance of their own but it is always performed after a war. At that time about forty of our people began this northern custom, and my brother-in-law Josiah Francis, who now says he is a prophet, was at the head of them. Their number has very much increased since; there are probably now more than half of the Creek nation who have joined them."

Sam continues, "Being afraid of the consequences of a murder having been committed on the mail route, I had left my home on the Federal Road and had gone down to my plantation on the river. I stayed there some time. I went to Pensacola with some steers during which time, my sister and brother, who have joined the war party, came and got off a number of my horses and other stock, and thirty-six of my negroes. About twenty or so days ago, I went up to my house on the road, and found some Indians camped near it whom I tried to avoid, but could not. An Indian came to me, who goes by the name of High-headed Jim, and who I found had been appointed to lead a delegation sent from the Autossee Town, on the Tallapoosa, on a trip to Pensacola. He shook hands with me, and immediately began to tremble and jerk in every part of his frame, and the very calves of his legs would be convulsed and he would get entirely out of breath with the agitation [an involuntary reaction of a believer touching a nonbeliever, according to the prophets]. This practice was introduced in last May or June by the prophet Francis, who says that he was instructed by the Spirit. High-headed Jim asked what I meant to do. I said that I should sell my property and buy ammunition, and join them. He then told me that they were going down to Pensacola to get ammunition, and that they had got a letter from a British general which would enable them to receive ammunition from the governor. That it had been given to the Little Warrior, and saved by his nephew when he was killed and sent down to Francis. High-headed told me that when they went back with their supply another body of men would go down for another supply of ammunition, and that ten men would go out of each town, and that they calculated on five horseloads for every town. He said that they were to make a general attack on the American settlements, that the Indians on the waters of the Coosa and Tallapoosa and on the Black Warrior were to attack the settlements on the Tombigbee and Alabama, particularly the Tensaw and Fork settlements. That the Creek Indians, bordering on the Cherokees, were to attack the people of Tennessee, and that the Seminoles and Lower Creeks were to attack the Georgians. That the Choctaws also had joined them and were to attack the Mississippi settlements. That the attack was to be made at the same time in all places where they got furnished with ammunition."

In answer to questions, Sam says, "I learned from my sister that the people at the Holy Ground are being treated very rigorously, and must conform to strict standards, and that many, particularly the women, were very desirous to leave but could not. Many of the women, including the daughters of the late General McGillivray, had been induced to join the war party to save their property. I found, from the talk of High-headed, that the war was to be against whites and not between Indians themselves—that all they wanted was to kill those who had taken the talk of the whites—Big Warrior, Alexander Cornells, Captain Isaacs, William McIntosh, the Mad Dragon's son, the little Prince Spoko Kange, and Tallassee Thicksico. They have destroyed a large quantity of my cattle, and burnt my houses on my river plantation, as well as those of James Cornells and Leonard McGee."

The stenographer reads back the testimony, offers it to Sam, and points out the place he is to make his mark. The document identifies Samuel Moniac as a warrior of the Creek nation. The statement contains enough truths to meld with what the white men already know and enough exaggerations to confuse the issue over what they do not know. If the whites believe Sam, they will consider the Creeks, with all their allies and no divisions in their own nation, to be as strong as Billy had tried and failed to make the Creeks with alliances. The truth is that the nation is on the brink of a civil war and that the handsome High-headed Jim, whom Americans describe as the "beau ideal," only dreams of getting ammunition in any quantity from the Spaniards.

As part of the artful espionage, Sam starts a rumor by telling a story of how he and Billy, returning from a trip into the Choctaw nation of the Mississippi Territory, where they had been trading in beef cattle, found several chiefs assembled on Tallewassee Creek, a mile and a half from the Alabama, taking the black drink. These chiefs told Billy and Sam that they must join them or be put to death. Sam refused and had mounted his horse to leave when his brother-in-law Josiah Francis grabbed the bridle. Sam snatched a war club from his hand, gave Francis a blow to the head, and raced away in a shower of rifle bullets. Billy consented to remain, telling the Indians that he disapproved of their course and that it would be their ruin, but that they were his people and he would share their fate, that in staying with them he hoped to prevent bloodshed. From person to person, white and mixed-blood, the story circulated, growing and contracting, then expanding again, until generations later it was accepted by many as truth.

More than any other American, Hawkins seems to be acutely aware of the impending Creek civil war, perhaps because he himself has done so much to start it. While he is urging the chiefs friendly to the Americans to work to avoid the civil war, white settlers and the mixed-bloods whose emerging society is the product of the government's Americanization program are hastily throwing up flimsy stockades in their neighborhoods. They expect to feel the wrath of the long-aggrieved Indians. If they understand the depth of the cultural betrayal the traditionalists believe has been committed, they disavow it. It is easier to blame everything on Tecumseh, to say that the problems started when he came into the country, that he was recruiting allies for a war against the United States, that he was a British emissary spreading revolt in the Indian nations at a time when the United States and Britain were entering a war. With Tecumseh to blame, the Americanized sector in the Creek nation did not have to accept any responsibility for the turmoil of the civil war.

The message Tecumseh brought to the Creeks, the words of the Open Door, gains added impact and meaning in the traditional-minded Creek community as the whites and U.S. government officials demand that Indians violate more and more of the most ancient and sacred of their laws in order to retain American friendship. The prophets and their followers are subjected to derision by the Americanized Indians. Big Warrior invites some prophets from an Alabama town to come to Tuckabatchee and give him and the Americanized Indians proof of their spiritual powers. In part, Big Warrior's message says, "You say the Great Spirit visits you frequently; that he comes in the sun and speaks to you; that the sun comes down just above your heads. Now we want to see and hear what you say you have seen and heard. Let us have the same proof you have had, and we will believe what we see and hear."

The mocking tone of the message rings loudly in the hearts of the Alabamas. They kill the messenger and send out their own dispatches saying that they will destroy Tuckabatchee and Coweta, as well as Hawkins, his deputy, Cornells, and all the chiefs who have accepted the Americanization program. The Americanized residents of Tuckabatchee and Big Warrior act surprised that the Open Door converts and traditionalists are serious about their beliefs. They say that they had thought the whole business was just a "sort of . . . amusement for idle people."

Though the insulted traditionalists have no ammunition and only war clubs and bows and arrows for weapons, they lay siege to Tuckabatchee, which is considered the capital of the Creek nation. The Americanized Indians inside the town lack enough ammunition to repel the siege. By the time a message gets through to the Lower Creeks, Tuckabatchee is also low on food. Finally, the Cusseta King, a chief at that town, rallies a force of two hundred warriors with guns and plenty of ammunition from the lower nation and enters the town without any violence, hostilities, or interference from the siege force. He escorts all the townspeople to the town of

Cusseta, which becomes the new capital of the nation. Tuck-abatchee is abandoned.

The prophets of the Open Door hold their religious services wherever they can find willing audiences. The people become more and more receptive as the executions of traditional Creeks dramatically demonstrate the warnings Tecumseh has spoken. The selecting and training of prophets lacks the process of a careful screening as well as the ancient traditions and methods of the firemaker's training. To be a prophet, one has only to give one's self over to the Open Door, to seek and receive a mystic experience, and to be able to go into trances at will. To doubt the sincerity of the prophets is disingenuous, but to recognize that sometimes unstable personalities are attracted to the position is common sense.

The powers and forces of the Spirit can be tools of enlightenment or weapons of self-destruction. Lateau, an eighteen-year-old boy, enters the darkness, the confinement required of those seeking to become a prophet. He trembles in the presence of the Spirit, and, after days and nights spent in confinement and darkness, he emerges, blinded by the daylight; as his eyes slowly readjust to the light, he is pronounced reborn. The secrets of the confinement, the communion with the Spirit, and the passage through the Open Door are the gifts that Lateau brings with him into his new life as a prophet. Devoted, perhaps even fanatical, Lateau soon has a cadre of eight subprophets. In July 1813, he and his followers go to the old town at Coosa and invite all the people from the nearby towns and villages to come for a spiritual service. Orations directed by the Spirit are followed by the music and motion of the dance of the lakes, at the end of which the prophets give a war whoop, race across the square into the crowd, and kill three chiefs who have actively supported the Americanization process within the nation. In the pandemonium that follows, the other chiefs at the Coosa square scatter, race for their nearby homes, collect a group of warriors, return, and kill Lateau and his eight cohorts, then continue to Little Ocfuskee and kill a number of the Open Door practitioners who live there, in keeping with the Indian code of exacting revenge on the family of murderers. During these troublesome days, traditionalists among the Upper Creeks and Alabamas claim the ultimate vengeance on nine members of the Hawkins death squad, but McIntosh still lives. Hawkins begins referring to the dissidents among the Upper Creeks as the "Red Sticks" for the war clubs painted red those Indians are displaying on their town squares.

Both Peter McQueen, a mixed-blood of Tallassee (son of the infamous James McQueen, a British seaman who had jumped ship at St. Augustine as a young man after striking a British officer and sought refuge in Creek country), and Hobothle Micco have been openly supportive of Tecumseh's talk at Tuckabatchee; now, as the civil war festers and erupts in the nation, they become more outspoken and begin to emerge as leaders of the traditional sector of the nation. Josiah Francis of the Alabamas early emerged as the principal religious adviser of the Open Door, and now High-headed Jim of the Autossees is recognized as the principal war chief of the dissident group. This group crosses the Tombigbee River and heads toward the concentration of Choctaw towns near the headwaters of Buckatunna Creek for the conference with the Choctaws that Billy and Sam have arranged with Mushalatubbee. The pro-American Pushmataha dominates the Choctaws at the conference, and the less-than-peaceful rhetoric of these Creeks does not change his mind. The council proceeds in the ancient prescribed manner for a length of three days—no conference or council can last less time than that—but the Choctaws will not be swayed. Buffered by the Creeks from the remote Georgia frontier, they do not have the extensive personal knowledge of American atrocities that the Creeks possess. Only the southeasternmost towns of the Choctaws, the Chickasawhays, those nearest the Georgians and the Tombigbee settlements, understand the Creeks' distress and openly support them.

The Creeks return to the Holy Ground and almost immediately set out for Pensacola. McQueen, High-headed Jim, Josiah Francis, and a group of about sixty warriors earnestly believe that the letter that has come into their possession by way of a nephew of the slain Little Warrior guarantees them ammunition and help from the Spaniards at Pensacola. Billy and Sam's visit with Manrique did not address the letter, from a British general in Canada, which had been acquired by Little Warrior during his travels to the north with Tecumseh. The nephew had hidden it from his uncle's executioners. The dissidents believe that, on delivery of the letter, each of their towns will be well supplied with ammunition with which to wage war against the Americans if it becomes necessary; in the meantime, there will be more than enough to exact the necessary amount of revenge on the executioners of Little Warrior and his party.

When the Indians reach Burnt Corn Springs, a crossroad for the Pensacola trail and the Federal Road, they burn the house of James Cornells, one of the principal executioners of Little Warrior's party, kidnap Cornells's wife, and carry her to Pensacola, where she is sold to a French lady (Madame Baronne) for a blanket. Cornells was away from home when the Indians arrived. Their behavior toward his property and wife was appropriate within the ancient code of exacting revenge. Cornells's black slaves, unharmed and left behind, eventually take a message to a neighbor telling of the Indians' activities. Though the mixed-bloods and nontraditionalists surely know and understand the code of retaliation, they react as if the dissidents' actions are unreasoned, illogical, and brutal. They quickly spread news of what they call an outrage to the white settlers. Most of these people claim to understand Indians and Indian ways well, yet none except the U.S. Indian agent Hawkins seems willing to accept the incident as an isolated one committed in reaction to another act.

These actions—the kidnapping and the burning of houses by an isolated group of Indians—are transformed into an impending Creek attack on all white and mixed-blood settlements in the Tombigbee and Tensaw region, and, most fantastically, the British fleet is "seen" off the coast unloading supplies, arms, and ammunition to be sent to Indians through the Spanish port at Pensacola. General Flournoy refuses to send out his troops to satisfy the rumors. But, hearing talk that a group of dissident Indians has gone to Pensacola, Colonel Joseph Carson asks David Tate, Billy's half-brother, and William Pierce to go there and investigate the matter.

The letter which the dissident Indians expect to bring them a bounty of arms and ammunition is just a letter of introduction and recommendation from a British general in Canada, according to the governor. He listens to the Indians explain what they believe the letter says. He says he cannot supply them with ammunition because he has so very little himself, scarcely enough to defend Pensacola should the Americans decide to annex any more of West Florida. He does agree to meet again at a later date with the delegation. The Indians make efforts to purchase ammunition and powder privately, but such commodities are difficult to come by from private sources in a Spanish colony. The British traders operating out of Pensacola are a possible source of powder and lead, but they hesitate to offer quantities larger than what would be normal for hunting without the local government's approval. Perhaps a behind-the-scenes deal between the traders and the dons was made.

In their next meeting with the governor, the Indians are issued three hundred pounds of powder and a limited amount of lead with which to manufacture bullets. At the Americans' request, David Tate quickly arrives at Pensacola to learn what he can of the Indians' activities and as quickly departs. He is an American spy. He tells the Americans that to secure this small amount of ammunition, Peter McQueen gave the governor a list of towns with forty-eight hundred warriors planning to take up arms in defense of their nation against the Americans. The small amount of powder and lead is a fraction of what the dissidents believe they need to make their towns safe from the Americans. Tate tells Colonel Carson that after the Indians received the powder they "openly" said that they were going to war against the Americans—that they would return to the Alabama, distribute the powder, and then move against the Tombigbee settlers.

Before departing from Pensacola, the Indians perform the dance of the lakes for the governor. High-headed Jim, a group of warriors, and the packhorse train loaded with the gunpowder and lead head home, while some of the warriors prolong their visit to the city.

The news from Cornells plus the report of the spies send the settlers and nontraditionalist mixed-bloods scurrying for the forts and stockades they have erected. Colonel James Caller, the senior militia officer in the area, calls out the militia. With three companies of local militia, he crosses the Tombigbee at Fort St. Stephens on Sunday, July 25. He marches south to Fort Glass, one of the stockades that has sprung up in the countryside, where he is joined by two other companies, one under the command of Sam Dale, the other under William McGrew. Members of the militia, mounted on their own horses, carry their own rifles and shotguns. They cross the Alabama and march southeast towards the cowpens of David Tate, where they halt and wait for another company, this one led by Dixon Bailey of the Tensaw district. Now with 180 men—Americanized Indians, mixed-bloods, and whites—Caller's men continue their march only after they reorganize and elect more officers. The militia unit is now top-heavy with officers. On July 27 scouts report that they have found the "war party" from Pensacola camped on a branch of Burnt Corn Creek a few miles ahead, and that the warriors are busy cooking and eating their midday meal. Caller divides the militia into three units and plans to lead a surprise attack into the Creek encampment.

With their packhorses scattered about the spring, grazing, the Creeks nonchalantly enjoy their midday respite. The men in the militia dismount, leaving their horses in the rear and sneaking around a hill in the pine barren that harbors the spring where the dissident Creeks are camped. The tumult of the sudden charge of the militia down the hill to the campground surprises the Indians. Many quickly grab their guns and begin returning the militiamen's fire before scattering into a nearby canebrake on Burnt Corn Creek. From the sanctuary of the dense cane, the dissidents see that the militiamen are more interested in capturing the packhorses and looting the camp than in pursuing the warriors and fighting. The dissidents rally, burst from the canebrake, charge the looting militia, and drive them from the camp. Unable to collect enough troopers to stand and fight the Indians, Colonel Caller orders the militia to fall back, to regroup and resume the attack. But the looters panic when they see the few fighting troopers retreating before the enemy and scramble from the camp, driving the Indians' packhorses before them. The officers have little control over the militia-men. Fewer than 80 of the 180 men respond to orders. In the open woods on the far side of the hill, the militia ex-changes gunfire with warriors under the command of Peter McQueen and High-headed Jim. In less than an hour the militia fully retreats. Many of the last Americans to go have lost their horses, driven off by their own fleeing men, and now run from the battleground on foot. The dissidents pur-sue the militiamen for about a mile, and then, in the south-eastern Indians' established tradition of seeing a battle as a limited engagement, give up the pursuit. The militia contin-ues its ragtag retreat until its members reach white settle-ments and stockades. The first battle of the war has been fought. Victory escapes the militiamen and costs the Red Sticks about two hundred pounds of their precious powder, some lead, and packhorses. Two militiamen lose their lives and fifteen suffer wounds, including the Mississippi Terri-tory's most boastful murderer of Indians, Captain Sam Dale. The Americans say, "Ten or twelve Red Sticks were killed and eight or nine wounded."

High-headed Jim, surprised at the attack, says he did not know that war had "fairly broke out." He frankly admits that, if the militiamen had not stopped to loot the camp and gather up the packhorses, the Indians, who were far out-numbered by the militia, could not have claimed a victory. He says that the Indians watching from the canebrake as the militia searched for plunder had only to fire a few guns in the air and the militia ran like scared rabbits.

Not waiting for a formal declaration of war, which would include posted notices in pictographs at the enemy frontiers, the militiamen surely understand that the Indians' code of justice now demands a revenge attack without warning on an American or Americanized settlement. Not all the American and Americanized citizens of the Mississippi Territory settlements in the vicinity of the Creek country appreciate the action of the militia. They criticize Caller and his troops for putting innocent people in harm's way and starting a war that might have been avoided. All the diplomatic and conciliatory measures that might have prevented bloodshed had not been tried, they say. Now there is no turning back; the dissidents will have to avenge the unprovoked attack at Burnt Corn.

The great storm of war has erupted. Billy sits in the quiet of its center as his name is firmly linked to the war party. "Weatherford" becomes a curse word when spoken by Andrew Jackson of Tennessee and the other Americans impatiently waiting to dismantle the Creek nation. Occasionally an American will refer to Billy as Red Eagle but never Lamochattee. With a name like Weatherford and a glint of red in his hair, Americans despise him as a traitor "to the white race." As the Americans wait for the vengeance that must come, they all agree that William Weatherford will be masterminding the Indian moves. The red club of war now stands in all the dissident town squares, and the Americans have begun calling their adversaries the Red Sticks.

Eleven

Massacre

Billy and I are the warriors returned from the council, from the declaration. Now we prepare. We paint our bodies black. We streak the blackness with vermillion lightning-shaped zigzags. On our blackened faces we paint circles of red around our eyes so that we may see more clearly, so that our vision will be sacred. We strap swan wings to our arms and fan the air. Inside the sanctuary of our souls we dance the circle of our own hearth, of our own inner fire, testing our wings as our spirits soar. We tune our souls. We prepare to go into battle. We make our peace with the universe. I have entered the vision to be here. I have become the unformed shadow to prepare for this time, to understand this moment.

I think that I cannot comprehend war or condone murder, that my mind-set is too advanced for such primitive responses. This is the fantasy with which I cushion my modern life. No matter that I live in a time of rage and destruction, when people are called to battle a never-seen enemy who is destroyed from a distance, a time and place in which humanity has

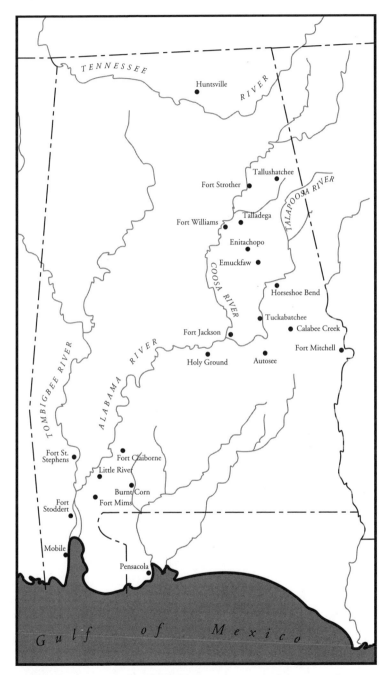

Prominent Creek War sites super-imposed on modern state of Alabama.

become an abstraction, a time and place that nurture the most savage wars the world has ever seen. No matter. This war must be noble, righteous. I cringe at the thought of blood on our hands; yet that is the road we must walk. That is the place we must go. Executioners. Slayers. I tell myself it is just a symbolic war, a ritual battle. There can be no balance until the people have their revenge and wrongs have been made right, until the unavenged warriors have been rescued from the realm of ghosts. I am sick, dizzy with the thoughts. I cannot turn back. I can only move forward. Duty. The dutiful must provide the peace through war. We are the warriors of the Master of Breath. We are on his mission. We must beg the forgiveness of those whom we will slay, as we prepare to die. Our own deaths can hold no fear. We have stopped needing. We have stopped wanting.

Billy and I sip the black drink, yaupon tea, until we purge our bodies of all impurities so that we can see the way with greater clarity. The songs we chant wrap us in the essence of the Master of Breath's embrace. We make our spirits invincible. The enemy may attack, maim, or kill our bodies, but our souls are inviolate. We have merged with the vision of the Spirit. We have sipped the sacrament of the dream. We have entered the altered state of the warrior. We are ready to battle the darkness that would devour the soul.

As the Red Sticks prepare for war, so do the Americanized mixed-bloods and settlers. They spend much of late July and August in their forts and stockades. Only two long-established forts, St. Stephens and Stoddert, really offer any formidable protection. Most of the other eighteen or so stockades that have sprung up on farms and around homes in the Tombigbee and Tensaw districts are rough timber and log palisades with primitive bastions around very small areas. During the summer, several of the communities that have moved into their neighborhood stockades hold religious revival services in the style of frontier camp meetings to pass the time and recall the recent earthquakes that were surely omens of the end time and second coming foretold in the New Testament, but, at other stockades, alcohol consumption, gambling, and rowdy-rustic entertainment is the order of the day. Frontier generals send detachments of regular soldiers and Mississippi Militia units to man most of the forts. The forts, as the stockades are called, are usually named for the family around whose home the walls have been raised.

Northward, on the east side of the Alabama, two miles below the Cut-off (the shortcut channel to the Tombigbee and upper Mobile rivers) and a quarter of a mile from the Tensaw boatyard, is the home of Samuel Mims, the ferry operator. The walls of Fort Mims encircle the family home and several other nearby buildings on a very cramped acre of land. A row of slave houses stands nearby, outside the walls, in a sweet potato field. Several other houses outside the walls make up the neighborhood stretching to the boatyard; then just one mile away stands Fort Pierce, a palisaded sawmill. Fort Mims lacks many finishing touches necessary for even a primitive stockade, and, when General Claiborne visits in early August, he orders the commander, Major Daniel Beasley, "to strengthen the pickets and build one or two additional blockhouses." Major Beasley does not vigorously comply with this or any other orders from Claiborne.

Beasley and a hundred and seventy-five Mississippi volunteers man the fort where seventy local militiamen, under the command of Captain Dixon Bailey (this unit of Americanized mixed-bloods and their captain were prominent in the battle of Burnt Corn), and sixteen regulars under Lieutenant Osborn are gathered. This force theoretically stands ready to protect about two hundred area civilians. Among the civilians are women, children, black slaves, and several

Spanish deserters from Pensacola. Life inside the fort is crowded and uncomfortable, but most of the inhabitants turn their confinement into a carnival. Shipments of whiskey arrive regularly. Alcohol consumption ranks high on the list of entertainment. Young women flirt and dance with the soldiers as black slave fiddlers play tunes throughout the day. The men inside the fort gamble and play cards with an obsessive devotion. Children run in and out the open gates to and from the river, searching tangles of thick vines for ripe muscadines, playing and courting mischief. The western gate has not been yet installed, and a secondary rough gate inside the western perimeter offers no obstacle to anyone entering the fort. Fine, white river sand blows against the east gate until dunes lock it into an open position. Beasley becomes angry when someone suggests that the gates be kept closed and movements into and out of the fort limited and monitored. Though Beasley receives communiques on the reported movements of the hostile Red Sticks, he ignores them. He apparently has nothing but contempt for the possibility of danger and the military ability of the Red Sticks. As the inhabitants of the fort carouse themselves into believing that there is no real danger, *we of the Red Stick army count the broken days, with a bundle of twigs from which a stick is taken each passing day, until we gather on the lower Tallapoosa near the Hickory Ground.*

Warriors from the towns of Hoithlewale, Fooshatchee, Cooloome, Ecunhutke, Oakchoicoochie, Pockuschatche, Ochebofa, Puckuntallahasse, Wewococ and Wocescoie, Alibamo (Alabama), Muklose, Souvanoga (Shawnee), and the other Red Stick towns purge their bodies, fast, and drink willow-bark tea as their leaders plot the vengeance necessary to rescue the unavenged from the realm of ghosts. Peter McQueen, High-headed Jim, and Far-off Warrior emerge as leading chiefs of this army, Josiah Francis and Paddy Walsh the main prophets, and Billy Weatherford the military advisor and planner. *I am but a phantom.* The main Red Stick army, led by High-headed Jim and Billy, begins its southwestern march on August 20, 1813. Peter McQueen leads a force of warriors from Tallassee, Autossee, and Ocfuskee eastward toward Coweta, homebase of McIntosh and the leaders of the Americanized Creeks, while Josiah Francis leads a small force of about a hundred Alabama warriors toward the fork of the Alabama and Tombigbee and the forts located there. These two groups plan to divert attention from the main force. Moving separately from the Holy Ground and trailing behind the main Red Stick expedition is a shadow army: northern Indians and Shawnees who have martial aspirations for a pan-Indian movement, runaway black slaves of white settlers and of Americanized mixed-bloods, and the black slaves-in-name-only of the traditionalists. Seekaboo and a group of black slaves known as the "McGillivray negroes" lead this army. The ancient rituals of limited warfare to exact revenge and to free the unavenged from the ghost realm will not satisfy the shadow army. The black men want the dreadful, apocalyptical vengeance of the god of Israel, the god the white men imposed on them, and they are willing to be his instrument of destruction against people embracing a philosophy that holds them in demeaning servitude. The northern Indians see themselves as grasping the last chance red men will have to free their native land. They shave their heads and paint their skulls red. The shadow army understands well the anarchic nature of all Indians, especially the Red Stick army, and will use this knowledge for their own purposes. (We would have only oral traditions to chronicle the actions of these passionate fighters without the memoirs of George Stiggins, a Creek-Natchez mixed-blood warrior, and the letters of General Thomas Woodward, both American partisans.)

The Red Stick army moved down the Alabama River, some by river, some overland on horseback in small groups, to one of Billy's plantations. At the nearby plantation of Zachariah McGirth, several of McGirth's black slaves who had been sent out to tend their stockaded master's cattle are captured. Making sure that they understand the gravity of the situation and the intent and purpose of the Red Stick expedition, the army allows those slaves who are so inclined to escape. Despite the Burnt Corn battle, where war was made on the Indians without just and proper notice and for which there must now be retaliation without a formal notice, the Red Sticks do not consider it morally correct to attack without giving any warning. The escaped captives will surely make their way to Fort Mims, where the McGirth family has taken refuge. (Mrs. McGirth, née Vicey Cornells, had been the second wife of Alexander McGillivray.) The slaves behave as Billy expects, and Beasley sends out a patrol which rides about the countryside for a short distance, returns to the fort, and reports that they have seen nothing. Joe, one of the McGirth slaves who has chosen to remain with the Red Sticks, explains in detail the lack of discipline and military order at the fort and the drunken carnival atmosphere that prevails among the troops and people there.

Billy, *the shadow-that-I-am*, and the Red Stick army scouts, who are painted for war and purified for the ritual, range through the woods stalking the fort, waiting and listening, so near that *we* easily hear the conversations going on inside the palisaded acre. At night *we* venture in so close that *we* can stoop and peer into the portholes which are strangely positioned four feet from the ground and four feet apart around the flimsy palisade. On August 29 a messenger from

General Claiborne arrives, announcing that grave danger is near and warning Beasley to be ever vigilant. Two black slaves belonging to different masters come out to tend cattle, only to run quickly back into the fort saying that they have seen in the woods a group of twenty or so Indians painted for war. Beasley immediately orders the slaves flogged for unduly alarming the fort with false reports. One slave's master intervenes and forbids the flogging, saying, "My man does not lie." Beasley orders the master, his family, and all of his slaves out of the fort by the next day. *We hear every word.*

The next morning—Monday August 30, 1813—a horseman races toward the open gate of the fort, pulls his mount up short, and shouts that he has seen a group of Indians painted for war headed that way. Beasley shouts back that all the rider has seen is a gang of red cattle. The rider replies, "Before evening that gang of red cattle is going to give you a hell of a kick," then speeds off. From *our* perch in a nearby thicket, hidden by a leafy green curtain of muscadine vines, Billy recognizes the horseman as James Cornells.

A new shipment of whiskey reached the fort just yesterday, and now the men and soldiers lull about, hung over or still drunk. During the morning, a black fiddler begins his tunes as ordered, and some of the young women dance with the soldiers. As noon approaches, *we* smell beef roasting, peas cooking, sweet potatoes and corn bread baking. The drum sounding the noon hour, the call to dinner, signals the warriors to attack. The sentry, his back to the gate, is absorbed in a nearby card game as a tomahawk dispatches him to the hereafter. Only as the war whoops sound and the red tide surges toward the fort does Beasley leave his card game to order the gates closed, but the sand has frozen the eastern gate into an open position. Red Sticks quickly cut through the secondary western gate. Black slaves inside the fort begin cutting down pickets to let the Red Sticks enter at other locations. The warriors pour through the open eastern gate. Billy leads the charge. On foot he races through the gates, discharging his gun and raising his war club. Cumbersome guns are not the weapon of choice for a warrior on foot seeking to cut a swath through the enemy soldiers. After the first surprise volley that sweeps *us* into the fort, loading and reloading rifles is too time consuming for the front ranks. In hand-to-hand combat, the ablest weapon is the tomahawk or war club. Arrows and bullets pellet the air. This ritual engagement requires few guns and little ammunition on the part of the Red Sticks. Unavenged warriors rescued from the realm of ghosts do not need the confusion of excessive gunfire. Traditional Indians led by the prophets do not put all their faith in the Americans' weapons. There is no ammunition to be wasted. There are no spare guns.

Beasley, with sword in hand, comes to the east gate and struggles to free it from the sand. A Red Stick warrior quickly dispatches him to the realm of ghosts. From five hundred to seven hundred Red Stick warriors swarm through the fort. *I race forward. I meet death face to face. Does death know who I am? Does death doubt the color of my heart?* Women screech, babies bawl, and men curse. When all the rhetoric is stripped away, this is a war of kinsmen, of brother against brother. In the midst of death and carnage, as desperate hand-to-hand combat rages, warriors take some of the women and children prisoners. Vicey McGirth and her eight daughters are rescued by the Red Stick warrior Sanota, her foster son. (Sanota takes his foster mother and sisters to his home, and they are eventually reunited with Mrs. McGirth's husband, Zachariah, who was absent from the fort at the time of the attack.) Mrs. Susan Hatterway (George Stiggins's sister), holding hands with two small girls, one white and one black, walks out of the fort toward a Red Stick warrior and announces, "We surrender." The warrior, Iffi Tustnuggee, leads them from the battle to a safe spot. Hester, a black slave woman, escapes from the fort, finds a canoe on the river bank, furiously paddles to Fort Stoddert at Mount Vernon, and gives General Claiborne the first news of the attack. Other black slaves surrender or are taken prisoner and removed to Red Stick strongholds.

The prophets, dressed in feathers and painted black but without the red lightning zigzags of the other warriors, run forward as standard bearers, chanting and dancing. As the soldiers grab rifles and begin firing, the prophets are the favored targets. With shouts of "That will teach them" as a prophet falls, the soldiers and Americanized citizens of the fort feel that they have proven some philosophic point, and that once the Red Stick warriors have seen a prophet succumb to rifle bullets, *we* will lose faith and retreat. That does not happen. Paddy Walsh is shot three times but survives and continues the dance of the lakes. Indians are at every porthole. Captain Middleton's company, stationed near the east gate, perishes in the first minutes of the battle. After Beasley falls, Captain Dixon Bailey, the Americanized mixed-blood, assumes command of the fort, urging his company to lie low and hang on, saying that Indians never fight for long periods of time but only make brief attacks and then quickly retreat. He is right, but by the time the brief attack is over the majority of his men are dead. In less than two hours, the Red Sticks win the battle. The surviving soldiers and militiamen, plus women and children, are barricaded in the blockhouse. Burnt Corn has been avenged. Enough revenge has been exacted. The warriors begin a retreat from the fort to care for our wounded and dead. *I am the phantom singing the death song. I did not close my eyes. I mourn. The feculent smell of the swamp mingling with the sweet scent of death is sickening. Blood stings the ground. Insects swim through the heavy, humid air, ready to devour. I sing, "Your mother who always was and always will be, your mother who is spun from star memories embraces you who have come to the end of one journey. Join your mother to begin another." This is my spontaneous song.* A lull settles over the fort. A group of about thirty-five men, including Captain Bailey, steal out from behind the walls, leaving their wives and children behind. Bailey soon dies of his wounds in the nearby swamp. *Over a pot of herbs, I sing, "Send your strength, your healing," breathing through the hollow reed tube into the medicine, imitating the essence of the Master of Breath's gift. Breath. I am the phantom. I can only sing. No one can hear me except those wounded hearts listening to the wind.*

Now Seekaboo, the "McGillivray negroes," and the shadow army arrive and prepare to renew the attack. The McGillivray negroes are whipping their force into an emotional frenzy, a hypnotic murdering madness. They ignore Billy's and High-headed Jim's recommendations and declaration that the battle is over and any further attacks unnecessary. They surge forward, out of control, threatening to kill any Red Stick who tries to stop them. Men, women, and children fall victim, are battered to death, then mutilated and scalped. The swollen bellies of pregnant women are slit with butcher knives, the unborn babies ripped from their wombs and slammed against the walls. Fiery arrows ignite the wooden shingle roofs of the buildings, and an inferno engulfs the last defenders of the fort.

The Red Sticks might fight only a ritual battle, but the shadow army of Seekaboo and the McGillivray negroes fights the type of war relished by American propaganda machines. The Red Sticks are branded as ruthless, and the propagandists of Tennessee, Georgia, and the Mississippi Territory have the fuel they need to rationalize a war that will be abated only by the destruction of the Creeks. A newspaper in Nashville gleefully reports that the Creeks have given the United States an excuse to dismember the Indian nation. The Americans attach but one name to the Red Stick uprising, to the Red Stick army, to the massacre at Fort Mims, to the murder and mutilation of women and children. It is William Weatherford. For the Americans, he is now the ultimate villain. They tell each other, "It isn't like he is a real Indian. He is more white than he is Indian. He knows better." They never consider the color of his heart or the disposition of his soul.

As the renewed battle rages out of control, Billy and High-headed Jim leave the fort with most of the Red Stick warriors. *On horseback Billy and I ride to his brother David Tate's plantation about twelve miles away, where Billy tells Davy of the retribution taken at the fort and how a renegade force had got out of hand, could not be controlled, and was bent on the destruction of every person in the fort. Smeared with paint, we smell of death, sweat, and horses. We return to Billy's plantation upriver from the destroyed fort. Hungry warriors provision their mess kits from the last supplies and livestock on the place. We bathe in the river and tend the wounded warriors resting here before they continue the journey upriver by canoe.*

Hiding in the swamp, a few escapees and survivors from the fort see a bonfire leaping towards the night sky at Weatherford's Landing as Billy piles his accumulation of Americanized accoutrements into his house and, with the cleansing fire, purges his life of material ties to the rejected culture. *We sit in the darkness at the edge of the water watching the flames consume his thoughts and purify his intentions.* The black slaves he owns who have chosen not to join him at the Holy

Ground are sent to David Tate. His Americanized brothers, David and Jack, claim all the property and land that have been allotted to him by the nation that the Americans say he owns. He owns nothing. *We own nothing. We are free. Our ritual at Fort Mims, our retribution for Burnt Corn and the unavenged dead of the nation is complete.*

For others, retribution has just begun. Zachariah Mc-Girth, one of the first to reach the devastated Fort Mims, had left the fort on the morning of the attack with several slaves for a quick trip to his plantation for supplies. He hid in the swamp with the slaves when he heard gunfire and stayed there until well after dark. The gunfire had long since ceased but the dense black smoke rising from the direction of the fort kept the frightened man from approaching, even though he had left his wife and children inside. Now the master and his slaves carefully moved through the swamp to the fort. Dawn came before they ventured close enough to see what had been the enclosure strewn with slain, mutilated bodies, many half-burned and others still slowly burning atop live coals. A search through the burned bodies turned up none of the McGirths. After spending a day and night in the swamp accompanied by his worst fears, and then assuming that his family had perished, McGirth became an express message rider for the Americans in the military actions that followed, always taking the most dangerous missions, the ones more reasonable men turned down. Months later when he was in Mobile, he received a message that a group of captured Indians being held on the docks had asked for him. He went to the wharf and found his family.

Forty to sixty Red Stick warriors had lost their lives in the attack on Fort Mims, according to the Creek chiefs reporting to the Americans, who, in turn, declared that over two hundred hostile warriors had perished. *We expect retaliation from the Americans and decide that it would be best to pick the next battleground ourselves. There is no separating me from them. We hold up in the dense green swamps and canebrakes north of Bear Creek.* Bands of Red Stick warriors range about the countryside, burning houses and sawmills. Runaway slaves arrive in the Red Stick camps regularly, full of news of the Americans' activities. The slaves delight in leading the Indians to spots where their masters have buried valuable household goods. *When we learn that the Americans are not going to materialize in a reasonable amount of time, Billy and I return to the Holy Ground.*

Major Joseph Kennedy leads a detachment from Mount Vernon to Fort Mims, arriving ten days after the massacre to bury the dead. As buzzards circle overhead, nauseated troopers, bandannas over their mouths and noses, count 247 bodies, but no one is sure of the exact identity of any body. Many are thought to be enemy dead. The mutilated, charred bodies have suffered decomposition and been ripped apart by starving dogs and scavenging birds. The troopers inter all the bodies in two large pits. In his report to General Claiborne, Kennedy writes, "The plains and the woods around were covered with dead bodies. All the houses were consumed by fire, except the block house and part of the pickets." Kennedy relates that the burned buildings were filled with bones. Newspapers and rumors report that a thousand Red Stick warriors have slain anywhere from four hundred to six hundred innocent Americans, but the part of the story that the authorities find most frightening never reaches the public.

The participation of the blacks in the battle strikes a deeper horror in the hearts of members of the Euro-American government—military, political, and financial leaders—than the news of an Indian uprising. If news of black involvement were to escape the frontier into the everyday gossip of the

American nation, enslaved black men and women throughout the South might take heart and rise up against their oppressors. The slave revolts in Haiti had brought refugees into the Mississippi Territory with firsthand stories of the horror of such enterprises. Knowledge of the Haitian terror, plus the unrest in Louisiana and Virginia slave communities, shade all the acts the American and territorial armies will be ordered to take against the Indians. The active role of blacks in the Creek War will be understated by historians for generations, for all the reasons one people offer for enslaving and demeaning another. Frontier historians a generation or two after the war will still be writing that the Creeks had stepped beyond the bounds of decency by letting the blacks fight with them.

I am at the Holy Ground. The sacred place. The prophets have built defenses beyond and around the circles of the villages. Walls of dry pine logs, thick with turpentine hungry for a spark, mark our outer defenses. These sacred barricades can be ignited to protect us from the Americans. Billy sleeps here within the circle. I am the inhabitant of a dream he is having, a pale shadow of who we are. "Firemaker, must I tend two fires?" I ask. Around us are swirling good and evil. Right and wrong are hiding behind identical masks.

Twelve

War

On July 3, 1813, the slave trader, lawyer, entrepreneur, and militia general Andrew Jackson wrote Tennessee's Governor Blount concerning the Creeks, saying that he did not need authority or reason to justify "laying waste their villages, burning their houses, killing their warriors and leading into captivity their wives and children." Though he does not require the Fort Mims massacre of August 30, 1813, to justify his bellicose plans, the incident there offers the self-righteous frontiersman a handy excuse for an invasion which the Tennessee legislature approves on September 24 by authorizing Governor Blount to enlist five thousand volunteers for three months of service and ordering General Jackson to call up two thousand militiamen immediately. Jackson plans to cut a swath from Tennessee to Mobile, where he will be poised to invade Pensacola. Naming Pensacola as their destination, the militiamen leave Nashville, expecting the Creeks to be a minor inconvenience.

Jackson suggests to the Chickasaw deputy agent that, as

a sign of solidarity with the Americans, the Chickasaws and Choctaws should attack the Creek town at the fall line of the Black Warrior River. Taking this suggestion as an order, a small group of Chickasaw and Choctaw men, mainly Americanized mixed-bloods, gather at Peter Pitchlynn's in the Choctaw nation and proceed to the Creek town, from which Oceeochee Emathla, the principal chief, has evacuated the people to a spot deeper in Creek country. A cavalry detachment of Tennessee Militia meets the Americanized Indians, and the joint force burns the deserted town. The Tennesseans, who have few provisions, confiscate three hundred bushels of corn at the town and proceed to forage about the countryside in an attempt to live off the land. The Americanized Indians go back to Pitchlynn's, where they disburse and return to their homes, thinking that they have completed their obligation to show the Americans their displeasure over Fort Mims. A few individual Chickasaws do decide to serve further in the war, while a small group of Choctaws enlist as a unit.

Pushmataha, the Choctaw Americanist, arrives at Fort St. Stephens on September 29, meets with the U.S. factor George Gaines (director of the government trading post), and offers five thousand Choctaw warriors in the fight against the Red Sticks. Gaines accompanies him to Mobile, where General Flournoy refuses the offer. Returning to St. Stephens, Pushmataha and Gaines encounter a small group of Choctaw warriors angry at the insult, but shortly a messenger arrives at the fort to say that the general has reconsidered and will welcome Choctaw help. Though Pushmataha claims that he can deliver five thousand warriors to the American cause, he actually recruits only a hundred and thirty-five for his Choctaw division, of which he is made lieutenant colonel. The majority of the Choctaws do not want to participate in war on anyone's side. Even as these events transpire, Billy and Ochille Haujo revisit Mushalatubbee, hoping for a last-minute change of heart that might ally some of the Choctaws with the Red Sticks. Though Billy finds sympathy, he does not gain the direct aid the Red Sticks need.

Gaines orders Pushmataha a fancy blue uniform trimmed with gold epaulets and excessive amounts of gold braid, as well as a top hat adorned with grand plumage, an ensemble that costs three hundred dollars in Mobile. Pushmataha models his behavior after that of the American officers at the fort, and, when he sees that they promenade around and about in the evening with their wives, he sends for his wife, who is soon dressed in the best feminine finery available, and the couple joins the evening walks. Pushmataha turns a blind eye and deaf ear to the mocking gestures, laughter, snide re-marks, and behavior of the American officers and their wives. Probably more fervently than any other Indian, Pushmataha wants to be an American and eagerly goes to great lengths to accomplish his goal.

Red Stick bands scatter about the countryside, destroy-ing crops, foodstuffs, and livestock. A scorched-earth policy from the earliest operations thwarts Jackson's plans to live off the land. In areas far from the American troops, Red Sticks turn hogs into the cornfields of abandoned farms to fatten for *our* larder. Messages reach Red Stick leaders that aid from the British will soon arrive. Governor Charles Cameron of New Providence in the Bahamas receives orders from Lon-don to give all possible assistance to the dissident Creeks and Seminoles, but tangible British aid, gun powder and lead, never reaches *our* warriors. Governor Manrique at Pensacola writes to Billy, congratulating him on the victory at Fort Mims and asking that the Red Sticks not attack Mobile, as that town rightfully belonged to the king of Spain; the governor hoped that it would soon be retaken by the Spanish and said that it would be unfortunate if the Red Sticks were to attack and destroy property that in reality belonged to that country's king. Attacking Mobile is not on the Red Stick agenda. Billy keeps the letter in his house at the Holy Ground.

Jackson and his militia join General John Coffee and thirteen hundred Tennessee cavalrymen below Huntsville at Ditto's Landing on the Tennessee River in the Mississippi Territory. A detachment marches twenty-four miles along the river to the mouth of Thompson's Creek, where they build Fort Deposit, the main supply base for the Tennessee troops. Jackson sends a detachment of two hundred cavalrymen twenty-two miles away to the head of Canoe Creek, where in the early hours before daylight on October 29, they attack and burn the village of Littefutchee. All the countryside around Fort Deposit is scoured for provisions. Other militiamen cut a fifty-mile-long road over Coosa Mountain to the juncture of Canoe Creek and the Coosa River at Ten Islands, where they establish Fort Strother, another supply base. The Americans wait for the arrival of provisions to stock the forts, Jackson declaring that he is more afraid of hunger than of the "hostile" Creeks. But he vows to live on acorns if necessary to accomplish his military goal. He personifies the American frontiersman—gruff, afflicted with chronic dysentery, and recovering from a recent dueling gunshot wound, he feeds on dreams of glory, greed, and conquest. Perhaps he needs to prove to himself that he can be just as rich, just as powerful, and just as ruthless as the British officer who slashed his face with a sword when he was a child in the Revolutionary War. The American frontier is so thickly populated with men like Jackson that they soon block, at least temporarily, his path to glory. All these men with the same agenda volunteer to fight the Creeks. Reputations for a dozen generals and for men such as Davy Crockett, Sam Houston, and Sam Dale have to be hacked out of the Creek nation. Jackson encounters other complications because the Creek nation lies partly in the U.S. Sixth Military District, under the command of General Thomas Pinckney, and partly in the seventh, under the command of General Flournoy. The War Department attempts to solve the problem by placing the war operation under the command of Pinckney while allowing Flournoy to make the day-to-day routine decisions of his district. The compromise works poorly if at all. The two generals feel stymied by the restrictions and what they consider interference with their commands. Besides the sixth and seventh district armies, Jackson's militia from western Tennessee, General John Cocke's militia from eastern Tennessee, General John Floyd's Georgia Militia, General Claiborne's third regiment of U.S. Army regulars, and the Mississippi Militia stand poised to rip the Red Sticks apart, if the groups can work out accommodations to each other's egos. Jackson, determined from the beginning to be the conqueror, gives no quarter.

McIntosh, the leader of Hawkins's death squad, recruits Cherokees to join forces with the Americans and Americanized Lower Creeks. After a visit to Coweta and a meeting with Hawkins, the Cherokee leader John Ridge agrees to aid the Americans. In battle the Cherokees wear white feathers and deer tails on their heads so the Americans can distinguish them from the enemy. In early October, McIntosh, Big Warrior, and Little Prince ambush 150 Uchees on their way to join the Red Sticks. McIntosh burns several Red Stick villages and the villagers' crops. Jackson promises the retribution-fearing Creeks at Coweta that the Red Sticks cannot harm them because his army will stop their advance. *Our enemy is relentless.* His campaign has just begun.

Thirteen miles from Fort Strother, the village of Tallussahatchee is targeted. The Tennessee troops under General Coffee's command split into two divisions and advance on the village with the Americanized Indian scouts being sent into the village to draw out the warriors. Amidst the gun fire, the drums summon the warriors to the defense of their homes. The Red Sticks charge toward Coffee's lines, but are caught in a cross fire and driven back into the town. They have little ammunition and use bows and arrows more than their rifles. Davy Crockett sees a woman sitting in the doorway of a house with a bow and an arrow, which she fires into the heart of a Tennessee volunteer. His companions are so enraged at the woman that they quickly pump her body full of more than twenty balls. A group of forty-six warriors run into a house for refuge. Crockett and his comrades are hot on their trail. He later brags, "We shot them like dogs; then set the house on fire." Many of the villagers are burned alive. Crockett writes of eating potatoes found in a pit under an Indian house, describing them as having been cooked in "Indian grease"—fat from burned Indian bodies.

A more sensitive man, Lieutenant Richard Keith Call, writes, "We found as many as eight or ten bodies in a single cabin . . . some of the cabins had taken fire, and half-consumed bodies were seen amidst the smoking ruins . . . heart sick I turned from the revolting scene."

Coffee makes a vain attempt to excuse the death of so many women and children. He blames the Red Stick warriors for retreating from the artillery cross fire into the village where the women and children were. On November 4, 1813, Jackson writes to Governor Blount, "We have retaliated for the destruction of Fort Mims" at Tallussahatchee. Troops under the command of General Coffee killed 186 people and took about 80 women and children prisoners. General Coffee reports, "Not one of the warriors escaped to carry the news."

After the battle, a baby boy is found sitting and crying beside his dead mother in a field at the charred village. The soldiers cannot convince any of the women captives to care for him. "Kill him, too," the women say. "He has no family, he has no one, you have killed his family. It is better that he dies now than live longer only to suffer." The soldiers bring the baby to Jackson, who expresses self-righteous shock and dismay at the women's attitude. Though short on supplies, Jackson finds brown sugar to nourish the boy until he can be delivered to Huntsville. His adopted son, ten-month-old Andrew, Jr., is about the same age as the Creek baby, Lyncoya, so Jackson sends him by express rider on from Huntsville to his wife in Nashville, where he is reared as a member of the family and is a companion for Andrew, Jr. Few, if any, of the other captives were treated so kindly. Food for the captives meant fewer supplies for the soldiers. There was nothing to spare.

Talladega, a town deep in Upper Creek country inhabited by 154 Americanized warriors and their families, is symbolic of Creek disunity. *In the midst of this madness cannot men with true vision see the Americans for what they are? Our own people who uphold the wrongs to the traditions, who do nothing to correct the disharmony in this middle world, must bear the costs of their incorrect actions. We besiege the town. Billy leads the siege force. We encircle the town, stopping movements into and out of the countryside. We are a thousand Red Stick warriors, a passive barrier through which there is no movement. We wait for the besieged to realize the error of their ways,* to understand that they are Indians—that their hearts are red. A Talladega man dressed in a hog skin, rooting and ranging with the hogs at night, makes his way through the Red Stick lines and reaches Jackson with pleas to come and raise the siege.

"Weatherford?" Jackson asks. "Is Weatherford there?"

Yes, Weatherford is there.

Jackson needs to hear no more. He promises his soldiers that they will engage Weatherford in battle, that they will meet the man he considers the mastermind of the Red Stick rebellion on the field in combat. The Tennesseans quickly move to Talladega, thirty miles below Fort Strother, crossing the Coosa in relays with each horseman carrying a foot soldier behind his saddle across the deep, stony river. On November 9, 1813, Jackson's force of twelve hundred infantrymen and eight hundred cavalrymen attack *our* siege lines in a crescent-shaped formation with mounted horsemen at each wing tip. *They plan to encircle us. The riflemen and artillery move forward to provoke us. When we move forward, they will fall back; the cavalry will close in behind us to spring the trap. Rifle balls rain in on us. The cannons roar. We fight with the conviction of the religiously sure, the spiritually inspired. We have little lead and less powder. Our weapons against the American rifles and cannons are bows and arrows, tomahawks and clubs. We fall back into the town. The American horsemen bear down on our bowmen, catching them in a cross fire. As the battle rages, many men and women of the town sit quietly, as if in a trance, unresponsive, seemingly unaware of the conflict and death that swirls around them. The Americans are bewildered. "What is wrong with these people?" they scream at each other. "Why don't they run? Why don't they get out of the line of fire?" They cannot grasp our conflict, the conflict that is separate and apart from their war.*

*We are in the cross fire of the cannons, the relentless ar-
tillery.* Then, without explanation, a segment of Jackson's
crescent retreats instead of advancing. The Indian scouts
who have led Jackson to Talladega misdirect units, making a
gap in the American lines, deliberately leaving an escape
route open for the Red Sticks. *We are soon gone. There is no
shame in survival; there is honor in living to fight another day.*
William Weatherford, Jackson's quarry, escapes into the
woods, where he will inspire guerilla actions, raids and attacks in which bows and arrows and cunning are more effective than cannons. *This is just one day in our life, in our
conflict. We live this moment without emotion.* Jackson has
spent much of the battle in a rage. The action is not moving
swiftly enough or being deadly enough for him. He says his
officers are refusing to obey his orders. He curses them and
attempts to run one of his colonels through with a saber.

The Americans have begun a war of extermination so ter-
rible that many of their Indian allies are appalled. This is not
the way wars should be fought. Even in the depths of battle
a warrior is a human being. A woman is a woman. A child is
a child. Jackson reports that his troops killed about four hundred of the siege force and delivered a severe blow to the
enemy. The Red Sticks fought with "religious frenzy" and
"Spartan valor" according to the Americans. Jackson curses
the failure of his men to kill or capture Weatherford.

Jackson writes from Ten Islands, "Could I have followed
up that victory immediately, the Creek war . . . would have
been terminated. But I was compelled by a double cause—
the want of supplies and the want of cooperation from the
East Tennessee troops—to return to this place." He claims
that his soldiers have found a Spanish flag in the possession of
a dead Red Stick. In the same letter relating the victory at
Talladega, Jackson writes, "It is not understood by the Gov-

ernment that this war is to be confined to mere temporary in-
cursions into the enemy's country—such movements might
distress them, but would produce none of those lasting and
beneficial effects which are designed to be produced. Perhaps, too, there are ulterior objects, not yet avowed, which
may be within the contemplation of Government."

Jackson's troubles with the rival Tennessee units increase
as the competing generals and officers look for a battle or action to establish their military reputations and wrap themselves in glory. General John Cocke of the East Tennessee
Militia orders a thousand men under his subordinate, General White, to march to Turkey Town, report to Jackson, and
receive further orders. Jackson orders White on to Fort
Strother. In the meantime Jackson negotiates a surrender of
several Red Stick Hillabee towns. On his march to Fort
Strother and under Jackson's command, White receives orders from Cocke to join him at the mouth of the Chattooga,
which he does, though he is now under Jackson's command.
The joint forces of Cocke and White move on Tallasse-
hatchee only to find that it already has fallen to Jackson. They
take prisoner about twenty wounded Red Stick warriors
they find recuperating in the area and move on to the Hillabee towns that have negotiated a peace with Jackson. The
startled and bewildered Indians of the first town in the eastern Tennesseans' path make no effort to defend themselves.
On November 18, 1813, the Tennesseans slaughter the Indians who have accepted Jackson's terms for peace. White
brags, "We lost not a drop of blood." The surviving Hill-
abees believe that they have been betrayed by Jackson. Other
Red Sticks take the lesson to heart. There can be no surrender, only a fight to the death.

McIntosh, Big Warrior, Mad Dog, Little Prince, and
Alexander Cornells write to General Floyd, begging him and

his Georgia troops for help in escaping Coweta, which they claim is besieged by Red Sticks. The men say that the hostile Indians are killing all the livestock and burning houses in the area, but that they themselves cannot fight "on account of our women and children." They go on to say that with a thousand of Floyd's men they are confident that they can defeat the Red Sticks in a nearby "open pine woods" where they are camped. McQueen's warriors have not laid siege to Coweta. At first they harass the area as a diversionary tactic for Billy's march to Fort Mims, then to render a scorched earth and make life difficult for the enemy. Floyd's Georgia Militia starts toward Coweta beset by fears that McQueen will pillage the baggage train of provisions. McQueen vows to do just that. The Americans offer the Red Sticks the most obvious source of ammunition, if and when the Americans themselves are being supplied. American officers in charge of procuring supplies often make personal financial gains at the expense of ill provisioning the troops, so that soldiers constantly find themselves short of supplies. By the time Floyd crosses the Chattahoochee into the Mississippi Territory, where his 950 militiamen are joined by McIntosh and 450 Americanized Creeks, the main group of McQueen's forces have returned to their towns. Abram Mordecai, the Jewish trader whom the Indians had convicted of adultery and punished by cropping his ears and burning his cotton gin, guides the force to the Tallapoosa River, moving them through the night over the last few miles to Autossee. Red Stick scouts have estimated the enemy's arrival at noon, but the nighttime march places them outside the town at dawn on the frosty morning of November 29.

Coosa Micco, the leading man of Autossee, and the prophet Tewasubbukle are in counsel that morning over the best defense the warriors can make when a warrior who has been camped out to hunt turkeys comes running into town to warn of the impending arrival of Floyd and the Georgians. Immediate evacuation of the infirm, aged, women, and children begins. They quickly disappear from the town into the caves and woods, any place of safety they can find along the river. The two leaders quickly decide that upper Autossee will be defended by Coosa Micco, Peter McQueen, and the Tallassee and Autossee warriors and that the command center will be near the mouth of Calabee Creek. Tewasubbukle will command the lower town with the aid of warriors from the small villages located between the fork of the Tallapoosa and Coosa. The hastily arranged plans are no sooner agreed to than a runner announces that the Georgians are in the woods bordering the town.

George Stiggins, a Creek warrior of mixed blood, tells us the story of the attack, which came at daylight, with the Georgians firing their small arms and cannons into the Indian town. "Coosa Micco . . . called for his men to arrange themselves properly and meet the enemy. He gave the war whoop and returned the Georgians' fire. He moved back and forth among the warriors in the front lines encouraging his men to fight bravely and calmly without shrinking back and not to waste their fire in fear. He tried to infuse in them his spirit of fighting, both by words and actions. While Coosa Micco was encouraging and exhorting his men, news was brought to him that Tewasubbukle was killed, that the warriors in the lower town were giving way to the Georgians. On hearing this, Coosa Micco mounted his horse and sped to the lower-town warriors to try to repair the damage. But the cause was scarcely retrievable; the greater part of them were retreating, making for the ponds of water by their houses. They were in a panic after they had been charged by the horsemen. Coosa

Micco rallied and stopped some of them; he saw that they were not willing to fight front to front. So he thought to turn to the left the rear flank of the American troop, hoping to cause the warriors to rally and fight. In trying to turn their flank, he said, he saw that the enemy would always present a solid front. By the time he reached the uppermost level [of the town] he began to see his own horsemen mix in mortal strife. They gave ground and ran into the big reed brake. This convinced him that he was overcome. He himself was badly wounded in two places from bullets, and chopped across the cheek by a sword, and his horse was shot through the neck and body. Being very faint from loss of blood, he dismounted at length and went into the reed brake and gave up Autossee to the conquerors."

Autossee, on the south bank of the Tallapoosa near the mouth of Calabee Creek, eighteen miles from the Hickory Ground and twenty miles above the junction with the Coosa, contains the most distinctive and elegant surviving styles of traditional Indian architecture. Now the Georgians set fire to more than four hundred buildings. Again the Americanized Indians fighting with the Georgians leave open a route of retreat for the Red Sticks by failing to cross the Tallapoosa to attack retreating warriors, as they have been ordered. A Red Stick marksman's rifle ball shatters Floyd's kneecap. The Red Sticks suffer eighty fatalities and more than a hundred casualties. The Indians who escape go into the swamps or take up residence in other towns. A few seek refuge at Pensacola. The Georgians move on to destroy Tallassee and Little Tallassee (the home of the late Alexander McGillivray, also called the Apple Grove) by fire. After their fiery, murdering spree, the Georgians march to Fort Mitchell on the Chattahoochee just inside the boundaries of the Mississippi Territory; from there, they form a forward defense for Coweta, the town of the Americanized Creeks.

The Red Sticks, desperate for ammunition, call a meeting of all the leading men, chiefs, and prophets to review their situation. *Billy and the unformed-shadow-that-I-am have retreated into the forest and closeted ourselves with nature; now, we answer the summons to Hoithlewaule.* Paddy Walsh and High-headed Jim make an inventory of powder and lead among the warriors and pronounce the supply too low for continuation of the war. The Indians will not be able to withstand another blow of the magnitude of Autossee. Billy is chosen to go to Pensacola and make a plea for ammunition. The prophets, the light makers, give the mission their blessings. With an escort of over three hundred horsemen, Billy and *the phantom-that-I-am* travel to Pensacola to make the Red Sticks' appeal.

The sandy streets of the town, the sprawling groves of seaside oaks, the smell of the sea, the house of Panton, Leslie and Company (now owned by Forbes) are so far distant from Red Stick desperation that the officials and people cannot grasp the circumstances: warriors armed with bows and arrows are going into battle against cannons and rifles, sacrificial slaughter on the altar of American greed. Pensacola still suffers from a lack of regular provisions. British aid for *our* cause has not arrived. Any day, they say, any day. Hold on. Just hold on.

Using all the resources available in the capital of West Florida, the governor is able to procure only three horseloads of lead and powder that can be spared. *We return with the horsemen, guarding the precious freight to the Tallapoosa.* The arrival of the meager supply of ammunition brings a tentative measure of hope to the Red Stick camps.

In October, Flournoy sends Claiborne out to escort and

guard citizens in the Tombigbee area of the Alabama as they gather their surviving crops and to harass any small bands of the Red Sticks that they might find in the field. Anxious for action and for his share of the military honors that will be bestowed on the victors in the Creek War, Claiborne is frustrated because Flournoy continually orders only defensive moves. Finally Flournoy dispatches orders that will carry Claiborne and the Mississippi volunteers into combat. From Pine Level (present-day Jackson, Alabama) on the Tombigbee, Claiborne and his force travel overland with Pushmataha and the Choctaws to the Alabama, cross to the right side, and, at Weatherford's Bluff (named for Charles Weatherford), about thirty-five miles above Fort Mims, construct a "strong stockade, two hundred feet square, defended by three block houses and a half-moon battery which commanded the river." It is finished in ten days and named Fort Claiborne. The Mississippi volunteers gleefully speculate that the army's next move will be to Pensacola. The Third U.S. Infantry has been ordered to cooperate with the Georgia Militia. Claiborne wants orders to "cooperate" with Jackson. In his report detailing the construction of the fort for the storing of provisions for Jackson's army, Claiborne writes that he sincerely hopes that he will soon be under Jackson's command and that the fort will effectively block the Red Sticks' communications with Pensacola. Pushmataha, fifty of his warriors, and Lieutenant Calahan of the volunteers move out towards Burnt Corn Creek to harass Creeks in the vicinity. Hoping to ingratiate himself with the general from Tennessee, Claiborne writes to Jackson, assuring him that much corn and other provisions can be obtained in the area of the fort and stored there for the Tennesseans' use. He knows that Jackson never stops worrying about provisions and famine. At the same time, he writes to Governor Blount of

Tennessee to inform him of the arrival of "English vessels" at Pensacola, saying he desires to be "authorized to take that sink of iniquity." He says he had been informed from Mobile that the British have arrived in Pensacola with "a large quantity of Indian supplies" and "many soldiers," but these nebulous facts are never quantified or verified. Guerilla Red Sticks burn several mills across the bay from Mobile, and from those actions Claiborne justifies regarrisoning Fort Pierce.

Flournoy has stressed restraint in pursuing the Red Sticks, but, as the end of the year approaches, he relents and authorizes an expedition into the Creek country that Claiborne has so ardently sought. Claiborne immediately announces his plan to march against the Holy Ground located 120 miles above Fort Claiborne. Twenty-six officers sign a memorial protesting the plan. The volunteer militia's enlistment will be up before the expedition can be completed, the men have no winter clothes or blankets (some lack shoes), there is no road or path across the wilderness to take them to the Holy Ground, supplies cannot be transported, and the wet winter weather has set in. Despite these formalized objections, Claiborne is determined to wage a fight for his share of the glory, which he believes the war will bring. On December 13, the army, which with Pushmataha's 135 Choctaws numbers 1,000, begins the move toward the Holy Ground. Despite the memorial, Claiborne reports that the officers "when . . . exposed in these swamps and canebrakes to an inclement winter, without tents, warm clothing, shoes or food; when every countenance exhibited suffering; then they were nine days without meat and subsisted chiefly on parched corn, these brave men won an important battle, and endured without a murmur the exigencies of the service."

A depot for the army's wagons, baggage, and the sick is established on high ground south of the Double Swamp along the Alabama. Claiborne leaves a hundred men to guard the spot he calls "Fort Deposite," as he continues with the main force through the woods toward Holy Ground. On the night of December 22, the army camps within ten miles of the Red Stick refuge. The main town, with two hundred houses at the Holy Ground, is situated on the south side of the Alabama, between Pintlala and Big Swamp creeks. Near the mouth of the Pintlala is a village of about eighty houses. The picketed main town covers about fifty acres. The Americans consider the main town the military headquarters of the principal chiefs and leaders of the Alabamas, a depot for provisions and military supplies, and a refuge for women, children, and wounded warriors. The consecration of the area to the Open Door by the light makers as a sacred place to rebuild lives and lost culture is an idea the invaders do not fully comprehend. Pine lightwood ready for a barrier of fire lies beyond the pickets as a defense line against invaders. The town, with its forward palisade, backs up on the high banks of the south side of the river. The Mississippi volunteers tell each other that the prophets have drawn "wizard circles" on the ground around the Holy Ground and that the Indians believe that a white man stepping onto it will fall dead.

Sam Moniac travels with Claiborne's army as a secondary scout. He manages to send a message to Billy that the Mississippi volunteers are on their way to the Holy Ground. *The word coming to us is not a surprise but still causes trepidation.* When the Americans arrive on the morning of December 23, the women, children, elderly, and infirm have been evacuated across the Alabama and hidden in the deep woods near Autauga. Claiborne divides his army into three columns and leads the center column of the Third Regiment of U.S. Infantry, with Lester's Guards and Wells' Dragoons acting as a corps of reserve; the Mississippi volunteers make up the right column; Pushmataha and his Choctaws, plus a battalion of militia under the command of Major Benjamin Smoot, compose the left column. Sam Moniac is positioned with Major Cassel's mounted riflemen, who are ordered to take a position on the river bank west of the town to prevent Red Sticks from escaping down the river. *Those in charge of our wall of fire are not able to ignite our pine wood barricade.*

Colonel Carson's detachment is to make the first assault on the enemy. Unable to cross the ground assigned to him and engage the Red Sticks because of a dense canebrake, he marches his men through freezing water—two feet deep in places—over a level piney woods. *By the time Carson's troops come in sight of the town we are assembling our defensive forces to the accompaniment of war whoops and a constant drum beat.* As Carson's men reach the Red Stick line, they meet a volley of gunfire. The soldiers return fire and the battle begins. The Americans' firepower from rifles and cannons renders the fight one-sided. Billy, mounted on his horse Abbanonair, leads the defense. With little ammunition, the Red Sticks rely on bows and arrows more than on guns. The first barrage of arrows is aimed too high and misses the target. The bowmen prepare a second. A Shawnee prophet with a buffalo's tail dyed red runs about in a frenzy of dance, becoming the favored target of many of the frontiersmen's rifles. *If we are to die, we die within the Master of Breath's grace.* The black men—slave, runaway, and free—fight the invaders fiercely. The white frontiersmen say that they are disgusted by the fact that the Red Sticks are letting the blacks join them in battle against the Americans; it is a sin of such magnitude that it cannot be forgiven.

Over half an hour passes before the other American columns join the battle. As the offensive, well-armed force presses forward against *us,* *our* defenses give way. The Americans swarm through the town. Sam Moniac deliberately misguides Major Cassels and his detachment so that they fall back on Carson's thrust, creating confusion. *Red Stick warriors quickly evacuate our wounded down and across the river and begin a retreat from the Holy Ground through the opening Sam Moniac has devised for us and our horses.* Many of the runaway slaves consider themselves to be in a fight to the death and will not quit the battle. Others join the warriors in escaping across the river.

Billy is among the last Red Sticks in the town. By the time he can see that the evacuation is virtually complete, he and his friend William McPherson, a mixed-blood warrior, find themselves trapped on a bluff between fifty and sixty feet high above the junction of the creek and river. Billy rides Abbanonair up to the edge of the bluff, lets the horse look over the edge, then rides back thirty paces, turns the horse's head towards the bluff, and, with a touch of the heel and a shout of "Ho ya," races to the bluff's edge and leaps to the river below. *The phantom-that-I-am flies through the air with them.* The horse seems to travel straight forward off the bluff for more than thirty feet, then turns nearly head down and keeps a curving flight until he strikes the water. Billy and Abbanonair separate in the flight. *We all land in the water and swim for shore.* The awestruck Mississippi volunteers regain their composure and send a hailstorm of bullets toward the horse and rider. *The lead balls splatter the water around us but miraculously no one is hit.* The soldiers speculate that the Great Spirit watches over Billy Weatherford, since none of the sharpshooters is able to hit him. When Billy reaches the far shore, just beyond the reach of the rifles, he removes Abbanonair's saddle and blanket and carefully examines the horse to see if he has been hurt by the bullets or the jump. A lock of the horse's mane, just above the saddle, has been shot off, but Abbanonair is not hurt. *As Billy wrings water from the horse's saddle blanket, we look to the high bluff and see McPherson repeat the desperate leap.* "Like a cormorant flying to pounce on a fish," Billy says. When McPherson and his horse reach the shore safely, Billy resaddles Abbanonair, and, with the Americans on the bluff across the river an attentive audience, remounts the horse, makes a universal sign of contempt to the soldiers, and rides into the refuge of the forest.

Pushmataha's detachment sacks the town. The Choctaws scalp the slain Creek warriors and blacks, and then, to appease the white men, discard the scalps of the blacks. A contingent of the white troopers cut long strips of skin from the bodies of the slain warriors, which they tan and make into bridles as souvenirs. The letters from the Spanish governor are found in Billy's house and translated into the conspiracy the Americans believe exists between the Spaniards and the Indians. Fifteen hundred bushels of corn found in storage are appropriated for the troops before Claiborne orders the town and its stores burned. Despite the intense defense put up by the Creeks, only one American was killed and twenty wounded, due largely to the Red Sticks' lack of ammunition and guns. Among the thirty-three slain Red Sticks are twelve blacks. They died infected with the mad dream of freedom.

Claiborne's army spends the next day destroying the towns, farms, villages, and boats in the area. Few hostiles are encountered. But when the troopers pursue three Shawnees, Claiborne himself is aroused and marches toward the sound of the gunfire. That night he camps in a cornfield that the militiamen say Billy Weatherford planted. Their only provisions are corn ears gathered from the field and parched for eating. Christmas day passes in "laying waste to the countryside." The army retraces its route back to the baggage depot and then to Fort Claiborne, with the artillery men periodically firing their cannons to discourage any Indians from trailing behind. At Fort Claiborne, the Mississippi volunteers and Pushmataha's Choctaws are mustered out of the service. Left with a skeleton force, Claiborne no longer commands an army. The white people of the southern portion of the Mississippi Territory feel that with the victory at the Holy Ground they have been freed from the Red Stick menace.

Early on the morning of January 22, 1814, near Emuckfau Creek, Jackson and nine hundred Tennesseans, with two hundred Indian warriors—Cherokees and Americanized Creeks—are marching southward, when Billy, Peter McQueen, and Josiah Francis lead a force of about five hundred Red Sticks in an attack as the American cannons and the artillerymen ford the stream. After a day of intense fighting Jackson retreats toward Fort Strother. *We dog his trail.* By January 24, Jackson has reached the Hillabee village Enitachopco, where *we attack.* Jackson falls back. Red Stick warriors report to their families, "We whipped Captain Jackson and ran him to the Coosa River." Hope is reborn—fragile hope, but hope nonetheless.

Meanwhile, Floyd and the Georgia Militia of seventeen hundred men augmented by McIntosh and four hundred Americanized Creeks move into the Calabee Valley, near the site of modern-day Tuskegee. Runners bring news to Paddy Walsh that the Georgians are moving over the Federal Road with their cannons. He calls for warriors to rendezvous at Hoithlewaule. When *we assemble, Walsh tells us* that the Georgians are forming a camp on the Calabee. Over a thousand Red Stick warriors stripped to their breechcloths, bodies painted black with smeared red lightning bolts jolting up their arms and legs, listen as the plans of the attack are proposed. The leading men and prophets agree to defer to the plans worked out by Walsh, High-headed Jim, Billy

Weatherford, and William McGillivray, a mixed-blood warrior. Walsh's proposal calls for the warriors to surround the Americans and attack after they have retired for the evening and are beginning to go to sleep. If the attack is making headway at daylight, the battle will continue; if not, the warriors will retreat. High-headed Jim agrees. McGillivray and Billy vote against Walsh's plan. Billy offers an alternative plan. His attack would be made at the same time that Walsh had suggested, just as the Georgians are retiring and going to sleep, but he suggests that three hundred warriors armed with rifles and tomahawks steal through the enemy camp to the center where the commanding officers' tents are located, give the war whoop, and strike the officers with the tomahawks. All of the officers must be killed. At the same time, the rest of the warriors will charge the camp at large. The three hundred warriors in the center will fight their way out of the encampment towards their own lines, which are fighting towards the center. Billy says that the white soldiers will not fight unless their officers give them orders to do so, and that in the confusion the American soldiers will run for the woods.

Walsh and High-headed Jim visibly shudder at the proposal. Walsh shouts that it is insane. High-headed Jim asks why Billy would want to see three hundred of his own countrymen gunned down without any chance. Walsh says Billy and McGillivray are trying to publicly force him to lead the three hundred so that he will be destroyed, that they are seeking his murder. Billy and McGillivray both jump to their feet and answer, "I volunteer to lead the three hundred!" in unison. Billy says, "Man is born to die. Death is preferable to neglecting to make every sacrifice for the people, for the nation."

The four men turn to the audience of warriors. Who will

volunteer to go with Billy and McGillivray into the middle of the Georgians' camp? Fewer than a dozen offer to make the excursion. The Indians cannot conceive of anything so bizarre as an army that operates by following officers' orders. Even the crazy Americans could not be that stupid! The warriors shout their disapproval of the plan. Billy cannot in good faith endorse Walsh's plan, so, in keeping with the Indians' policy, he and those who agree with him mount their horses and leave the meeting. McGillivray stays. *I go where Billy goes.*

The Red Sticks, led by Paddy Walsh and High-headed Jim, attack the Georgians according to Walsh's plan, springing from their camouflaged positions in the undergrowth at Calabee Creek in the night. At daylight on January 27, Walsh realizes his plan has failed. The Red Sticks scramble for their horses and make a wild ride to the freedom of the woods. The Georgians report that High-headed Jim has been killed, that Walsh has been wounded again, and that the Red Sticks' campaign has failed. Paddy Walsh and his warriors move to Pensacola. If aid did arrive they would be there to convey it into the nation; if it did not come, they would have the Spanish frontier between them and the Americans. *Billy and I begin a desperate journey, hoping to rendezvous with a British emissary, needing to procure ammunition and supplies for the remnant faction of warriors who still hold out.* The emissary offers only words and promises. He cannot move ships across the ocean any more quickly than London will allow. Help is being assembled in the Bahamas. *If we can lie low and hang on, hold out, maybe aid will arrive in time.*

The last stronghold of the Red Sticks, *our last stronghold*, is the sacred precinct of Tohopeka at a bend in the Tallapoosa River the Americans call the Horseshoe, where a thousand warriors from the towns of Hillabee, Ocfuskee, Oakchoie, Eufaulahatchee, New-Yauca, Hickory Ground, and Fish Pond have fortified themselves. The Horseshoe becomes the Americans' target.

When Jackson is told that the fortifications are across the neck of the bend, enclosing about a hundred acres, with the only possible escape route on the river a point where hundreds of canoes are tied up along the banks, he says that the Indians have "penned themselves up for slaughter." General Coffee fords the Tallapoosa two miles below the Horseshoe peninsula, and, with his cavalry and Jackson's force of American allied Indians, effectively closes off the escape routes. When Coffee signals Jackson that his force is in place, Jackson marches towards the Red Sticks' log breastwork and stations two cannons eighty yards from the nearest Red Stick defensive post. On the morning of March 27, 1814, Jackson sends a flag of truce toward the Red Sticks' breastwork. The Hillabee warriors fire on it. The American cannons open fire. Bullets pepper the air after the hurdled cannonballs and add to the tumult with noise but actually do little damage. While the main force of the Red Sticks responds to the attack on the breastworks, the Cherokees, along with with Coffee, swim the river, steal the canoes, and move them across the river. On the far banks, Tennessee militiamen and Americanized Indians hop into the canoes and quickly paddle back over the river to the village at the bottom of the bend and torch it. Jackson orders his troops to storm the breastwork. With Coffee's men coming up from the rear, the Red Stick warriors, most of whom are armed only with bows and arrows, are trapped between two lines of fire. The battle rages until nightfall. The Red Sticks will not surrender. Sam Houston, one of Jackson's junior officers, determines to carve his destiny from the Indians' hopeless situation at the Horseshoe and, with no real effort, emerges from the twilight as an American hero.

Menawa, the leader of the Red Sticks at Tohopeka, his body riddled by bullets, hides in the river, under water, by clinging to a root near the shore and breathing through a reed cane with one end held in his mouth and the other above the water. Only after the deep dark of the night has settled is he able to make his escape. Another warrior escapes by hiding under the slain bodies of his Red Stick comrades. The Americanized Indians estimate that only twenty Red Sticks have escaped. Jackson's troops cut the tips of the noses off the slain warriors, saying it is their method of counting the dead.

Jackson receives word from his scouts that William Weatherford is not, was not, at the Horseshoe. He curses. Even with this devastating blow to the last Red Stick stronghold, he fears that without Billy's death or capture the war will not be over. *A few days earlier Billy and I, his shadow companion, had left Tohopeka to go to Hoithlewaule to reinforce morale and shore up the lines of communication among the Red Stick factions.*

The morning after the battle, Jackson moves his army toward the junction of the Tallapoosa and Coosa rivers. At the small village Fooshatchee, Jackson captures a few Red Sticks, but most of the warriors in the nearby villages and in the sizable town of Hoithlewaule have fled across the Tallapoosa. Much to Jackson's dismay, militia troops from the Carolinas at their newly established Fort Decatur on the eastern side of the river make no effort to stop the escaping Indians. Jackson proceeds to the Hickory Ground, and, near the site where the French had built Fort Toulouse, his men erect Fort Jackson. The battle at Tohopeka is the Red Sticks' last stand in the Mississippi Territory. A great number of the surviving dissidents, led by Josiah Francis, Peter McQueen, and Sandy, John, and Peter Durant, escape into Spanish Florida. Among the women and children seeking refuge with the Seminoles are many of Billy's kinsmen, including the young boy Billy Powell, who will become Osceola. The war and the Americans will follow them south in several years. A few Red Stick warriors come into the Hickory Ground, accept the terms Jackson offers, and surrender. The land is ravaged; crops, farms, and towns are destroyed. Men, women, and children are starving.

Thirteen

Billy Comes In

We join the burial details. We commend our brothers and sisters and children to the Master of Breath. We dig their shallow graves, cover them with a blanket of earth. We whisper, "Your death is not meaningless. We will remember your sacrifice. Thank you for your faith in the vision. We will keep your dream of freedom. We will survive and with us the dream, the vision, that will be your unbreakable bond with the future." We take the oath on silenced hearts. We have smelled the stench of death, tasted horror, swallowed pride. We know the terror of spilled blood. We have sat beside the dying and sung their last songs. We have claimed the fear, we have opened the door to the next dimension on the endless spiral. Billy is the firemaker, the warrior who stands between the dead and the dying. I am the un-formed shadow. The promises he makes are the promises that I must keep. Our song will not end, he tells the warriors; our hearts will be remembered. The circle does not lose its shape, the spiral does not cease to make its loop. We are one with the dead

warriors, the slain grandmothers, the murdered children. We all belong to the earth, the sun, the stars.

So we walk the land. We hide in the swamps.

We are here, we are now. We go on, we continue. We hear the cries of hunger and hurt. We see people sleeping in the grass, on the ground. There is no shelter. Their clothes are tattered rags. They have fought the war and lost. They have not gone to Florida. They have not fled the oppressor. They do not abandon the land. There are ties that cannot be broken.

Jackson says that Billy must surrender. He tells the Red Stick warriors who turn themselves in that he will not consider the war ended until Weatherford surrenders. "If you want peace," he says, "bring me Weatherford! Bound and at my feet." His secretary writes the words down on paper. Food has reached the Americans; long supply lines have stocked their forts. The Americans could feed the starving women and children of the nation if only Weatherford were Jackson's prisoner. Jackson wants the satisfaction of hanging the Truth Speaker, of silencing him forever.

The road to Florida is open, but how can the firemaker, the mystic warrior, serve the people who remain,who have survived, from there? The Americans will swallow up the land, pushing the people into the swamps. With their small, mean hearts and shriveled souls, they do not understand the rules of war. For them there are no rules. For them victory is hollow unless the enemy nation is completely destroyed. The warriors must be spared the humiliation of having to bring the Truth Speaker-Lamochatte-Red Eagle-Weatherford tied and bound to the Americans.

Billy mounts Abbanonair and begins the journey that honor dictates, the route that will serve the people, the journey from the deep woods into the camp of the enemy, the path that must be traveled. Into a glade across the trail, a deer runs, stands and waits, poised for the encounter. Billy loads his rifle, slowly, deliberately takes aim. "Thank you for your sacrifice, brother," he whispers. With the deer slung behind his saddle, he has the gift that will gain him admission to the American compound. He is bringing a gift of venison for the general. The sentries outside the American bastion at the Hickory Ground see an Indian, shirtless and dressed in buckskin breeches and worn moccasins, riding toward the new fort. The American soldiers and frontier militiamen cannot tell the difference between a friendly Indian and a hostile Red Stick. They tell each other, "All Indians look alike." In combat the Americanized Indians had worn special badges on their headdresses so the Americans would not attack them. Now, in the relaxed postcombat atmosphere, an Indian was an Indian. Indians are continually riding in and out of the camp.

Billy calls out to the first militiaman he sees, "Where is Jackson?"

The surly frontiersman answers, "Now, why do you want to know?"

"Yeah?" his companion asks and spits.

"I have a gift for General Jackson," Billy says, motioning to the slain deer behind the saddle. The militiamen taunt the Indian on the grey horse. The Indian does not respond.

An older militiaman, in a coonskin cap, standing a little apart from the young soldiers, watches and listens. He sees the dignified Indian, a man with bearing, being harassed by punks. He steps forward, holding his hand up to silence the younger men. "General Jackson's tent is there." He points to the large marquee inside the palisade and nods.

"Thank you." Billy nods, and Abbanonair prances for ward. No one challenges him as he rides across his childhood playground. He dismounts in front of the marquee.

Big Warrior, lounging outside the entrance, shouts, "Ah, we've got you now, Billy Weatherford!"

Billy quickly dismounts and moves forward with his rifle in his hand. "You damn traitor, one word of insolence from you and I'll put a ball through your cowardly heart."

Jackson and Benjamin Hawkins rush out of the tent. "Weatherford? How dare you ride up to my tent! You! The murderer of the women and children of Fort Mims!" Jackson shouts.

Billy moves away from Big Warrior toward Jackson. These are his words, according to Major John Reid, Jackson's secretary: "General Jackson, I am not afraid of you. I fear no man. I am a warrior. I have nothing to request on behalf of myself; you can kill me, if you desire. I have come to beg you to send for the women and children of the war party, who are now starving in the woods. Their fields and cribs have been destroyed by your people, who have driven them to the woods without an ear of corn. I hope that you will send out parties who will safely conduct them here in order that they may be fed." Billy's voice did not waiver. "I tried to prevent the massacre of the women and children at Fort Mims. My efforts were in vain. Creek warriors do not kill women and children. I am now done fighting. The Red Sticks are nearly all killed. If I could fight you any longer, I would. I am asking you to send for the women and children, they never did you any harm. Don't let them starve. Kill me if you want."

Rowdy militiamen attracted by the shouts of Big Warrior crowd around the marquee. Pushing forward, they scream, "Kill him! Kill him."

"Silence!" Jackson orders. He appears to be mesmerized by Billy. As the soldiers grow quiet, he says, "Any man who would kill as brave a man as this would rob the dead!" The soldiers grumble; they have made a recent practice of robbing the dead. A noncommissioned officer disburses the crowd. The soldiers sullenly turn from the marquee. Jackson watches Billy intently, saying, "Come in." He motions into the tent. "Come, sit with me and talk."

"I have a gift for you." Billy gestures toward the deer behind Abbanonair's saddle. Good manners must never be forgotten. The gracious Indian always arrives with a gift.

Surprised and admiring of his adversary, Jackson says, "I will not ask you to lay down your arms and become peaceable. The terms on which your nation can be saved, and peace restored, have already been disclosed: in this way, and none other, can you obtain safety. If you want to continue the fight you are at liberty to leave and rejoin the war party. If you are captured later in those circumstances you will pay for your crimes with your life."

Billy says, "I desire peace. I want relief for my people. You may address me with threats and taunts now, it does not matter. There was a time when I had a choice, and could have answered you: I have none now—even hope has ended. Once I could inspire my warriors to battle, but I cannot animate the dead. My warriors can no longer hear my voice: their bones are at Talladega, Tallushatchee, Emuckfau, and Tohopeka. I have not surrendered myself thoughtlessly. While there was a chance of success, I never left my post, nor asked for peace. But my people are gone, and I now ask it for my nation, and for myself. On the miseries and misfortunes brought upon my country, I look back with deepest sorrow, and wish to avert still greater calamities. If I had been left to contend with the Georgia army, I would have raised my corn on one bank of the river, and fought them on the other; but your people have destroyed my nation. You are a warrior, a brave man: I rely upon your generosity. Whatever your terms for peace it would now be madness and folly to oppose them. Those who would still hold out can be influenced by a mean spirit of revenge and to this they must not, shall not sacrifice the last remnant of their country. You have told us where we might go and be safe. This is a good talk, and my nation ought to listen to it."

Jackson realizes that enlisting Billy in a bid for peace and an end to the war is in his best interest. He sends Billy out with a small party of Americanized Creeks to speak to the Red Sticks who have not come in. Billy persuades them that the war is over, that they must seek peace with the Americans, and that they must save what portion of their nation they can. They must turn themselves in at Fort Jackson. A warrior does not turn from humiliation if it serves the people. For the warrior, humiliation does not differ from adoration. When Billy has completed his peace mission, he visits the site of his burned-out home at Little River. The neighbors rise up in outrage. They vow to kill him. In a few days he continues on to Fort Claiborne, where he turns himself in to the commanding officer. He is imprisoned immediately in a tent adjacent to the commanding officer's marquee.

According to family stories, the following interaction takes place:

James Cornells, one of the militiamen assigned to guard the prisoner, has sworn that he will kill Billy Weatherford for the indignities suffered by his wife when she was kidnapped from their home at Burnt Corn and sold as a slave at Pensacola. Now Billy asks Cornells straightforwardly, "Do you plan to kill me while I am under your charge?"

Cornells answers, "No, I will take no advantage of you while you are here and I am guarding you. But when this time is over I intend to kill you."

Billy smiles. "Well, if you will take no advantage of me on

this occasion, I will trust myself to you." In time, Cornells learns that Billy had not been at Burnt Corn and had nothing to do with his wife being taken captive by Peter McQueen and sold as a slave at Pensacola. He has a change of heart. Like Jackson, Cornells soon seems mesmerized by Billy and declares himself his friend.

The tensions of having Billy Weatherford as a prisoner at Fort Claiborne are overpowering. Military order is strained with the constant threats on the prisoner and his jailers. After about two weeks, Colonel Russell, the commandant, announces that he is going to send Billy back to Fort Jackson. Around midnight of the same day, Russell sends his aide with Billy to the watch station of Captain William Laval, officer of the guard.

"Captain Laval," the aide says, "the commanding officer says you must take Weatherford to yonder mulberry tree, beyond the compound, under which you will find a horse tied, and that he must mount the horse and make his escape." The aide salutes and leaves Billy with the captain.

The captain tells Billy to follow him. They walk past the sentries, the captain giving the password when challenged. Laval leads him to the mulberry tree under which Abbanon-air waits. Billy unties the reins from the tree limb, throws them over the horse's head, reaches out, shakes hands with the captain, says the classic Alabama blessing, "May the Spirit be with you," mounts the horse, and rides away. Laval listens to the hoofbeats fading into the distance. When the song of the locusts claims the silence, he returns to his post.

Billy disappears into the forests and swamps. No one knows where he is. In the quiet stillness, he seeks the peace that can only come from within. Rumors proliferate about his whereabouts. Many people think he is with Jackson at the Hickory Ground, that they have become good friends, with

Jackson admiring the bravery and genius of his former adversary so much that when the Tennessean leaves for home toward the end of April Billy goes with him to Nashville, to the Hermitage, where he is a secret guest for over a year. People imagine the two horsemen comparing notes on breeding techniques and on various horseracing tracks and experiences. Gossips say Billy has the eye of an eagle and moves with the regal air of a king, that he is fearless, high-toned, noble, that he is the most handsome man anyone has ever seen. He is becoming a legend. Many white men are now calling him Red Eagle. For every person who idolizes him, a dozen still speak the word "Weatherford" as a curse; they, too, are making a legend. None of the words means anything.

For the shadow-that-I-am, the battle at Fort Mims and the war have just been preliminaries for this moment, an introduction to the lesson the Spirit teaches. Now, here in the forest, I learn the message that I must take to another time. Billy tells me with grave certainty that we must not let other people dictate who we are, how we view ourselves, or how we react in calm or crisis.

How do we do this? I ask.

He says we must refuse to be provoked. We must keep our souls sacred. Our spirits are our temple, our minds are our monasteries, our hearts are our holy book. We do not leave the Path. We choose the Path. We are the force, the essence, that brings balance and harmony to the middle world. The need for harmony and balance will not abate. We must never doubt who we are. If we doubt who we are, we may forget our purpose. We are spiritual beings. We are awake to the Spirit. We commune with the Master of Breath with each measure of air that enters our lungs. For us there are no barriers between here and there. We remember that day is renewed with the sunrise. In the noisy

*nights, with quails calling and frogs croaking, the light
promises to return. Hope can begin again.*

*In the quietness of the swamps and secret places of the forest,
the lessons of the firemaker can be remembered and a new vision
sought. Billy and I stop at the abandoned cornfields in the
night. The smell of the soft damp earth is hope gestating. We
keep faith with the Master of Breath. He supplies the seeds, leading us to a forgotten ear of dried corn where we believe there is
none. We plant. In the cornfield we make an affirmation of life.
In the day, in the deep forest, we sleep within the leafy walls of a
hut disguised by a tangle of brush. In our fitful sleep we pray for
a vision. We of the blackened soul, we who have embraced darkness seek the light. And the vision eludes us. We have not spent
enough time in this new shallow grave of the soul. The fire has
not burned our funeral mound clean. We live in the place between thoughts, and, at night, in the abandoned fields, we plant
the corn. Even without a new vision we can keep the faith.*

*Sam comes into the forest and swamps, passing by us with-
out seeing, searching for Billy. Billy makes no response. His
brothers ride past us in the daylight and we keep silent. We have
this time to spend in nothingness together.*

The British land troops at Apalachicola in Florida below
Pensacola. The Apalachicola runs up to the Chattahoochee
and Flint rivers. British ships bring "Indian supplies" into
Pensacola. But the war in the Mississippi Territory is over. A
British colonel disembarks from another ship at St. Augustine with supplies and support intended for the Red Sticks,
but there are no Red Sticks to claim them. The British can
only conduct meaningful rendezvous with those who have
abandoned their homeland and sought refuge in Florida.
Emissaries from the British king move through the forests
and swamps that have become burial grounds for the Red
Sticks. Too late.

Benjamin Hawkins begins to let some of the Upper Creeks return to their former homes and farms. The frontier politicians are outraged. In a few months Jackson comes back from Nashville to the Hickory Ground, where he is the sole commissioner of the peace treaty to be made with the Creeks to end the Red Stick war. The politicians trust him to be firmer than Hawkins. His firmness devastates his former allies. Big Warrior, McIntosh and the Lower Creeks, and the Americanized Creeks of Georgia are to be punished as severely as the Upper Creeks of the Mississippi Territory. The entire Creek nation must pay all the expenses incurred by the United States in fighting the war. Land is to be the medium of exchange—a payment of twenty-three million acres. In addition, the United States will retain the right to establish and maintain roads and the right to navigate on the rivers within the boundaries of whatever land remains in the Creek nation. The Treaty of Fort Jackson demands that the Creeks break off all communication with the Spanish and the British and that all the prophets who have participated in the war be surrendered to United States authorities for just punishment—hanging. The treaty is signed on August 9, 1814, less than a year after the massacre at Fort Mims. None of the major Red Stick leaders signs. William Weatherford does not sign. Jackson does not ask that he sign. Only the friendly Creeks are ordered to sign. Big Warrior suggests that the peace treaty and payment demanded by the Americans is premature; after all, he says, the Red Sticks have not been conquered but have merely escaped and might return and resume the war at any time. Red Stick warriors who decline to appear at Fort Jackson ask the Americanized Creeks why they should do so, saying that they now have friends and arms and are ready to "spill blood" rather than submit to the Americans. Big Warrior seems baffled that he and the Americanized Creeks who have gone to such great lengths to remain friends with the Americans must be punished.

Though Jackson brags of the harsh terms he demands of his allies in the treaty, he is aware that the Creeks' current economic condition is about to push them all into rebellion. The war prevented Upper Creeks and Lower Creeks from being able to maintain their farms and hunting practices. He asks that about eighty-two hundred Creeks be clothed and fed at the government's expense until they can plant and harvest again, adding that, even so, the government has made an excellent bargain and will gain much profit from the rich, newly acquired lands. At the same time, Jackson writes threatening letters to the Spanish governor at Pensacola demanding the arrest and extradition of Peter McQueen and Josiah Francis. McIntosh now becomes Jackson's flunky, raiding into Spanish Florida and attacking refugee settlements.

In the woods where we have taken refuge, Billy says, "My war is over. Now I choose peace." The way of the warrior is not always war. The warrior priest presides over the fire, the sacred flame. He keeps the vision. He preserves the faith. The warrior transforms his time as a living person into whatever force the people need.

In the forest of our minds and under the summer mornings' faded blue skies, we sing the songs and say the words of the chants. The wild grasses stoop, seed pods gleaming, under a coat of dew. We cross the willow bogs, touch the blooming mallow, walk under the canopy of the dogwoods. The hungry land swallows the remnants of what has been, the muscadine vines shroud the trees at the edge of the swamps, the forest comes and goes. Any vegetation neglected for a short time makes a jungle of dense brush. A few more years and the forest will reclaim the places that boasted towns and villages just last year. Cedars, sweet gum, live oaks, and pines—we walk among the trees. Our spirits mingle. In the thick, hot smell of July we find a green cornfield and flocks of yellow butterflies and black moths. Green grass laps at our legs. Wildflowers, yellow and lavender, thrive under the pines. The purple heads of the ironweed staunchly claim their ground. Wild tobacco plants poke their spikes skyward. Water lilies dot ponds and lakes. Ferns hover in the shadows. We linger in the thick shade of trees a hundred variations of green. We bathe in the cold creek. Wild sunflowers— Jerusalem artichokes—send up shots of flowers to mark where their tubers may be found. We see the red earth exposed. Sometimes we spy horses cavorting in fields of lush grass. We find sparse volunteer patches of melons and peas. The canebrakes offer refuge should we need it. We are brothers with the bears who live there in secret, never revealing themselves until the right moment.

In time, the lost time, the time when no one knows where Billy is, the fury of the neighbors at his old home on Little River lessens. Soon cotton captivates their imaginations with promises of fortunes that shuffle everything else to the back of their minds. *My lessons are learned. My apprenticeship in the other time served.* Billy turns his attention to his own immediate future. As the Americans carve up the Indian country, his brothers retain the land along the lower Alabama in the Tensaw district long ago allotted to them and their wives by the nation, now claiming it in the manner of the Americans. Jackson has gone on to fight the British at New Orleans, and, as the Americans claim Florida under the Adams-Onis Treaty, he moves into Florida to take up the old fight with the Creeks who have escaped and become Seminole.

Josiah Francis had gone to Pensacola, then on to England with the late-arriving British emissaries to plea the cause. He returns to Florida with supplies and support. His path leads back to Jackson in Florida. Jackson captures him and carries out the death sentence issued back in the Mississippi Territory. Prophets die by hanging. The remnant of the Red Sticks with the Seminole will continue to fight the United States for years. Menawa vows he will execute McIntosh for his treachery. The list of grievances against McIntosh grows as he continues to betray the Creeks to gain personal favor with the Americans. His execution is accomplished after several years. The dead of Tohopeka are avenged, the cost of honor paid.

Billy comes back to the land that had been his plantation at Little River, and, with his brothers' help, slowly and quietly rebuilds his life as a farmer. Within the family the communal bonds have not been destroyed. In time, he marries again. His wife, Mary Stiggins, is the sister of George, the chronicler of a Creek version of the war. His neighbors seldom see Billy, as the fields and forests of the old Creek nation become the cotton factories of the American entrepreneurs. But needy and destitute Indians find their way to his home with no difficulty. None is ever turned away. His brothers say he can easily become wealthy again if he will just stop giving away so much to the Indians and learn to be a white man. *He finds that the warrior's path leads back to the priesthood and to the knowledge that the ultimate priest is the farmer who plants the seeds and nourishes the earth.*

Unnoticed, he travels to Tuckabatchee to the grave of his mother, Sehoy, to the land that the Americans have claimed from the people. He collects her remains and carries them back to his plantation at Little River. There he prepares a new grave for her. She sleeps beside his cornfield.

In the fall of 1824, Billy joins some kinsmen on a ritual bear hunt in a canebrake, a sacred bear hunting ground, near his home. *In a dream he calls me to come with him. We slip into the pathless jumble of the cane; when we are a few feet into the dense growth, we no longer feel the wind. Above us the fronds rise to block the sun. Our feet struggle to find cane-free ground. We stumble, wedging our way deeper into the brake, pushing canes aside only to have them snap back and slap us. How can we know where we are going? Briars grab at our ankles. The sharp edges of the mature cane fronds slice our hands. In the thick cane, separated from the other hunters, we find places here and there where animals have beat down a small spot within a fortress of giant cane roots and nested under sheltering thatches of fronds. Though the first frost of the season has come, they have been warm and dry in their nests on the canebrake floor. Moving silently through the cane is scarcely possible. The cane snaps and pops when bent or stepped on. If we venture too far into the brake will we be able to find our way out? We bend back the next frond and come face to face with the bear. For an instant, all three of us are suspended in time and space. The bear waits and watches Billy carefully for a few seconds, then slowly turns and disappears into pathless wilderness. Billy stares after the bear.*

"Do you understand?" *he asks the shadow-that-I-am.* "If you come to your death and do not know who you are, what will you have accomplished? We have walked this Path to know who we are. We have journeyed through time to encounter our true self, our spirit. We must not let other people dictate who we are. You must not forget who we are." *He shivers slightly, then leads me out of the canebrake, announcing that he has a yearning for home and a fire. At home he tells his wife that he is overwhelmingly tired. He goes to bed, closes his eyes, and dies. This is just one day in our life. In my phantom world I paint my body black, encircle my eyes with vermillion so that my vision will be sacred, strap swan wings to my arms, and then raise the wings in the flight of dance around the circle of fire on the hearth. I sing the warrior's song, chant the words of death. This is my spontaneous song for Billy: This is where we cross the divide, where we change form, where our bodies become irrevocably earth.*

Billy's family buries him beside his mother. Six generations later, I sit on the ground by Billy's grave at Little River. Death sends an emissary. The wind is his voice, whispering the never-ending refrain: "If you don't know who you are, your life is without meaning. All the lessons of the grandmothers add up to identity. The teachings are a way to define yourself."

A blackjack oak, wild and ragged, is growing at the foot of Billy's grave, nurtured by his bones. I touch it. I have followed the Path, performed the work my childhood vision required. I have traveled across the old Creek nation and have seen the cleared fields and forests of the American frontiersmen over-grown and abandoned. I have seen the places where the white men worshipped cotton defiled by time. I have seen the deer in the pine woods running wild and free. I have seen the cane-brakes returning inch by inch, foot by foot, on the abandoned bottoms and heights. I have seen the sacred bear hunting ground reborn. The panther has crossed my path. I have but one heart, and it is of the Spirit. I know who I am.

I am the straight-haired girl who became the deer, the six-year-old who never doubted her identity, the child who heard the stories of William Weatherford from her uncle and understood the moral, the time-traveler who invited you along on a mystic journey. Thank you for going with me, for listening to the words of the grandmothers, for remembering the warriors, the men, the women, the children who have become earth. Thank you for recognizing who they were and what they believed. I am bringing you a gift from them—the knowledge that you can choose who and what you will be. You can even choose to be a true human being.

Notes

Chapter One

3 death date: 1824 appears on the tombstone, though grandson Charles Weatherford wrote in a letter to T. H. Ball on October 7, 1890, that his grandfather died in 1826 (Halbert and Ball, *Creek War*).

4 Regarding Indian mixed-bloods in the American experience, Professor Herbert Hoover of the University of South Dakota says that on nearly every white frontier, no more than two generations passed before a noteworthy component in the society was of mixed biological heritage. He goes on to point out that no one in an official capacity seemed to care until a time came to compensate tribes for land by annuity payments and other benefits. Then it became essential to address the issue. In the 1830s, two steps were taken. One was the announcement of a federal policy to label all people of mixed Indian-white heritage as "half-breeds," whatever the blood quantum happened to be, and this remained the official label in federal vernacular until at least the end of the century. The second was an experiment with two "half-breed" reservations,

seemingly modeled on the British Canadian policy of naming a third category of people, called *Metis*, which still exists. This experiment led to confusion, and the two reservations closed by the end of the 1850s. Thereafter, a person was an "Indian" if tribal leaders said it was so—for some purposes, even if it was a white man who had married into the tribe. This had become official federal policy by 1905, but soon the matter of federal benefits got in the way. Finally, in 1918, Congress set the "quarter-blood" rule, which is still in place. According to this rule, only persons who have a quarter-blood quantum or more are eligible for benefits such as education and health care delivery which are owed to the tribes. Otherwise, the matter of who is or is not a tribal member has been the decision of each tribe. Today the terms "mixed-blood" and "full-blood" have cultural, not biological, meaning (private communication).

5 Thomas Jefferson wrote in *Notes on the State of Virginia* that he believed all Indians (he does not offer geographic qualifiers) were already racially mixed with blacks. Samuel J. Wells, in his master's thesis "The Evolution of Jeffersonian Indian Policy," delineates and examines Jefferson's documented ideas that, through intermarriage with whites and other means of the "American civilization" process, the Indians on the southern frontier could be turned into yeoman farmers and a ready militia against foreign intrigue. Several generations earlier, the French had decided that when white people married Indians they became Indians and were lost to the colony (*Mississippi Provincial Archives: French Dominion 1701–1729*; hereafter referred to as *MPA:FD*).

5 "native communism": Eggleston, *Red Eagle*.

7 Mobile, Nanibia, and Tohomé: Cushman, in *History of the Choctaw, Chickasaw and Natchez Indians*, says that the Mobile Indians are "an ancient clan" of the Choctaws. The Mobile Indians are first documented in *The De Soto Chronicles* (Tuscaloosa: University of Alabama Press, 1993), which are the journals of three members of the 1539–43 expedition through the Southeast. The Nanibia, Tohomé, and Mobile Indians all spoke Choctaw or a

dialect of Choctaw (Swanton, *Indians of the Southeastern United States*). When the French established their headquarters on Mobile Bay in 1702, the Mobile, Nanibia, and Tohomé had villages along the western banks of the Mobile and Tombigbee rivers from above the new French fort upward to the modern location of McIntosh. In Roulett's census of 1730 the three nations are counted as Choctaws (*MPA:FD 1729–1740*). Some scholars speculate that these people "disappeared"; however, their descendants are living in the same general locations today and are usually referred to as mixed-bloods (many of their ancestors intermarried with early colonists) or are erroneously called "creole" or "cajun" by local white people. Jay Higginbotham lists primary documents mentioning the three nations in *The Mobile Indians* (Mobile: Sir Rey's, 1966).

9 mixed-blood enclaves: Hudson, "scattered enclaves," in *Southeastern Indians.*

8 "mixed with a little African": from Benjamin Hawkins's letters in *Sketches* (Reprint Company edition) regarding Benjamin Durant. Henri, in *Benjamin Hawkins and the Southern Indians*, interprets this to mean that Durant is a mulatto.

9 *Weaver et al. v. State* (1 Div. 756, 757.): *The Southern Reporter*, vol. 116 (St. Paul: West Publishing Co., 1928); also *Corpus Juris Secundum: A Complete Restatement of the American Law*, Francis J. Ludes and Harold J. Gilbert, eds., vol. 58 (Brooklyn, NY: American Law Book Company, 1948).

19 For an overview of customs, behavior, and beliefs, see Swanton, *Indians of the Southeastern United States* and Hudson, *Southeastern Indians.*

21 Regarding the importance and validity of oral tradition preserved in oral history, Professor Herbert Hoover points out that the Holy Bible is largely oral history and that the Roman Catholic fathers, having regarded it as "plausible allegory" for some two thousand years, have used it as one basis for a globally important denomination. Hoover says that for half a century or more, oral history has been embraced as a necessary means of gathering information

about the past and that oral tradition is the basis for every spiritual and philosophical tradition in the world (private communication).

Chapter Two

The mystic thought-world of Native America is considered in Carl Jung's *Memories, Dreams, Reflections* (New York: Pantheon Books, 1961) pp.246–53; Claude Lévi-Strauss's works are all recommended reading for general background information, as are the works of Swanton and Schoolcraft for specifics. Francisco Guerra, in *The Pre-Columbian Mind* (London: Seminar Press, 1971), examines how Native Americans saw themselves, their world, and their relationship with the tangible and intangible world. In *The Hero with a Thousand Faces* (Princeton, NJ: Princeton University Press, 1949), Joseph Campbell explains in psychological and scholastic terms the universality of the mythic journey (the quest, spirit guides) and of mystic experiences. His remarkable work places myth and mysticism on a scientific grid without destroying any lyric component.

26 The quotation is from *Black Elk Speaks* as told through John G. Neihardt (Lincoln/London: University of Nebraska Press, 1979) p. 204.

Chapter Three

Family stories and information from the Stout Collection and from Wind clan traditions are major sources for this chapter.

39 French interaction with the Alabamas and Creeks that led to the building of Fort Toulouse: *MPA:FD 1704–1743*; Giraud, *Company of the Indies*; Thomas, *Fort Toulouse*; French, *Historic Collection of Louisiana*.

40 early meetings with English: Wells, *Native Land*; Moore, *Nairne's Muskhogean Journals*; Cotterill, *Southern Indians*; Cockran, *Creek Frontier*; Crane, *Southern Frontier*.

40 early Creek (Alabama) dealings with the Spanish: Cockran, *Creek Frontier*; Cotterill, *Southern Indians*; Crane, *Southern Frontier*; John Francis Bannon, *Bolton and the Spanish Borderlands*.

42 Yamasee War: Wells, *Native Land; MPA:FD 1704–1743.*

42 Natchez uprising: ibid.; *MPA:FD 1729–1740;* Giraud, *Company of the Indies.*

43 descriptions of houses, customs, etc: Bartram, *Travels;* Swan in Schoolcraft; Romans, *Concise Natural History of East and West Florida;* Hudson, *Southeastern Indians;* Swanton's several works.

45 French-Indian marriages: *MPA:FD 1701–1729;* Giraud, *Company of the Indies.*

48–49 McGillivrays: Cashin, *Lachlan McGillivray, Indian Trader;* Peter Brannon, *The Southern Indian Trade* (Montgomery: Paragon Press, 1935); Caughey, *McGillivray of the Creeks;* John R. Alden, *John Stuart and the Southern Colonial Frontier: A Study of Indian Relations, War, Trade, and Land Problems in the Southern Wilderness, 1745–1755* (Ann Arbor: University of Michigan Press, 1944); Stout Collection; family stories.

50 travelers: Mereness, *Travels in the American Colonies;* Clark, *Travels in the Old South;* Wells, *Native Land.*

50 John Tanner: report to the trustees of Georgia cited in Wells, "Choctaw Mixed Bloods"; Cashin, *Lachlan McGillivray.* Wells also cites Spanish sources of similar accounts of the British traders' many mixed-blood children at later dates, as does information in Mississippi Provincial Archives: Spanish Dominion (MPA:SD); Holmes, "Archivo de Indios"; Mississippi Provincial Archives: English Dominion (MPA:ED).

51 Taitt: Mereness, *Travels in the American Colonies.* Spellings vary; Taitt, Tate, and Tait are used interchangeably.

Chapter Four

53–56 customs: family stories; Stout Collection; Swanton; Schoolcraft.

57–60 myths: author's version of family stories. See Swanton, *Myths and Tales of the Southeastern Indians;* Hudson, *Southeastern Indians.*

62 Boskita (Green Corn Festival): Bartram, *Travels;* Swanton; Hudson; Romans; Schoolcraft; Adair.

66 black drink: ibid.; Charles Hudson, ed. *Black Drink: A Native American Tea* (Athens: University of Georgia Press, 1979).

67 striking the post: Iberville in French, *Collection of Historic Louisiana*; Swanton; Schoolcraft; Bartram.

Chapter Five

70 childcare: Romans; Bartram; Swanton; Schoolcraft; Hudson.

71–72 sacred traditions, buildings, and people: ibid.

72 Panton, Leslie and Company: Coker and Watson, *Indian Traders*; Prucha, *American Indian Policy in the Formative Years*; Cotterill, *Southern Indians*; Wright, *Britain and the American Frontier*; Mobile (Alabama) Public Library (special collections); Pensacola (Florida) Historical Society (Seville Square); Pace Library (special collections), University of West Florida in Pensacola; papers of Panton, Leslie and Company.

72–73 American Revolution: O'Donnell, *Southern Indians in the American Revolution*; Cashin, *Lachlan McGillivray, Indian Trader*; Caughey, *McGillivray of the Creeks*; Cotterill, *Southern Indians*. The aftermath is discussed in Reginald Horsman, *The Frontier in the Formative Years* (New York: Holt, Rinehart and Winston, 1970).

72–73 Alexander McGillivray: Caughey's *McGillivray of the Creeks*, a fine biography, contains primary documents including correspondence from, to, and about Alexander McGillivray; Cotterill, *Southern Indians*; Whitaker, "Alexander McGillivray, 1783–1789"; see also Prucha, *Bibliographic Guide to the History of Indian White Relations*, for other journal articles concerning Alexander McGillivray.

74 Charles Weatherford: *American State Papers*, hereafter referred to as *ASP*; Griffith, *McIntosh and Weatherford*; Wells, "Choctaw Mixed Bloods"; Caughey, *McGillivray of the Creeks*; Hawkins, *Sketches* (Reprint Company edition).

74–80 William Weatherford's boyhood: family stories; Stout Collection.

Chapter Six

83, 93 Sophia: family stories; Stout Collection; Caughey, *McGillivray of the Creeks*; Hawkins, *Sketches* (Reprint Company edition); Pickett, *History of Alabama*.

84 skin trade: Hudson, *Southeastern Indians*; Cotterill, *Southern Indians*; Usner, *Indians, Settlers, & Slaves in a Frontier Exchange Economy*; Coker and Watson, *Indian Traders*; Wright, *Anglo-Spanish Rivalry in North America*; Wells, *Native Land*; Giraud, *Company of the Indies*; Prucha, *Documents of United States Indian Policy*; *ASP*; *MPA:FD*; MPA:ED; MPA:SD.

85 alcohol: Coker and Watson, *Indian Traders*; Prucha, *American Indian Policy in the Formative Years* and *Documents on United States Indian Policy*; Usner, *Indians, Settlers, & Slaves in a Frontier Exchange Economy*; Wells, *Native Land*; *ASP*; *MPA:FD*, MPA:ED and MPA:SD.

88 slaves: Usner, *Indians, Settlers & Slaves in a Frontier Exchange Economy*; Littlefield, *Africans and Creeks*; *ASP*.

89–91 Le Clerc de Milfort: *Memoirs* by same; Woodward, *Reminiscences*; Coker and Watson, *Indian Traders*; Wright, *Britain and the American Frontier*.

91–94 Bowles: *Authentic Memoirs* by same; Wright, *William Augustus Bowles*, *Britain and the American Frontier*, and *Anglo-Spanish Rivalry in North America*; Cotterill, *Southern Indians*; Griffith, *McIntosh and Weatherford*; Hawkins, *Sketches* (Reprint Company edition); *ASP*.

Chapter Seven

95–99 William Weatherford: family stories; Stout Collection.

98 customs: Swanton; Schoolcraft; Bartram; Hudson.

100 Americanization: *ASP*; Hawkins, *Sketches* (Reprint Company edition); Wells, "Choctaw Mixed Bloods"; Sheehan, *Seeds of Extinction*; Prucha, *American Indian Policy in the Formative Years*.

102 Quakers: Hawkins, *Sketches* (Reprint Company edition); Griffith, *McIntosh and Weatherford*; Henri, *The Southern Indians and Ben-*

jamin Hawkins; Henry Warner Bowden, *American Indians and Christian Missions* (Chicago/London: University of Chicago Press, 1981); Prucha, *American Indian Policy in the Formative Years*, *ASP*.

102, 104 Moravians: Hawkins, *Sketches* (Reprint Company edition); *ASP*.

108 gifts to Indians: ibid.; Cotterill, *Southern Indians*; Henri, *The Southern Indians and Benjamin Hawkins*.

108 British merchants: Coker and Watson, *Indian Traders*; Prucha, *American Indian Policy in the Formative Years*; Usner, *Indians, Settlers, & Slaves in a Frontier Exchange Economy*; *ASP*.

109 Georgians: *ASP*; Coker and Watson, *Indian Traders*; Prucha, *Documents of United States Indian Policy*.

108 31st parallel: Hawkins, *Sketches* (Reprint Company edition); Ellicott, *Journal of Andrew Ellicott*; *ASP*; Woodward, *Reminiscences*.

110 capture of Bowles: Hawkins, *Sketches* (Reprint Company edition); *ASP*; Wright, *William Augustus Bowles*; Griffith, *McIntosh and Weatherford*; Holmes, "Archivo de Indios"; Woodward, *Reminiscences*.

Chapter Eight

113 Weatherford's racetrack: Hawkins, *Sketches* (Reprint Company edition); family stories; tradition; Stout Collection.

114 treaties: Prucha, *Documents of United States Indian Policy*; *ASP*.

122 details of White Sapling Conference: *ASP*.

127 United States claim to West Florida—West Florida incident: *ASP*; Hamilton, *Colonial Mobile*; Claiborne, *Mississippi as a Province, Territory, and State*; Pickett, *History of Alabama*; Territorial Governor's Records, 1798–1817, Record Group 2, MDAH.

128 Washington County: ibid.

130 Federal Post Road: Southerland and Brown, *Federal Road*; Cotterill, *Southern Indians*; Pickett, *History of Alabama*; Griffith, *McIntosh and Weatherford*; Hamilton, *Colonial Mobile*; *ASP*.

Chapter Nine

144 runaway slaves: Hawkins, *Sketches* (Reprint Company edition); *ASP*; Henri, *The Southern Indians and Benjamin Hawkins*, Woodward, *Reminiscences.*

145 horse stealing-trading: Hawkins, *Sketches* (Reprint Company edition); *ASP*; Henri, *The Southern Indians and Benjamin Hawkins*, Martin, *Sacred Revolt.*

146 Tecumseh: Edmunds, *Tecumseh and the Quest for Indian Leadership*; Martin, *Sacred Revolt*; Stout Collection.

146 Tenskwatawa: ibid.; Edmunds, *Shawnee Prophet.*

147 Shakers: ibid.; Stephen J. Stein, *The Shaker Experience in America* (New Haven/London: Yale University Press, 1992); Flo Morse, *The Shakers and the World's People* (New York: Dodd, Mead and Company, 1980).

148 Hoentubbee story: Choctaw tradition; Halbert and Ball, *Creek War.*

149 Tecumseh speech: Choctaw tradition; Cushman, *History of the Choctaw, Chickasaw and Natchez Indians.*

149 Pushmataha's reply: ibid.

150 Seekaboo: Stiggins, *Creek Indian History*, Halbert and Ball, *Creek War.*

151 meeting with Seekaboo: One family story relates that William Weatherford met with Seekaboo to ask the prophet's aid in spiritually contacting Alexander McGillivray in order to seek the dead man's advice on the course the Creeks should follow.

155 Big Warrior's words: Stout Collection; Claiborne, *Life and Times of Sam Dale.*

159 Captain Isaacs: Stiggins, *Creek Indian History*, Martin, *Sacred Revolt.*

158 Josiah Francis and prophets: *ASP*; Stiggins, *Creek Indian History*, Nunez, "Creek Nativism"; Halbert and Ball, *Creek War*, Griffith, *McIntosh and Weatherford*; Martin, *Sacred Revolt*, Cotterill, *Southern Indians.*

160 New Madrid earthquake: Hawkins, *Sketches* (Reprint Company

edition); Halbert and Ball, *Creek War*; Claiborne, *Mississippi as a Province, Territory, and State*. For accounts unrelated to the Creek War, see John Bradbury, *Travels in the Interior of America* (USA: Readex Microprint Corp., 1966, reprint); Horsman, *The Frontier in the Formative Years*.

150 comet: Halbert and Ball, *Creek War*; Pickett, *History of Alabama*; Henri, *The Southern Indians and Benjamin Hawkins*; Edmunds, *Tecumseh*.

162 Holy Ground: family stories; Stout Collection; Stiggins, *Creek Indian History*; Halbert and Ball, *Creek War*; Griffith, *McIntosh and Weatherford*; Martin, *Sacred Revolt*.

Chapter Ten

164 Little Warrior: *ASP*; Halbert and Ball, *Creek War*; Wright, *Britain and the American Frontier*; Cotterill, *Southern Indians*; Griffith, *McIntosh and Weatherford*; Pickett, *History of Alabama*.

165 Mrs. Crawley: *ASP*; Halbert and Ball, *Creek War*.

165 Tandy Walker: ibid.; Hamilton, *Colonial Mobile*; Pickett, *History of Alabama*.

165 William McIntosh: Griffith, *McIntosh and Weatherford*; Halbert and Ball, *Creek War*; Pickett, *History of Alabama*; Cotterill, *Southern Indians*. Pickett identifies McIntosh as the grandson of the man for whom the town of McIntosh and the bluffs along the Tombigbee were named. Hamilton, in *Colonial Mobile*, writes that the spot on the Tombigbee that became known as McIntosh Bluffs was named for a British Indian interpreter named James McIntosh who lived there, and also that this spot had formerly been called Tomeehettee Bluffs for the Indian tribe (Tohomé) who lived there.

166–167 deaths of Thomas Meredith and William Lott: Woodward, *Reminiscences*; Halbert and Ball, *Creek War*; *ASP*; Henri, *The Southern Indians and Benjamin Hawkins*.

167–170 cattle drives: tradition; Stout Collection; Halbert and Ball, *Creek War* (Sam Moniac's deposition); Woodward's *Reminiscences*.

168 meeting with Mushalatubbee: tradition; Stout Collection; Halbert and Ball, *Creek War*; Cotterill, *Southern Indians*. Although Americanized family members protest this, Eggleston, in *Red Eagle*, says that Weatherford actively participated in plans for the war against the Americans and that his only regret was that the war came too quickly for the Red Sticks to procure the aid they needed to insure victory, a thesis that is supported by Wright in *Anglo-Spanish Rivalry in North America* and *Britain and the American Frontier*.

169 United States takes possession of Mobile: Halbert and Ball, *Creek War*; Pickett, *History of Alabama*; Hamilton, *Colonial Mobile*; Wright, *Anglo-Spanish Rivalry in North America*; Claiborne, *Mississippi as a Province, Territory and State*; Holmes, "Archivo de Indios" (includes a summary of the court-martial of Perez on charges of surrendering Mobile to Americans); Coker and Watson, *Indian Traders*.

170 visit to Pensacola, Spanish offer: Stiggins, *Creek Indian History*; tradition; Stout Collection; Holmes, "Archivo de Indios"; Halbert and Ball, *Creek War*.

171, 175 Wilkinson at Sam Moniac's and the latter's deposition: Halbert and Ball, *Creek War*; Claiborne, *Mississippi as a Province, Territory and State*; Carter, *Territory of Mississippi*; ASP.

173 Judge Toulmin: ibid.; Mrs. Dunbar Rowland, *Andrew Jackson's Campaign*; Clark and Guice, *Frontiers in Conflict*.

174 attitudes and actions of Moniac and Weatherford: tradition; Stout Collection.

177 espionage: tradition; family stories (some of which are conflicting).

179 "amusement for idle people": ASP; Halbert and Ball, *Creek War*.

179 siege of Tuckabatchee: ibid.; Cotterill, *Southern Indians*; Pickett, *History of Alabama*; Griffith, *McIntosh and Weatherford*; Stiggins, *Creek Indian History*.

180 Lateau and murder at Coosa: Halbert and Ball, *Creek War*; Martin, *Sacred Revolt*; Griffith, *McIntosh and Weatherford*; ASP.

178 civil war: Hawkins's position as late as September 30, 1813, ASP.

181 Peter McQueen meeting with Choctaws: tradition; Stout Collection; Halbert and Ball, *Creek War*; Cotterill, *Southern Indians*.

184 David Tate at Pensacola: Halbert and Ball, *Creek War*.

184 Burnt Corn battle and preceding trip to Pensacola: Stiggins, *Creek Indian History*; Woodward, *Reminiscences*; Halbert and Ball, *Creek War*; Pickett, *History of Alabama*; Claiborne, *Life and Times of General Sam Dale*; Cotterill, *Southern Indians*; Mrs. Dunbar Rowland, *Andrew Jackson's Campaign* (correspondence between officials in Mississippi Territory and Spanish West Florida and from Mississippi Militia officers to their commander); Coker and Watson, *Indian Traders*; Owsley, *Struggle for the Gulf Borderlands*.

186 fair notice of war: Romans, *Concise Natural History*; Wells, *Native Land*.

183–186 lack of British and Spanish aid: Cotterill, *Southern Indians*; Wright, *Anglo-Spanish Rivalry in North America* and *Britain and the American Frontier*.

Chapter Eleven

188 warriors' rituals: Moore, *Nairne's Muskhogean Journals*.

190 forts: *ASP*; Halbert and Ball, *Creek War*.

191 Samuel Mims's fort: Halbert and Ball, *Creek War*.

192 warriors prepare: ibid.

193 shadow army: tradition; Woodward, *Reminiscences*; Halbert and Ball, *Creek War*.

194 McGirths: ibid.

194 Weatherford scouts fort: Stiggins, *Creek Indian History*.

195 attack on Fort Mims: ibid.; Woodward, *Reminiscences*; Halbert and Ball, *Creek War*; tradition; Stout Collection. See Claiborne, *Mississippi as a Province, Territory and State*, and Pickett, *History of Alabama*, for American partisan views.

198 Seekaboo, "McGillivray negroes": tradition; Woodward, *Reminiscences*; Halbert and Ball, *Creek War*; Stout Collection; Stiggins, *Creek Indian History*.

199 Weatherford's Landing: tradition; family stories; Stout Collection.

201 Major Kennedy's detachment: Halbert and Ball, *Creek War*; Carter, *Mississippi Territory*; Mississippi Territorial Archives, MDAH; Pickett, *History of Alabama*.

201 white reaction to black involvement: tradition and interpretation. Correspondence from Holmes, governor of Mississippi Territory, to General Wilkinson on October 19, 1812, documents fears about a "negro insurrection"; Carter, *Territory of Mississippi*; Clark and Guice, *Frontiers in Conflict*.

Chapter Twelve

203 Jackson's reaction to Fort Mims: The Papers of Andrew Jackson; Reid and Eaton, *Life of Andrew Jackson*; see also Cotterill, *Southern Indians*, regarding sentiments of Tennessee whites.

203 newspaper: Nashville *Clarion* editorial, April 12, 1814.

204 Chickasaws and Choctaws: The Papers of Andrew Jackson; *ASP*; Mississippi Territorial Archives, MDAH.

204 Pushmataha: *ASP*; Mississippi Territorial Archives, MDAH; Cotterill, *Southern Indians*; Halbert and Ball, *Creek War*; Carter, *Mississippi Territory*.

206 Jackson and Tennessee volunteers arrive in Mississippi Territory: The Papers of Andrew Jackson; Reid and Eaton, *Life of Andrew Jackson*; Cotterill, *Southern Indians*. Remini, in *Andrew Jackson* (New York: Harper & Row, 1966), says that on Jackson's arrival he "unleashed a widespread assault of savagery against the Indians."

207 McIntosh/Cherokees: Cotterill, *Southern Indians*; Griffith, *McIntosh and Weatherford*; Reid and Eaton, *Life of Andrew Jackson*.

208 Tallusshatchee: Davy Crockett, *Life of David Crockett*; Reid and Eaton, *Life of Andrew Jackson*; Richard Keith Call quoted in Remini, *Andrew Jackson and the Course of American Empire, 1767–1821*.

209 Lyncoya: The Papers of Andrew Jackson; Remini, *Andrew Jackson*.

209 Talladega: Stiggins, *Creek Indian History*; Woodward, *Reminiscences*; The Papers of Andrew Jackson; Reid and Eaton, *Life of Andrew Jackson*; Halbert and Ball, *Creek War*.

212 Hillabee massacre: Halbert and Ball, *Creek War*; Stiggins, *Creek Indian History*; The Papers of Andrew Jackson; Reid and Eaton, *Life of Andrew Jackson*.

213 Coweta "siege": *ASP*; Halbert and Ball, *Creek War*; Southerland and Brown, *Federal Road*.

213 Abram Mordecai: Halbert and Ball, *Creek War*; Hamilton, *Colonial Mobile*; Pickett, *History of Alabama*.

214 Autossee battle: Stiggins, *Creek Indian History*; Remini, *Andrew Jackson*; Halbert and Ball, *Creek War*; Pickett, *History of Alabama*; Cotterill, *Southern Indians*.

215 Autossee architecture: Bartram, *Travels*; Pickett, *History of Alabama*.

216 second trip to Pensacola: Stiggins, *Creek Indian History*.

217 Claiborne and Mississippi troops: Mississippi Territorial Archives, MDAH; Mrs. Dunbar Rowland, *Andrew Jackson's Campaign*; Halbert and Ball, *Creek War*.

219 Sam Moniac sends message to Holy Ground: tradition; family stories; Stout Collection; in other stories an unknown person sent a runner with a message. (Moniac's wife, son, brother, and other family members were at the Holy Ground voluntarily.) Stiggins says that William Weatherford found out about the approach of the Mississippians, rode to the Holy Ground to warn the people there, and got "trapped" into leading the battle. Mrs. Dunbar Rowland, in *Andrew Jackson's Campaign*, has this comment about such a version of Weatherford's involvement: "preposterous!"

220 Sam Moniac misdirects troops: A military court of inquiry composed of Captain Woodruft, Captain J. E. Denkins, and Lieutenant H. Choutard found Moniac responsible for misdirecting Major Cassels and allowing the Red Sticks to escape. Mississippi Territorial Archives, MDAH; (General) Claiborne Papers, MDAH; Pickett, *History of Alabama*.

220 Holy Ground battle: Mississippi Territorial Archives, MDAH; (General) Claiborne Papers, MDAH; Halbert and Ball, *Creek War*; Stiggins, *Creek Indian History*.

221 leap over river: tradition; family stories; Stout Collection; Stiggins, *Creek Indian History*; Halbert and Ball, *Creek War*. In our family stories the horse's name was Arrow; in Stiggins, it is Abbanonair.

223 Emuckfau Creek—Jackson's retreat: The Papers of Andrew Jackson; Reid and Eaton, *Life of Andrew Jackson*; Halbert and Ball, *Creek War*; Pickett, *History of Alabama*.

224 plan Calabee attack: Stiggins, *Creek Indian History*.

225 Battle of Calabee Creek: ibid.; *ASP*; Halbert and Ball, *Creek War*; Cotterill, *Southern Indians*. Stiggins says that High-headed Jim, a.k.a. Jim Boy, was killed at this battle. Historians often confuse the Jim Boy of the Creek War with the Jim Boy of the Seminole wars. They were two different men.

225 Paddy Walsh moves to Pensacola: Stiggins, *Creek Indian History*.

225 Tohopeka (Horseshoe Bend): *ASP*; The Papers of Andrew Jackson; Reid and Eaton, *Life of Andrew Jackson*; Stiggins, *Creek Indian History*; Halbert and Ball, *Creek War*; Pickett, *History of Alabama*. Note: New-Yauca was named for New York by warriors who had visited there with Alexander McGillivray in 1790.

227 escape to Florida: Woodward, *Reminiscences*; Stiggins, *Creek Indian History*; Halbert and Ball, *Creek War*; Coker and Watson, *Indian Traders*; Wright, *Anglo-Spanish Rivalry in North America* and *Britain and the American Frontier*.

Chapter Thirteen

230 Jackson demands: tradition; Stout Collection; Woodward, *Reminiscences*; Reid and Eaton, *Life of Andrew Jackson*.

232 Weatherford sues for peace: family stories; tradition; Stout Collection; Reid and Eaton, *Life of Andrew Jackson*; Pickett, *History of Alabama*.

234 Weatherford at Fort Claiborne: family stories; tradition; Stout Collection; Eggleston, *Red Eagle*; Pickett, *History of Alabama*.

236 rumors Weatherford goes to Hermitage: Eggleston, *Red Eagle*;

Remini, *Andrew Jackson and the Course of American Empire*, in which the author says Weatherford and Jackson became such good friends that Weatherford "occasionally" visited Jackson at the Hermitage. In his earlier work, *Andrew Jackson*, Remini says that Jackson was "mesmerized" by Weatherford.

237 British troops land at Apalachicola, supplies arrive: Coker and Watson, *Indian Traders*; Wright, *Anglo-Spanish Rivalry in North America* and *Britain and the American Frontier*.

238 aftermath of war: *ASP*; Reid and Eaton, *Life of Andrew Jackson*; Remini, *Andrew Jackson*; Henri, *The Southern Indians and Benjamin Hawkins*.

238 treaty: *ASP*; Prucha, *Documents of United States Indian Policy*; Henri, *The Southern Indians and Benjamin Hawkins*.

239 letters to Spanish: Holmes, "Archivo de Indios"; Remini, *Andrew Jackson and the Course of American Empire*.

240 Jackson in Florida: Reid and Eaton, *Life of Andrew Jackson*; Wright, *Anglo-Spanish Rivalry in North America* and *Britain and the American Frontier*.

241 Josiah Francis execution: ibid.

241 McIntosh's assassination: Griffith, *McIntosh and Weatherford*.

242 ritual bear hunt and death: family stories; tradition; Stout Collection. One story in the Stout Collection says that William Weatherford went on a ritual deer hunt, saw a white deer, took a chill, went home, and died.

Bibliographical Essay

For interested readers I offer this discussion of some documented sources influential in forming the basic structure of my knowledge of the world, culture, and era of William Weatherford. My own book *Native Land: Mississippi 1540–1798* (Jackson: University Press of Mississippi, 1995), a narrative history from a Native American point of view (my own), based on primary documents, formed a solid base from which to launch my research into the documented world of William Weatherford. Michael Green's *The Creeks: A Critical Bibliography* (Bloomington/London: Indiana University Press for the Newberry Library, 1979) offered me an overview of many scholarly works published about the Creek Indians and was a source I frequently referenced in my search for material about them.

For general background information on the Indians of the Southeast, especially the Creeks and Alabamas, there is no better source than the works of John R. Swanton. His *Early History of the Creek Indians and their Neighbors,* Bureau of American Ethnology Bulletin, No. 73 (Washington, D.C.: GPO, 1922) and *Myths and Tales of the Southeastern Indians* (Norman/London: University of Oklahoma Press, 1995) are especially insightful. A compilation of Swanton's other works and research of primary material related to the topic appears in *The Indians of the Southeastern United States* (Washington, D.C.: Smithsonian Institution Press, 1979). Albert S. Gatschet's *A Migration Legend of the Creek Indians, with a Linguistic, Historic, and Ethnographic Introduction*, 2 vols. (Philadelphia: Daniel G. Brinton, 1884) is also necessary reading. Charles Hudson's *The Southeastern Indians* (Knoxville: University of Tennessee Press, 1976) builds on Swanton's and other scholars' works to offer more insight into the topic in an easy-to-read narrative. *Travels of William Bartram* (New York: Dover Publications, 1928, reprint) by William Bartram and edited by Mark Van Dorn offers sensitive, poetic information gained from Bartram's travels and sojourns in the region, especially those with the Creeks, before the American Revolution. Bernard Romans, an eighteenth-century botanist and surveyor, offers views of the region and people in *A Concise Natural History of East and West Florida* (New Orleans: Pelican Publishing Company, 1961, reprint) through the lens of a British colonial official in pre-Revolutionary times. The British trader James Adair also wrote of such Indian tribes as the Creeks, Choctaws, Chickasaws, and Cherokees from firsthand experience in *History of the American Indians* (New York: Promontory Press, 1986, reprint) but was so obsessed with his personal prejudices and religious views that he must be read with caution. The book can help a grounded researcher understand the many prejudices through which modern Americans view American Indian history and culture.

Another work that offers insight but must also be read in context is H. B. Cushman, *History of the Choctaw, Chickasaw and Natchez Indians* (New York: Russell & Russell, 1972, reprint). Cushman, the son of missionaries, was born in the Choctaw Indian country of Mississippi at the Mayhew Indian Mission in the decade before Indian removal began. His book was first published in 1899. Angie Debo in *And Still the Waters Run* (Princeton: Princeton University Press, 1972, reprint) and *The Road to Disappearance* (Norman: University of Oklahoma Press, 1967) and Robert Spencer Cotterill in *The Southern Indians*

(Norman: University of Oklahoma Press, 1954) also offer overviews of Creek and southeastern Indian history. Among the modern scholars who have used a scientific approach in presenting an overview of the Indians of the region are Fred B. Kniffen, Hiram Gregory, and George A. Stokes in *The Historic Indian Tribes of Louisiana* (Baton Rouge: LSU Press, 1987). Peter Farb's *Man's Rise to Civilization: The Cultural Ascent of the Indians of North America* (New York: E. P. Dutton, 1978) offers summaries of indigenous societies of North America as they were first seen by Europeans.

The observations of French explorers and colonists in Pierre Margry's six-volume *Découverte et Établissement des Français dans l'ouest et dans le sud de l'Amérique Septentrionale* (Paris: D. Jouaust, 1879–88) and in B. F. French's five-volume *Historical Collections of Louisiana* (New York: Wiley and Putnam, 1846-75) are necessary reading for the researcher who would understand the era of early Louisiana, a region that once encompassed a part of the Creek confederacy and greatly affected the Alabamas' culture. French's *Historical Collections* is now available on CD-ROM from LSU Press. Also now available on CD-ROM is Henry Rowe Schoolcraft's six volumes of encyclopedic information on American Indians published as *Historical and Statistical Information, Respecting the History, Conditions and Prospects of the Indian Tribes of the United States* (Philadelphia: Lippincott, 1851–57) and the index compiled by Frances S. Nichols, *Index to Schoolcraft's Indian Tribes of the United States,* United States Bureau of American Ethnology Bulletin 152 (Washington, D.C.: GPO, 1954). Schoolcraft's work is also known by the title *Archives of Aboriginal Knowledge*. The CD-ROM entitled *The Indian Question* (Indianapolis: Objective Computing, 1994) also contains Schoolcraft's autobiography, *Memoirs of Thirty Years with the Indian Tribes*, as well as United States Indian Treaties, Bureau of Indian Affairs Statistics, Civil Rights Commission Report, Indian Resource Guide to the National Archive, and Indian Microfilm Guide to the National Archive, among other documents related to American Indians. United States Army Major Caleb Swan's "Topical History" of the Creeks, compiled from his journey with Alexander McGillivray back to Indian Country after the signing of the New York Treaty of 1790 and his sojourn there, can be found in Schoolcraft, vol. 5, pp. 251–83.

The trader and British agent Thomas Nairne offers early, poignant word-pictures of native lifestyles and sensibilities in the letters contained in *Nairne's Muskhogean Journals*, edited by Alexander Moore (Jackson: University Press of Mississippi, 1988). Later, letters of British soldiers, agents, and travelers, which add various dimensions to the knowledge of the region's Indians, are scattered throughout a number of travel anthologies, one of the more notable being Newton D. Mereness's *Travels in the American Colonies* (New York: Antiquarian Press, Ltd., 1961). David Taitt's journal from his travels as a British agent in Creek country is included in this work.

Memoirs; or, A Cursory Glance at My Different Travels and My Sojourn in the Creek Nation by Louis LeClerc Milfort (Savannah, GA: Beehive Press, 1972, reprint) was first published in 1802 by Milfort in an attempt to convince Napoleon Bonaparte to back a scheme for Milfort to return to America, where he had been friends with the Creek leader Alexander McGillivray and, in fact, had married McGillivray's sister (William Weatherford's aunt) and lead the Creeks in a pro-French alliance. The *Memoirs* failed to persuade the French leader, and many scholars have dismissed Milfort's accounts as fanciful story-telling, but valid ethnographic material can be gleaned from the book. *Authentic Memoirs of William Augustus Bowles* (New York: Arno Press, 1971, reprint) is a facsimile copy of the original book published in London in M.DCC.XCI (1791) and carries a flyleaf notice that the author William Augustus Bowles is ambassador from the United Nations of Creeks and Cherokees to the court of London. A fantastic actor, showman, and politician, Bowles brought more drama to the Creek country than any other single individual documented by history. J. Leitch Wright, Jr.'s *William Augustus Bowles: Director General of the Creek Nation* (Athens: University of Georgia Press, 1967) offers some balance to Bowles's "authentic" memories. Well-written and researched biographies of Alexander McGillivray (John Walton Caughey, *McGillivray of the Creeks* [Norman: University of Oklahoma Press,

1938]) and his father Lachlan (Edward J. Cashin, *Lachlan McGillivray, Indian Trader* [Athens/London: University of Georgia Press, 1992]) help round out knowledge of the direct influences that came together to create the mixed-blood world of William Weatherford.

In the late 1700s and early 1800s, there was no more influential force in Creek Indian country than Panton, Leslie and Company, later purchased by John Forbes. A condensation of the Panton, Leslie story is contained in William S. Coker's and Thomas D. Watson's *Indian Traders of the Southeastern Spanish Borderlands: Panton, Leslie & Company and John H. Forbes & Company* (Pensacola: University of West Florida Press, 1986). Special collections at the Mobile (Alabama) Public Library and the University of West Florida's Pace Library (Pensacola) contain copies of many primary documents related to this trading company.

Information from British archives available on microfilm at the Mississippi Department of Archives and History, Jackson, adds more pieces to the jigsaw puzzle we can put together for a picture of this era. The MDAH records are entitled "Mississippi Provincial Archives: English Dominion, collection of transcripts of archives in Public Records Office, London, England." One volume from these records, edited by Dunbar Rowland, has been published as *Mississippi Provincial Archives: English Dominion, 1763–1766* (Nashville: Press of Brandon, 1911); the other transcripts are on microfilm. The Cook Library at the University of Southern Mississippi is also a rich source of data from Spanish records (on microfilm) from part of the period (1780–1813) of Spanish dominion in the area in the records collected by Jack D. L. Holmes and entitled "Archivo de Indios. Papeles Procedentes de Cuba. Selected Records." *The Spanish in the Mississippi Valley, 1762–1804*, edited by John Francis McDermott (Urbana: University of Illinois Press, 1974); *The Spanish-American Frontier: 1783–1795* by Arthur Preston Whitaker (Lincoln: University of Nebraska Press, 1969); *The Southern Colonial Frontier, 1607–1763* by W. Stitt Robinson (Albuquerque: University of New Mexico Press, 1979); *The Southern Frontier, 1670–1732* by Verner W. Crane (Durham: Duke

University Press, 1928) and *Anglo-Spanish Rivalry in North America* by J. Leitch Wright (Athens: University of Georgia Press, 1971) explore the topics of Spanish, British, and Anglo-American interactions.

The most pressing interests of the first French emissaries to the Creek and Alabama country, the ancestral home of William Weatherford, were economic. The Europeans wanted to establish a trade with the Indians as well as to start colonial enterprises and exploit the bounty of the land. The details of those plans are contained within the Mississippi Department of Archives and History's five-volume *Mississippi Provincial Archives: French Dominion*. The first three volumes (1729–40, 1701–29, 1704–43) were edited and translated by Dunbar Rowland and A. G. Sanders (Jackson: MDAH, 1927–32). The last two volumes (1729–48 and 1749–63) were edited by Patricia Galloway, Rowland, and Sanders (Baton Rouge: LSU Press, 1984). Nancy Miller Surrey, *The Commerce of Louisiana During the French Regime, 1699–1763* (New York: AMS Press, 1968) examines in detail the primary documents relating to the economy of the era. Marcel Giraud's five-volume *History of French Louisiana* offers details gleaned from many primary French sources, including those of the Archives des Colonies (Archives Nationales, Paris), Bibliothèque Nationale, Paris, Archives of the Port of Lorient, and the Louisiana State Historical Museum, New Orleans. The venerable Giraud, a renowned French scholar of Louisiana history, tells the story of the founding, planning, and running of the colony from a decidedly French point of view. To date, only three of the five volumes have been translated into English and published by LSU Press, but the other volumes are forthcoming. *Volume One, The Reign of Louis XIV, 1698–1715* (1974); *Volume Five, The Company of the Indies, 1723–1731* (1991), and *Volume Two, Years of Transition, 1715–1717* (1993) are truly delightful narratives. Daniel H. Thomas's *Fort Toulouse* (Tuscaloosa/London: University of Alabama Press, 1989) a well-researched and admirably scholarly work, tells the story of the fort that was built at the heart of the Alabama country in 1717 with information that complements data in Giraud's works and the *MPA:FD* volumes.

Back at the Mississippi Department of Archives and History are many unpublished records grouped as the Mississippi Provincial Archives, in French and Spanish dominion (as well as the previously mentioned English dominion) subgroups, which are available on microfilm to researchers who visit the Jackson facility. These records contain official correspondence, censuses, ledgers, and journals—all primary documents. Especially fascinating are the detailed records of the official meetings of each group of Europeans with the Indian nations. Clerks carefully recorded the words spoken by the Indian representatives, as well as those of the white men and the details of the ceremonies the Indians thought necessary for these gatherings. The Territorial Governors' Records (Record Group 2) MDAH; Dunbar Rowland's many works edited from primary documents on Mississippi territorial and provincial history; Clarence E. Carter, *Territorial Papers of the United States*, 26 vols. (*The Territory of Mississippi*, vols. 5 and 6) Washington, D. C.: GPO, 1937–38 and *The American State Papers*, 38 vols. (Washington, D. C.: Gales and Seaton, 1832–61), especially *Indian Affairs*, vol. 1 and 2 of ASP, take up where the European provincial records leave off. The *Annals of Congress, 1789–1824* (Washington, D. C.: Gale and Seaton, 1834–56) is a source of information on the government's debates on federal Indian policy.

Francis Paul Prucha, editor of *Documents of United States Indian Policy* (Lincoln/London: University of Nebraska Press, 1975) and *A Bibliographical Guide to the History of Indian-White Relations in the United States* (Chicago/London: Newberry Library/The University of Chicago Press, 1977), as well as the author of *American Indian Policy in the Formative Years: The Indian Trade and Intercourse Act, 1790–1834* (Lincoln: University of Nebraska Press, 1962) addresses the particular problems facing the researcher/writer of American Indian history in "Doing Indian History," a paper read at the national Archives Conference on Research in the History of Indian-White Relations, Washington, D.C., June 15, 1972, and printed in *Indian-White Relations: A Persistent Paradox*, Jane F. Smith and Robert M. Kvasnicka, eds. (Washington: Howard University Press, 1976). Prucha stresses that historical events are complex and cannot be simplistically linked in a single chain of cause and effect, that history is a continuum, in which some events appearing to be unique phenomena are examples of a continuing pattern that researchers who are ungrounded in the two separate cultures of the past misinterpret, and that many mistakes enter the "record" and become difficult to correct because generation after generation of historians build their knowledge, especially their conclusions, on secondary sources. Most important, Prucha says, is understanding that the two diverse cultures existing in the historic period are not the same cultures that exist today; just as Indian cultures have undergone change, so has white culture, and the values held by whites in the early republic cannot be transposed with those of whites in modern America. Despite Prucha's advice, the major faults and weaknesses found in American Indian-white histories continue to be results of the unwillingness of Eurocentric historians to delve into the thought-world and culture of the American Indian in the past or present and these scholars' fondness for accepting as fact the often faulty conclusions of preceding generations of historians. Historians must always remember that primary documents are not pristine jewels of truth and that to have real meaning they must be read through the cultural lens of the past.

Histories of the region which must be read with a wry eye include J. F. H. Claiborne's *Mississippi as a Province, Territory and State* (Spartanburg, S.C.: The Reprint Company, 1978) originally published in 1880, and Albert James Pickett's *History of Alabama* (Tuscaloosa: Willo Publishing, 1962, reprint) originally published in 1851. Both authors lacked access to primary documents that are easily available now; still, both deserve a thorough reading for an understanding of how regional history was generally perceived in their day and how that view has continued to influence modern historians. (Author Claiborne was the son of the Creek War Mississippi Militia general F. L. Claiborne.) Attorney Peter Hamilton's classic work *Colonial Mobile* (University: University of Alabama Press, 1976, reprint) has stood the test of time since it was first published in 1897 and remains one of the finest examples of regional history despite the author's highly prejudicial version of the Creek War.

David H. Cockran, in *The Creek Frontier 1540–1783* (Norman: University of Oklahoma Press, 1967), addresses political and regional tensions, while James H. O'Donnell III discusses alliances in *Southern Indians in the American Revolution* (Knoxville: University of Tennessee Press, 1973). After the revolution, from 1791 to 1795, James Seagraves served as an agent to the Creeks, and his tenure is documented in the *American State Papers*. In 1796 Benjamin Hawkins was appointed "temporary" American agent to the Creeks (as well as to the Choctaws, Chickasaws, and Cherokees). Shortly afterward, he arrived among them and set up his headquarters in Creek country, where he would remain for sixteen years. He is the subject of Merrit B. Pound's *Benjamin Hawkins, Indian Agent* (Athens: University of Georgia Press, 1951) and Florette Henri's *The Southern Indians and Benjamin Hawkins* (Norman: University of Oklahoma Press, 1986). Hawkins himself is the author of *Sketches from Creek Country* (1846), which, with a selection of his correspondence, *Letters of Benjamin Hawkins 1796–1806* (a 1916 publication of the Georgia Historical Society), has been joined in publication in one volume by The Reprint Company, Spartanburg, SC, 1974. A primary document such as this is always to be valued for the insight it offers. A person knowledgeable of Creek and Alabama customs and culture can only marvel at how little Hawkins understood the people he was trying so valiantly to turn into Jeffersonian yeoman farmers. He rages, for example, against Sophia Durant and Sehoy Weatherford for claiming their brother Alexander McGillivray's estate at his death and sending his children to live with their maternal relatives. We can only ask whether he ever understood even the basic concepts of the Alabama matrilineal culture that dictated this behavior as proper and correct.

Mrs. Dunbar Rowland, in *Andrew Jackson's Campaign Against the British, or the Mississippi Territory in the War of 1812* (New York: The MacMillan Company, 1926), addresses even more cultural prejudices, though often inadvertently. More recently, scholars who have published books on the Creek War and events leading up to it include Henry DeLeon Southerland, Jr., and Jerry Elijah Brown, *The Federal Road* (Tuscaloosa/London: University of Alabama Press, 1989) and Frank L. Owsley, Jr., *Struggle for the Gulf Borderlands: The Creek War and the Battle of New Orleans, 1812–1815* (Gainesville: University of Florida Press, 1981).

Theron A. Nunez, Jr.'s article "Creek Nativism and the Creek War of 1813–1814" in *Ethnohistory* 5:1–47, 131–75, 292–301 (1958) is one of the most insightful pieces ever written on the causes of the Creek War. (See Prucha's *Indian-White Relations* for bibliography of journal articles.) Joel Martin's *Sacred Revolt* (Boston: Beacon Press, 1991) examines the religious and spiritual aspects of the war from the perspective of a Euro-American religious scholar. David R. Edmunds's two books *The Shawnee Prophet* (Lincoln: University of Nebraska Press, 1983) and *Tecumseh and the Quest for Indian Leadership* (Boston: Little, Brown, 1984) are necessary reading for immediate background on native religious influences.

The Creek War of 1813–1814 by H. S. Halbert and T. H. Ball (Tuscaloosa/London: University of Alabama Press, 1995, reprint), first published in 1895, remains the best-written and most enduring history of the Creek conflict. In most cases the authors' professionalism steers them through the minefield of primary documents, secondary sources, and moral attitudes of their day, but they do perpetuate the myth that the Creeks "forced" black slaves to fight the Mississippi Militia at the Holy Ground. Usually when unanswerable questions and contradictions arise, Halbert and Ball say so. They treat the renewed attack at Fort Mims in this manner, referring to the traditional stories and reports which claim that, after the first attack on the fort, when the Red Sticks had decided they had won and had withdrawn, a second force arrived (led by Seekaboo and the "McGillivray negroes") and renewed the battle. These traditional stories support my belief that blacks freely took an active role in fighting the Americans.

Thomas Woodward, a soldier in the Georgia army that invaded Creek country, wrote his *Woodward's Reminiscences of the Creek or Muscogee Indians, Contained in Letters to Friends in Georgia and Al-*

abama, first published in book form in 1859 (Mobile, AL: Southern University Press, 1965, reprint), when he was an elderly retired gentleman living in Louisiana. The book presents letters he wrote to a newspaper recalling his glory years, the Creek War, and bits of information he had gleaned from an elderly black slave woman who had been part of Alexander McGillivray's household until his death, at which time she moved with the McGillivray children to their mother's family (Moniac) household. Scholars question much of Woodward's information. The book is colored by the ethnocentric views of its author (for example, he says he personally does not believe that Alexander McGillivray was a scholar because McGillivray "paraded around New York" in an American uniform in 1790—a "scholar" in the cultural jargon of the time meant a person who could read and write), but, examined in context, much useful information can be discerned from Woodward's work. He, too, reports that Seekaboo and the "McGillivray negroes" led a newly arriving force in a second attack on Fort Mims after the Red Sticks had considered the battle won and ceased their attack. Woodward offers this information as fact, not "tradition."

George Stiggins's narrative, published as *Creek Indian History* (Birmingham Public Library Press, 1989, reprint), deserves careful consideration. (Microfilm of Stiggins's original longhand manuscript is on file in the Linn-Henley Research Library of the Birmingham Public Library and is from the Lyman Draper Manuscript Collection, series V, vol. 1, at the State Historical Society of Wisconsin.) Stiggins became William Weatherford's brother-in-law after the war, and, in this book, he offers a clear view of the conflict from the perspective of an American partisan but also relates Creek partisans' versions of battles. Understanding the racial attitudes of the dominant culture of the time and that culture's absolute refusal to view enslaved blacks, or anyone of African descent, as human beings with unalienable rights is a beginning step in the struggle to gain a true perspective on events that took place. The Creeks had dared to defy the dominant culture by offering refuge to runaway slaves, by recognizing them as fellow human beings, and by allowing them to join the fight against the Americans. It is necessary to understand that, in this important document, Stiggins was trying to convince the Americans that his brother-in-law William Weatherford was not such a bad fellow by saying he was forced to join the Red Sticks. Under a critical cultural lens, in tandem with Woodward's *Reminiscences* and Halbert and Ball's *Creek War*, Stiggins allows details of events that have been clouded in mystery to emerge. His work supports my thesis that blacks joined forces with the Indians to fight the Americans willingly, perhaps even eagerly, at Fort Mims and elsewhere.

Davy Crockett also wrote about the war in *The Life of David Crockett* (Knoxville: University of Tennessee Press, 1973, facsimile), as did several other American combatants. Crockett's aim seems to have been self-glorification, but his telling descriptions of death and destruction are portraits of the soul of the frontiersmen (not a pretty sight). Claiborne wrote a biography of Sam Dale (*The Life and Times of General Sam Dale, the Mississippi Partisan* [New York: Harper and Brothers, 1860]) and in the same vein includes that rowdy frontiersman's version of his actions in the war and his highly questionable report of the speech Tecumseh made to the Creeks on his visit to their towns in 1811.

Andrew Jackson's Papers, from the series "Presidential Papers on Microfilm," recorded by the Library of Congress, 1961, Washington, D. C., and The Papers of Andrew Jackson on microfilm, edited by Sam Smith and Harriet Chappell Owsley; Robert Remini, consulting editor; Sharon MacPherson, assistant editor, recorded by the University of Tennessee Press, Knoxville, plus myriad biographies of Andrew Jackson (major biographers include James Parton, John Bassett, and Robert Remini) detail bits and pieces of the Creek War and Jackson's actions during that time. John Reid and John Henry Eaton's *The Life of Andrew Jackson* (University: University of Alabama Press, 1974, reprint) is primary documentation. Reid, Jackson's secretary during the war, started the work but died before it was completed, and Eaton was brought in to finish the book. A list of all the great American heroes who carved out their reputations in the Creek War and went on to have biographies written about them is frightfully long. Few do the war or the Creeks justice. Benjamin W. Griffith, Jr.'s *McIntosh and Weatherford, Creek Indian Leaders* (Tuscaloosa/London: University of Alabama Press, 1988) offers an admirable portrait of American partisan and Lower Creek division leader William McIntosh and his activities in the war, but a clear portrait of Weatherford, though promised, never emerges.

Race relations—black, white, and red—are an undercurrent addressed in many of the above books, usually in an offhand manner. Dwight W. Hoover, in *The Red and The Black* (Chicago: Rand McNally College Publishing Company, 1976), offers background, in-depth research and commentary on the topic of how Indians and blacks were and are perceived in America. Editors Bruce A. Glasrud's and Alan M. Smith's anthology *Race Relations in British North America 1607–1783* (Chicago: Nelson-Hall, 1982) outlines the context of the problem during the stated era, and, in the volume's essay by Charles Hunter, "The Delaware Nativist Revival of the Mid-Eighteenth Century," the Indians' concerns with spiritual matters are brought into focus. Many historians see the Delaware movement as foreshadowing all the American Indian spiritual revivals of the next century and beyond. Daniel H. Usner, Jr., in *Indians, Settlers, & Slaves in a Frontier Exchange Economy* (Chapel Hill/London: University of North Carolina Press, 1992), examines the economic and cultural interactions among the complete population of colonial Louisiana and West Florida. K. W. Porter addresses a large area in *The Negro on the American Frontier* (New York: Arno Press and the *New York Times*, 1971). Daniel F. Littlefield, Jr., in *Africans and Creeks: From the Colonial Period to the Civil War* (Westport, CT: Greenwood Press, 1979) reports documented contacts and interactions between blacks and the Creeks, relying heavily on the partisan Mississippi Militia and General Claiborne's records for information on the role blacks played in the Creek War. The specifics of the relationship between the two peoples must be put together by the researcher from multiple sources, of which the *American State Papers* and the letters of Hawkins are among the most prominent. Thomas D. Clark and John D. W. Guice briefly address white concerns about a black insurrection in the Mississippi

Territory at the time of the Creek War in *Frontiers in Conflict* (Albuquerque: University of New Mexico Press, 1989). The roots of slavery in the region, the coming of black slaves, and the attempts to enslave Indians are addressed in the Mississippi Provincial Archives, French, English, and Spanish periods. Thomas Jefferson addresses the issue of black slavery as well as assimilation and acculturation of Indians in *Notes on the State of Virginia* (New York: W. W. Norton & Company, 1972, reprint) and in correspondence. In his master's thesis, "The Evolution of Jeffersonian Indian Policy with the Choctaws of Mississippi" (University of Southern Mississippi, 1981), Samuel J. Wells examines Jeffersonian policy, plans, and near-policy for the intermarriage of Indians and whites as a method of providing a frontier militia force for the southern boundaries with Spanish Florida and dissolving the Indian nations and culture. Wells further explores the topic in his doctoral dissertation, "Choctaw Mixed Bloods and the Advent of Removal" (University of Southern Mississippi, 1987). Each work incidentally includes the Creeks. Bernard W. Sheehan also addresses Jeffersonian policies and the American Indian in *Seeds of Extinction* (New York: W. W. Norton & Company, 1973).

The Wilber Stout Collection of Papers at the McCain Library, University of Southern Mississippi, Hattiesburg, includes works by Frank G. Speck on Creek medicine and music; copies of pertinent information from the Lyman Draper Manuscript Collection (State Historical Society of Wisconsin) include the Dreisbach papers, which are considered an excellent source for information on William Weatherford's family and kinsmen and their recollections of the man and the Creek War. The Stout Papers are not indexed and consist of cartons of miscellaneous information sorted and boxed at random. For someone without a solid background knowledge of the history of the region, the culture of the Creek Indians, and the era of William Weatherford's life, much of this collection would appear meaningless and contradictory. Apparently, Dr. Stout collected everything he could find said or written about William Weatherford.

Finally, there are two published biographies of William Weatherford. Alexander R. Meek's *The Red Eagle* (Montgomery, AL: Paragon

Press, 1914) is based largely on George Cary Eggleston's *Red Eagle and the Wars with the Creek Indians of Alabama* (New York: Dodd, Mead 1878). Eggleston offers an honest, intellectual assessment of the few documented facts of Weatherford's life. I had an opportunity to read a copy of this rare book in the Choctaw Tribal Archives at the Choctaw Museum in Philadelphia, Mississippi.

Selected Bibliography

Unpublished sources:

Jackson, Andrew. *Andrew Jackson's Papers.* From the series "Presidential Papers on Microfilm." Washington, D.C.: Library of Congress, 1961.

———. *The Papers of Andrew Jackson.* Edited by Sam Smith and Harriet Chappell Owsley; Robert Remini, consulting editor; Sharon MacPherson, assistant editor. Knoxville: University of Tennessee Press, 1980. Microfilm.

Mississippi Provincial Archives: English Dominion. Mississippi Department of Archives and History, Jackson, microfilmed from the transcripts of archives in the Public Records Office, London, England.

Holmes, Jack D. L. "Archivo de Indios. Papeles Procedentes de Cuba. Selected Records." Cook Library, University of Southern Mississippi, Hattiesburg. Microfilm.

Stout, Wilber. Collection of Papers. McCain Library, University of Southern Mississippi, Hattiesburg.

Wells, Samuel J. "The Evolution of Jeffersonian Indian Policy with the Choctaws of Mississippi, 1800–1830." Master's thesis, University of Southern Mississippi, 1981. McCain Library, University of Southern Mississippi.

———. "Choctaw Mixed Bloods and the Advent of Removal." Ph. D. diss., University of Southern Mississippi, 1981.

Published contemporaneous sources:

Adair, James. *History of American Indians.* Reprint, New York: Promontory Press, 1986.

American State Papers: Documents, Legislative and Executive, of the Congress of the United States. 38 vols. Washington, D.C.: Gale and Seaton, 1832–61.

Annals of Congress, 1789–1824. 42 vols. Washington, D.C.: Gale and Seaton, 1834–56.

Bartram, William. *Travels of William Bartram.* Edited by Mark Van Dorn. Reprint, New York: Dover Publications, 1928.

Bowles, William Augustus. *Authentic Memoirs of William Augustus Bowles.* Reprint, Arno Press, Inc., 1971.

Crockett, David. *The Life of David Crockett.* Reprint, Knoxville: University of Tennessee Press, 1973.

Ellicott, Andrew. *The Journal of Andrew Ellicott.* Chicago: Quadrangle Books, 1962.

French, B. F. *Historical Collections of Louisiana.* 7 vols. New York: Wiley and Putnam, 1846–75.

Galloway, Patricia Kay, ed., Dunbar Rowland, and A. G. Sanders, eds. and trans. *Mississippi Provincial Archives: French Dominion 1729–1748* (vol. 4) and *1749–1763* (vol. 5). Baton Rouge: LSU Press, 1984.

Hawkins, Benjamin. *A Sketch of the Creek Country in the Years 1798 and 1799* (1848). *Letters of Benjamin Hawkins, 1796–1806* (1916). 1 vol. Reprint, Spartanburg, SC: Reprint Company, 1974.

Milfort, Louis le Clerc. *Memoirs, or a Quick Glance at My Various Travels and My Sojourn in the Creek Nation.* Translated and edited by Ben McCary. Reprint, Savannah: Beehive Press, 1959.

Nairne, Thomas. *Nairne's Muskhogean Journals.* Edited by Alexander
  Moore. Jackson: University Press of Mississippi, 1988.
Reid, John, and John Henry Eaton. *The Life of Andrew Jackson.*
  Edited by Frank L. Owsley, Jr. Reprint, University: University of
  Alabama Press, 1974.
Romans, Bernard. *A Concise Natural History of East and West
  Florida.* Reprint, New Orleans: Pelican Publishing Company,
  1961.
Rowland, Dunbar, ed. *Mississippi Provincial Archives: English Domin-
  ion, 1763–1766.* Nashville: Press of Brandon, 1911.
Rowland, Dunbar, and A. G. Sanders, eds. and trans. *Mississippi
  Provincial Archives: French Dominion 1729–1740, 1701–1729,
  1704–1743.* 3 vols. Jackson: Mississippi Department of Archives
  and History, 1927–32.
Stiggins, George. *Creek Indian History: A Historical Narrative of the
  Genealogy, Traditions and Downfall of the Ispocoga or Creek In-
  dian Tribe of Indians by One of the Tribe, George Stiggins.* Edited
  by Virginia Pounds Brown. Birmingham: Birmingham Public
  Library Press, 1989.
Woodward, Thomas. *Reminiscences of the Creek, or Muscogee Indians.*
  Reprint, Tuscaloosa: Alabama Book Store, 1939.

Other sources and references:

Bannon, John Francis, ed. *Bolton and the Spanish Borderlands.* Nor-
  man: University of Oklahoma Press, 1974.
Cashin, Edward J. *Lachlan McGillivray, Indian Trader.* Athens: Uni-
  versity of Georgia Press, 1992.
Caughey, John Walton. *McGillivray of the Creeks.* Norman: Univer-
  sity of Oklahoma Press, 1938.
Claiborne, J. F. H. *Mississippi as a Province, Territory and State.* Spar-
  tanburg, SC: The Reprint Company, 1978.
Clark, Thomas, ed. *Travels in the Old South, 1527–1783.* Norman:
  University of Oklahoma Press, 1956.
Coker, William S., and Thomas D. Watson. *Indian Traders of the
  Southeastern Spanish Borderlands: Panton, Leslie & Company and*

John H. Forbes & Company, 1783–1847. Pensacola: University of West Florida Press, 1986.

Cotterill, R. S. *The Story of the Civilized Tribes Before Removal.* Norman: University of Oklahoma Press, 1954.

Debo, Angie. *The Road to Disappearance.* Norman: University of Oklahoma Press, 1941.

Drake, Benjamin. *Life of Tecumseh and His Brother the Prophet.* Cincinnati: E. Morgan, 1841.

Edmunds, R. David. *The Shawnee Prophet.* Lincoln: University of Nebraska Press, 1983.

———. *Tecumseh and the Quest for Indian Leadership.* Boston: Little, Brown & Company, 1984.

Eggleston, George Cary. *Red Eagle and the Wars with the Creek Indians of Alabama.* New York: Dodd & Mead, 1878.

Green, Michael D. *The Creeks: A Critical Bibliography.* Bloomington: Indiana University Press, 1979.

Griffith, Benjamin W. *McIntosh and Weatherford, Creek Indian Leaders.* Tuscaloosa: University of Alabama Press, 1988.

Halbert, H. S., and T. H. Ball. *The Creek War of 1813 and 1814.* Edited by Frank L. Owsley, Jr. Reprint, University: University of Alabama Press, 1969.

Hamilton, Peter J. *Colonial Mobile.* Edited by Charles G. Summersell. Reprint, University: University of Alabama Press, 1976.

Henri, Florette. *The Southern Indians and Benjamin Hawkins.* Norman: University of Oklahoma Press, 1986.

Hudson, Charles. *The Southeastern Indians.* Knoxville: University of Tennessee Press, 1976.

Martin, Joel W. *Sacred Revolt: The Muskogees' Struggle For a New World.* Boston: Beacon Press, 1991.

Meek, Alexander R. *The Red Eagle.* Montgomery: Paragon Press, 1914.

Neihardt, John G. *Black Elk Speaks. Being the Life Story of a Holy Man of the Oglala Sioux.* Lincoln: University of Nebraska Press, 1932.

Owsley, Frank L., Jr. *Struggle for the Gulf Borderlands: The Creek*

War and the Battle of New Orleans. Gainesville: University of
Florida Press, 1981.

Pickett, Albert James. *History of Alabama and Incidentally of Georgia
and Mississippi.* Reprint, Spartanburg, SC: The Reprint Company, 1988.

Remini, Robert V. *Andrew Jackson and the Course of American Empire, 1767–1821.* New York: Harper & Row, 1977.

Rowland, Mrs. Dunbar. *Andrew Jackson's Campaign against the
British, or the Mississippi Territory in the War of 1812.* New York:
Macmillan, 1926.

Schoolcraft, Henry Rowe, ed. *Historical and Statistical Information,
Respecting the History, Conditions and Prospects of the Indian
Tribes of the United States.* 6 vols. Philadelphia: Lippincott,
1851–57.

Southerland, Henry DeLeon, Jr., and Jerry Elijah Brown. *The Federal
Road through Georgia, the Creek Nation, and Alabama,
1806–1836.* Tuscaloosa: University of Alabama Press, 1989.

Swanton, John R. *The Indians of the Southeastern United States.*
Reprint, Washington, D.C.: Smithsonian Institution Press, 1979.

———. *Myths and Tales of the Southeastern Indians.* Reprint, Norman: University of Oklahoma Press, 1995.

Thomas, Daniel H. *Fort Toulouse: The French Outpost at the Alabamas on the Coosa.* Tuscaloosa: University of Alabama Press, 1989.

White, Richard. *The Roots of Dependency.* Lincoln: University of Nebraska Press, 1983.

Wright, J. Leitch. *Anglo-Spanish Rivalry in North America.* Athens:
University of Georgia Press, 1971.

———. *The Only Land They Knew.* New York: Free Press, 1981.

Index